ABOUT A GIRL

Rebekah Robertson is an Australian actor who has appeared on television and on stage. In 2012, she founded Transcend, the first parent-led peer-support group and information hub for transgender kids and their families in Australia. She advocates for transgender kids and has been nominated for numerous awards for her work.

ABOUT A GIRL

A Mother's Powerful Story of Raising Her Transgender Child

Rebekah Robertson

With a foreword by

Georgie Stone

VIKING
an imprint of
PENGUIN BOOKS

VIKING

UK | USA | Canada | Ireland | Australia
India | New Zealand | South Africa | China

Penguin
Random House
Australia

Viking is part of the Penguin Random House group of companies whose addresses can be found at
global.penguinrandomhouse.com.

First published by Viking, an imprint of
Penguin Random House Australia Pty Ltd, 2019

Cover photograph: Brendan Doyle, Broken Yellow, for the National Australia Day Council
Cover design by Alex Ross © Penguin Random House Australia Pty Ltd
Author photograph by Sanjeev Singh
Typeset in 12.5/18 pt Adobe Garamond by Midland Typesetters, Australia

Printed and bound in Australia by Griffin Press, part of Ovato, an accredited
ISO AS/NZS 14001 Environmental Management Systems printer

NATIONAL
LIBRARY
OF AUSTRALIA
A catalogue record for this
book is available from the
National Library of Australia

ISBN 978 0 14378 515 6

penguin.com.au

MIX
Paper from
responsible sources
FSC FSC® C009448
www.fsc.org

This book is dedicated to the young people affected directly in the years between 2004 and 2018 by the Family Court of Australia's approval process for the rightful, appropriate and life-saving treatment for gender dysphoria. You paid the price with your bodies, your mental health and your personal agency and autonomy for the discrimination that this law visited upon you and your human rights. You are heroes, and I honour you and your courageous families – ordinary people, dealing with extraordinary and overwhelming circumstances.

May your lives ever be blessed.

To my beautiful children,
Georgie and Harry,
you have delighted me from the moment you took breath.

And to Kathleen and Madeleine, you are so missed.

'To thine own self be true'
– *Hamlet*, Act 1, Scene 3

Contents

Preface
by Associate Professor
Michelle Telfer

It's not uncommon as a paediatrician to be told that you've made an impact on the life of a young person and their family. We are in a position of privilege, being trusted enough by people for them to express their deepest thoughts and greatest fears, their hopes and dreams for the future. Less frequently articulated is the deep and lasting impact a young person and their family can have on their doctor, as happened to me during the process of looking after Georgie Stone.

Georgie was a young girl when she came with her parents, Rebekah and Greg, to my clinic at the Royal Children's Hospital, Melbourne, in 2012. She had already seen many doctors before me, and had commenced her puberty-suppressing treatment for gender dysphoria after taking the legally mandated steps through the Family Court. Despite Georgie's quiet, reserved demeanour, an underlying confidence and sense of wisdom were evident the first time we spoke about her experiences. She captured my attention, eloquently describing what it was like to have to try to understand oneself at such a young age: having to convince the world that she didn't feel how she was expected to feel, and that she wasn't the person she was assumed to be.

Like many trans and gender-diverse young people I have met since, Georgie had needed to navigate childhood in a society that not only didn't understand her but also outwardly feared her. In this book, Rebekah brilliantly captures Georgie's vulnerability and sense of isolation. The hurt and rejection experienced by transgender children and adolescents affect their family life and everyday experiences. It can be devastating. For some young people I look after, it breaks them. But Georgie and Rebekah found incredible strength and solidarity, rising with a force of purpose that changed them as individuals as well as the entire system, making life easier for every trans child and adolescent who came after them.

I am incredibly lucky to be part of Rebekah and Georgie's story. Although I first met them in a clinical context, guiding them through medical treatment, I came to know them well in our five years of working together to advocate to change Australia's laws for transgender adolescents. Their strength of character and our shared unrelenting determination to change a situation that perpetuated discrimination and harm brought us together as a persuasive and powerful team.

About a Girl is more than a story about a transgender child. It's about love: the story of a mother and the pure, unconditional and boundless love she has for her two children. Held at all times by their mother's love, both Georgie and her brother Harry now appear free from the limitations that others create, and we see them growing up to change the world for the better.

I have taken enormous inspiration from Rebekah and Georgie, and at the same time have given much of myself to them, being forced to question and consider my own place in the world. I have been profoundly changed, and for this I will always be grateful.

Associate Professor Michelle Telfer
Director, Gender Service
The Royal Children's Hospital, Melbourne
September 2019

Foreword
by Georgie Stone

When Mum told me she would be writing a book about our story, I was over the moon: finally, I thought, people will understand how *hard* it has been! But now that I've read this book, I've realised that *About a Girl* goes much deeper. It is a story about a mother and her children, and what she will do to protect them from harm. What struck me are the vivid memories of parenthood, love and the strong bond between mother and daughter. I know for sure that I would not be the happy, driven and passionate person I am today without the support of my mum and dad. And my brother would not be where he is now without their support, either.

Something I must make clear is that everything Mum has talked about in this book – things I have said, done and experienced – I have given her permission to include. I know that it is important that trans and gender-diverse young people tell their own stories with their own voices. But parents have something

to say too. How do we support our children? What do we do in
this or that situation? We will not have trans kids standing up and
telling their stories if they don't have that support behind them.
Allies are everything.

The way my mum has supported me, and fought for me,
inspires me immensely. When I become a mother one day, I will
strive to be there for my kids the same way my mum is for me.
I will love them unconditionally, no matter who they are. Mum
fought for me in the courts to get puberty-blocking medication.
My case, *Re: Jamie*, was pivotal in helping other transgender kids.
I now have the right to identify myself as the person at the centre
of that case – and I'm proud to. I'm proud of my mother for
helping me, for sharing my story.

What I have learned so far in my (almost) two decades on
this earth is that, as clichéd as it sounds, love is the answer. Love
helps people listen; love helps people empathise. It was love that
fuelled my mum's support of me. It was love that helped my
dad accept me for who I am. We will not get anywhere with
contempt and prejudice. Love will not fix all our problems, but
it will help us open up and listen to each other. That's a start.

I feel so lucky to have had the childhood I did. There were
struggles and hardships, but there were so many beautiful things
too. Through it all, my brother has been a constant, providing the
laughs as a reprieve from the outside world. Amid all the political
turmoil, the media attention and the stress of everyday life, Harry
has been there. I love him so much.

All families fall on hard times. That is just how life works. It's
messy, arduous, chaotic, scary, surprising. All you can really do is
work with what you have. My family is a family like any other:

we've had to deal with things as they've come. And that's okay. It is all part of the learning process, as we are all constantly growing. My dad, who was at first scared at the prospect of having a trans daughter, is now my biggest supporter. He loves Harry and me so much. I'm proud of him.

I hope you will get something out of this book. Thank you for wanting to learn more. Thank you for being open. I'll let Mum take it from here.

September 2019

Prologue

All I can do now is wait. A short while ago, I gave Georgie a big hug and a kiss, and we said we loved each other. She walked into theatre for her gender affirmation surgery and I walked back to her room, to where Greg, Harry and I are now trying not to watch the clock too obsessively.

I imagined I'd want to cry, but I'm just really tired and need a decent cuppa. Perhaps I'll feel more when Georgie comes out of recovery in a few hours. I've sent out a message to family and friends to say she's now in theatre. It helps to know we have the love and support of so many near and dear to us.

Harry and Greg go for a walk and I'm left by myself. It's kind of nice to be alone. What I'm recognising, perhaps for the first time with clarity, is the enormity of our family's story. So many of the events that unfolded gave me no space for reflection, no time to catch my breath. I'm observing myself, at once living the experience and witnessing it from a slight distance. It's an odd sensation, but I'm not fighting it.

The sounds of the hospital envelop me: squeaking doors, instructions by nurses to the day patients on admission, keys rattling, cupboards shutting, the soft tear of medipacks being opened, the buzz of the ward bell. Lunch smells, hot and heavy, waft through the halls then recede. With a newly delivered gift of sweet-smelling peonies beside me on the bedside table, I'm soon engrossed with replying to texts wishing Georgie all the best.

While Georgie's surgery is a big deal, this is not a triumphant day as such, and it feels prosaic in many ways. She has waited for the surgery for so long now that the few hours' wait this morning were merely a little boring. There were a couple of procedural things, the anaesthetist and surgeon did their rounds, her bloods were taken. But there is nothing mundane about the manner of the staff, who are beautiful, professional and kind. Georgie was tired and hungry from her fast, but she was so ready.

Once in a while I've stopped and wondered where they are in the procedure, but right now I'm not worried. I've learned that many of the things I've spent too much time fretting about have never come to pass, so I've surrendered to this day with love and respect. This is a time of renewal; Harry and Georgie are adults now, school is done and my relationship with them is changing. I'm going to be learning a new way of being, a new way of experiencing my life and a new way of experiencing my children. These relationships will grow and evolve over time, the more independent Harry and Georgie become.

The window is slightly open and I can hear a dog barking in the distance, cars zooming by. The sun is shining. I watch the clouds; they're moving slowly. The hospital have their Christmas decorations up, which Georgie and I have found comforting. I feel as though this experience is sitting gently within me. There's no struggle, no defiance, no battle to win, no fear to overcome. Acceptance has made me at once open and strong.

I'm going to remember and love. You're welcome to join me. But we'll need tea, and lots of it.

A few things before we start: please don't expect me to go into graphic details about the surgery or share intimate aspects of Georgie's experience. Those experiences are hers to tell, not mine. You'll notice I use the female pronoun from early on in the story. This reflects and respects Georgie's innate sense of herself from a very young age, not how I understood her to be at the time. I didn't begin to use female pronouns for her until she was around eight years of age.

I am the parent of a wonderful transgender girl and her remarkable brother. This is my personal account of being mother to my lovely children. It is my perspective, and I do not speak for anyone else. I do not pretend to know all there is to know about raising a transgender child, or to represent all the possible experiences. That would be unhelpful. There may be aspects of my story you connect with and others you may not. There's quite a lot I want to share with you.

To start, I need to think back to 'before kids'. I'm sometimes asked if I ever imagined I'd become the parent of a transgender child. The obvious and unequivocal answer is no: never, in my wildest fantasies, of all the scenarios I could have invented, was this even remotely one of them. Parenthood itself had not been high on the list of priorities, and I was never clucky, although I did know that I wanted to be a mother one day. I loved kids: my nephews and nieces gave me lots of pleasure; they were so much fun! But I was in no hurry, and besides, I hadn't met anyone I wanted to have babies with. Then Greg and I happened, and I was thrilled when I discovered I was pregnant.

Over the past few days, memories have been flooding back to me of my two sweet babies, of two adorable toddlers, of playful schoolkids. Our twins were determined to make an impact from the start, and we could not have known then how often we would be faced with our strengths and our inadequacies in the years to come. Unexpectedly, we became part of a much wider social conversation about gender, politics and parenting. Back then, I never could have imagined having the discussions I've had both with my kids and with the broader community. We were engaged with each moment, each fresh realisation; still are.

Parents are constantly in unknown territory – especially new parents. When we start out, none of us can envision how our children will teach us new things, hard things, awkward, challenging and wondrous things. None of us can fathom the depth of love and strength we will need to call on to keep our babies safe in this world. Nor can we foresee developing the resilience to not be driven mad by fears, real or imagined. One of my favourite memes reads, 'What doesn't kill you gives you a set of unhealthy coping mechanisms and a very black sense of humour.' This can sometimes describe parenthood and childhood perfectly.

My parenting road wasn't on the map, there were few signposts for directions and it was unsealed. There was certainly no GPS signal! Nevertheless, as with every loving parent, the star I've navigated by has a flashing neon sign on it: *I want my children to be safe, healthy and happy.*

There are several reasons I'm recounting my parenting journey. It would be great if others in similar situations could obtain the information I wish I'd had, and if they could feel less alone. There's also the fact that my family has been featured in many media stories – with our full cooperation – but the narrative has sometimes been massaged to fit the medium. Much is ignored or the nuance is lost for the sake of a specific message. This book is an opportunity to tell the story completely from my perspective. On a personal note, I'm interested in taking the opportunity to reflect. Frankly, even now it's hard to find the time. But my kids have become young adults, and I want to try to grasp what raising them has taught me.

Above all, it's my fervent hope that people with open minds and hearts can read this book and better understand the issues surrounding transgender people, and realise that this is the story of an ordinary family doing their best. I want readers to understand the power of authenticity, of being true to yourself. Transgender people are human beings. Their rights, dignity and humanity need to be protected by family, friends, schools, medical practitioners, people of faith and governments. To do any less is shameful. But more importantly, being trans or gender diverse is only one aspect of a much bigger life. To reduce folks to their gender reduces their humanity, and denies the full scope of their reality.

I'm not just a mother. I am a fully rounded human being with dreams, hurts, strengths and weaknesses. My daughter is so much more than her gender identity, yet at key moments in her life her humanity has been reduced to this one fact. Those who have done so have overlooked her sweet and funny nature, her loyalty as a friend, her beautiful songwriting and love of singing, her uncontrollable laughter, her gentle wisdom, her intelligence, her courage.

What I'd dearly love is for you to see past what you think you know about young trans people – past the headlines, the rhetoric, the politics – and understand that the things that may seem to divide us are created by fear and nothing more. We're all on this planet for such a short time. Let's make it a kinder place for one another.

As I wait in the hospital room for Georgie to return from theatre, and for Greg and Harry to return from their walk, these reflections start to take shape. I begin to see the people first and foremost: two hopeful parents raising their children, twins growing up together, a young woman finding her place in the world and her mother doing everything she can to help her do that. This is our story.

1

An acting career

Sometimes people ask me where my strength comes from. I've been fighting hard for the past nineteen years, pushing through challenges that felt at times overwhelming. It's probably fair to say that my resilience was developed early on because, as a kid, I had to be self-reliant emotionally. My childhood was idyllic in many ways, and I was loved and provided for. Dad, though, was a complicated maverick character. He could be whimsical and playful, but he could also be scary and authoritarian, and his changeable nature could be disorientating. I learned to deal with this by developing a sense of humour; some quick banter could sometimes help diffuse an uncomfortable moment. Even now, if I'm feeling uncertain, I'll try to jolly my way out of it.

I was fortunate to have all my material needs met, but I was confronted by the truth that adults don't always have their shit together. That engendered in me two things: a sense that I needed to figure out the world by myself and a cynical attitude towards authority. While I can't say I rebelled, I did make a point of addressing all the authority figures in my life by their first name: for example, the school principal and our parish priest, who noted my sisters had much more respect for the clergy than I apparently did (which was true). I took to calling my dad 'Gordon', as his mother had done. I'd tell him off, saying, 'Gordon! You're being naughty. Stop it!' or 'All right, Gordon, you know best.' It was my coping mechanism, my winning formula for dissipating the tension, and most of the time it worked. Dad found me at once amusing and confounding.

Comfort for me was knowing my mum was around, even though when I became a teenager I was champing at the bit to grow up and get out into the world. Home was Mum. Wherever Mum was, I wanted to be.

People and human nature were fascinating to me, and I found the perfect outlet for my observations through school drama classes. It's every parent's hope that there will be one teacher who really inspires their child, and a subject they can excel in. For me, it was Deirdre de Blas and her speech and drama classes.

Mrs de Blas had been a talented actress and had studied at the London Academy of Music and Dramatic Art, but life had taken over. She'd married Alfredo, her Spanish husband, had become a mother and upon returning to Tassie had channelled her energies into teaching. She was the most sophisticated and elegant teacher in the whole school. There was a quality of worldliness and wisdom that shone out of her. Mrs de Blas talked to us about important matters and spoke to us as if we were adults. We burrowed into beautiful texts and discovered worlds way beyond our own. She saw something in me and nurtured it, as she did with many of her students. Even though I was involved in everything going at school – hockey, debating, choir, squash, ballet – drama became my passion.

Perhaps, early on, drama was a kind of therapy. I had some big emotions stored inside me, some burning questions and sharp observations. Drama allowed me to explore and ventilate all kinds of feelings and ideas, and it was liberating to inhabit a reality that wasn't mine. Acting teaches you what it might feel like to live in another's shoes. It demands that you not judge the character you play, that you are faithful to their truth and present their perspective. Drama actually helped me maintain my innocence in some ways. I played. I had fun. Acting preserved my sense of wonder, becoming a protective force.

My school, St Michael's in Hobart, put on fabulous plays. In the rehearsal and performance space, nothing and nobody could touch me. At one point I played Tiresias in *Oedipus Rex*. Standing in the wings, about to go on for the first show, I experienced my first overwhelming rush of adrenaline. I became scared and doubted myself, but moments before my cue I made a decision to commit to the story. I walked on, still terrified, but the longer I was out there the better I felt. It was exhilarating. I relished the stakes, and the breathtaking sensation of holding an audience enthralled in a story.

Once I discovered drama and theatre, I knew I had found my path in life. Theatre showed me a way to exist in the world alongside people who were like me and with whom I could connect. Theatre gave a beautiful form to all the devastating complexity of humanity.

In Year 12 I fell in love for the first time, and dreamed of performing on big stages on the mainland and maybe even in England. I set about making my dream a reality.

I finished school in 1984, seventeen years old and ready for anything. Harry and Georgie are around that age and stage now. It's exciting, that heady feeling of possibility. I involved myself in as much local theatre as possible, studied in Launceston for two years, then landed some major roles at Zootango Theatre Company, the main adult theatre company in Tasmania at the time. I toured *Soft Targets*, a play about the AIDS epidemic written by the Soft Targets Collective and performed first at Griffin Theatre Company. Instrumental in its development was actor and activist Timothy Conigrave, who later wrote the memoir *Holding the Man*. We toured in a state that still criminalised homosexuality – it wasn't decriminalised in Tasmania until 1997 – and whose parliament was responding to the AIDS epidemic with callous disdain.

The tour was a big learning curve for me. I had never come across the level of prejudice the gay community were facing, nor had I yet come to understand my own unconscious biases. I was so naive. Still, we had some laughs on tour. One night we found ourselves in Stanley, a small town on the north-west coast of Tasmania, a region sometimes referred to as the 'Edge of the World' – and it certainly felt like that to a young actress. We hadn't expected a big audience, so we were surprised when it seemed like much of the town had turned up. Although we were a bit worried about how it was all going to go down, at interval we were relieved that the audience seemed receptive. When Act 2 was about to start we realised our entire audience had absconded, having disappeared across the road to the pub. The stage manager had to pop across to get them back for the second half. They stayed to the end and put on the best spread for us after the show. People can really surprise you.

In 1995, I moved to Melbourne. The move came about because Roger Hodgman, the Artistic Director of the Melbourne Theatre Company at the time, was asked by the Australia Council to conduct a review of adult theatre in Tasmania and saw a couple of shows I was in. Along the grapevine, I heard that he liked my work, so I got in touch. He gave me some good advice and said to look him up if I found myself back in Melbourne again. When I did just that, he promptly cast me in *Lady Windermere's Fan* by Oscar Wilde.

I was to play Lady Agatha Carlisle, a young obedient girl of marriageable age who simply replies 'Yes, Mama' to all her mother's questions. The cast was star-studded: Robyn Nevin, Max Gillies, Frances O'Connor, Gerry Connolly and Sue Ingleton, along with a bunch of us jobbing actors. It was a brilliant opportunity to watch and learn from the best.

An actor named Greg Stone was cast as Mr Hopper, a jackaroo from Australia come to find a wife. I'd met Greg a month or so before at Playbox Theatre. A friend of mine was directing him in a Nick Enright play, *Good Works*, and I was introduced at drinks after rehearsal one Friday. I'd certainly found him handsome and he seemed nice, but my focus that evening was his castmate Helen Morse, an absolute acting hero of mine. I'd gone to see *Good Works* once it was playing and watched this man, Greg Stone, tear up the stage. His intensity was incredible, and I came away from the show with a massive crush. What a spunk! So it was a tiny bit of a thrill to be cast opposite one another in *Lady Windermere's Fan*, by which time we'd both independently released ourselves from any previous romantic attachments and began rehearsals as free agents.

The concept of Greg and me as an item was still not a fait accompli, and we flirted around one another for some time. In one scene on a balcony, the director gave us a note to make more of our Wildean flirtations. I blushed crimson at the suggestion and the director laughed at me, saying, 'They did flirt in those days, Rebekah.' I had desire written all over me in bold primary colours.

Greg was eager, but noncommittal; kind and respectful, but self-contained. He was hard to read. After six months of going out, I'd fallen in love with him, and I honestly couldn't be bothered being in a one-sided relationship. I told him I loved him and that I wanted to say so without fear of frightening him off. That I wanted to know how he felt, no matter what it was. I didn't want to invest more of myself than he was willing to give of himself. He proclaimed his love and we moved on from there.

Greg was in demand as an actor. Often he'd be working day and night, or he'd be on tour somewhere. Our love affair was dotted with trips interstate so I could see him in this show or that, and it was thrilling and adventurous.

Meanwhile, I was beginning to question my own dedication to acting, the result of some unhappy experiences and the greater competition for jobs in Melbourne. The theatre world is full of astoundingly good people: warm-hearted, generous folk. Often they're individuals who've been outsiders in their own lives and consequently are very accepting of others. There's nothing like the camaraderie of a cast backstage, with support, love and laughter, trust and friendship. But just one negative person can suck the joy out of a cast, and my tolerance for unnecessary drama is low. I prefer to save the drama for the stage, where I get paid for it.

I began to think of other occupations that would be fulfilling and settled on massage therapy. I enrolled at the Southern School of Natural Therapies, and I loved the study. The walls of my flat in Elwood were soon plastered with hundreds of notes recording muscle names, along with their origins and attachments. All the modalities of massage appealed to me; shiatsu, Swedish, reflexology and aromatherapy were all so enjoyable to learn and to give. I found myself really wanting to excel at my new profession.

Once I graduated, I promptly got a job at a day spa in St Kilda and rented a massage room above a flower shop in Glen Huntly. I worked six days a week, and loved the work and the clients. They'd often share with me their worries or concerns, hopes for their children or their relationships, and while I never gave advice, I would always look forward to their next visit to see if they'd resolved the issue or found another perspective. It was an obvious expansion of my interest in people, and in creating a space for reflection and temporary escape from the world's trials and tensions. To me, massage sessions weren't that different to performing. I liked helping people feel better, less alone, more connected to their hearts.

I still miss the grounding, centring calmness of being in that small, quiet space, focused on the wellbeing of another person. But there was a very good reason I put my massage career on hold: Greg and I were about to become parents.

2

Great expectations

Greg and I were married in our backyard in January 1999 by a lovely civil celebrant, Don Grant. Amazingly, we discovered many years later that Don was the father-in-law of Georgie's doctor, Associate Professor Michelle Telfer. Small world. That September, I became pregnant. I was thirty-two, and it felt very right.

My pregnancy progressed normally. A check-up by my doctor revealed I was having quite a big baby – or so she thought. I travelled to Perth to visit Greg's family and already had quite a pronounced baby belly at seventeen weeks. I felt mostly fine, but cigarette smoke and the smell of sausages were completely toxic to me and would make me dry-retch. I developed a passion for garlic bread and watermelon. I was also bone-tired, more profoundly tired than I had ever been.

On our return to Melbourne, I had an eighteen-week check-up with an obstetrician at the Monash Medical Centre not far from home. I'd been excited by the prospect of a water birth with as little intervention as possible. Greg and I arrived feeling a bit nervous, anticipating hearing our baby's heartbeat for the first time and checking out the facilities. It almost felt like an audition, as you had to fulfil certain criteria in order to birth there. If you were in a high-risk category for complications then it was simply not going to happen. The obstetrician, who by some stroke of luck we managed to have throughout my pregnancy and delivery – I was a public patient – was incredibly thorough, as you'd expect, but even so the consultation was less warm and fuzzy than I'd thought it'd be. I found myself taken aback by the barrage of questions.

The moment arrived for me to hear my baby's heartbeat. I hopped up onto the bed and, after palpating my stomach, the doctor held the Doppler to my belly. Quietly, she moved it from one spot to another. All the while, the soft, persistent swirl of a foetal heartbeat was audible. Proof of life. My own heart filled with pride. *Well done, bubba. You're doing great.* But the doctor kept moving the Doppler around. 'Okay,' she said, 'you either have your dates wrong, you have a growth on your uterus or there's more than one baby.'

Right, well, that was unexpected. If I was having a multiple birth, it pretty much guaranteed I wasn't going to be having that water birth. I was certain I had my dates right. Greg had been away on tour and we'd started trying for a baby when he got home, so unless it was an immaculate conception, my dates were rock solid. I wasn't fazed by the possibility of a growth on the uterus either. I just didn't feel that was it. By process of elimination, the slightly terrifying option of a multiple birth remained. We were duly booked in to have an ultrasound a few days later to confirm or rule out any of these possibilities.

Back home I perched myself on the toilet and cried. It was a lot to take in. I pored over my diary, checking and double-checking the dates. I simply couldn't have got it wrong. But as the days passed, Greg and I grew attached to the idea of having more than one baby. In fact, we both agreed it would now be a disappointment if we found out it wasn't so.

We arrived for our ultrasound with no small amount of anxiety and hope. Our technician was friendly and talkative, and put us at ease. I caught glimpses of a baby shape on the screen, only for it to morph into another unrecognisable curve or mass, another sweep of leg or spine or skull, then a different angle of the bulkhead that was my uterus. Honestly, I couldn't make head or tail of it. Then the technician slowly moved from one perfectly formed baby skull to another. Back and forth. 'Do you see what I'm seeing?' he said.

'Yes, two heads!' It was a relief to see them in their safe, warm bubbles, their little hearts pumping away. They were clearly fraternal twins. When I say clearly, we could see they weren't identical once it was pointed out. Both babies had their own placenta and their own amniotic sac. We didn't ask what sex they were. That was going to be a surprise.

Greg and I left the hospital on cloud nine. So overwhelmed was Greg that he couldn't find his way out of the car park. He had me in fits of laughter as we drove around and around the roundabout looking for the exit even though it was obvious. Each time he drove past the exit again, it would set me off. Thank god I was continent! We had such joy in our hearts. Two babies. A complete family, ready to go. It still makes us laugh to remember that day.

*

In February 2000, just after we discovered I was carrying twins and we were feeling full of excitement for our future, Greg's work called him away again. Greg has always said that acting is the best and worst job in the world. It can turn on a dime in curious ways. One week, you could be broke with no prospects; the next week you land an ad and are flown to some exotic location, put up in a five-star hotel. When the terrific roles come up, it's hard to turn them down, and if touring is involved then you go. This is harder to accommodate when you have children.

This show was *The Beauty Queen of Leenane,* by Martin McDonagh. Happily, Greg was to be finished and back before the babies' due date at the end of May. I stayed home, close to my regular doctors, and continued with my massage business.

Everything progressed well. The second trimester was terrific, and I felt healthy and energetic. Come 3 pm every day, though, I'd have to nap for a couple of hours. There were no two ways about it. My body and brain simply would no longer function and I had to rest. My belly was rapidly expanding. With two babies using me as a jungle gym, when they moved it looked as though I'd hidden a sack of wild kittens in there. It felt something like the scene from *Alien* just before poor John Hurt has a little creature burst out of his thorax. My cat Ollie would drape herself across my girth and I'd watch her undulate with the movements of these two floating universes. Ollie never batted an eyelid.

At some point Greg and I took a couple of antenatal classes, which were informative but not in the way we'd anticipated. The instructor would declare sagely that such and such would happen in labour, then turn to Greg and me and say, 'Of course, it will be different for you.' Having twins set our experience apart from the start, and – perhaps counterintuitively – because we had a high-risk pregnancy we were more relaxed about our birth plan, which became: 'Do whatever is necessary to bring two live babies into the world.'

A few things struck us as funny during these classes, the main one being that nobody could bring themselves to say the word 'vagina'. It absolutely staggered me that grown men, who'd quite literally put themselves into a vagina to create a baby, couldn't say the word. 'Down there' was the muffled phrase of choice. The women were coy, too. There we all were, pretending that what was about to happen to us wasn't the most visceral, raw, physical and genital-centric moment of our lives. Regardless of how you conceive or deliver your child in the end, a vagina is pretty central to the story. Greg and I entertained ourselves by mentioning vaginas as often as possible. You have to get your kicks somehow.

By the third trimester, my belly had become uncomfortably large, my feet began to swell and my hands lost their feeling. The only shoes I could wear were moccasins, and the lovely Pam at the Monash Medical Centre gave me wrist guards to help with my numb hands. I had to stop work. My clients were beginning to feel guilty about getting a massage from such a heavily pregnant woman anyway. Getting around and looking after myself became harder and harder. Then I developed awful heartburn and reflux, and needed to sleep sitting upright. Quite frankly, if I lay down, I couldn't get out of bed anyway.

Ollie the cat was getting mean. She knew something was up and started to lash out. One morning, I woke feeling someone looming over me. It was Ollie with her paw paused, ready to strike. She did, and caught me in the lip deep enough that I had trouble disengaging her claw. From then on, she was locked in the laundry at night. Filthy cat claws are a danger to pregnant women and I was taking no chances.

The bigger I got, the more isolated I became. Without clients coming to my house every day, I had very little contact with people. Although I missed Greg terribly, on doctor's advice I couldn't travel to be with him. Thankfully, I had lovely friends who'd pop in for a cuppa and bring cake. Even so, I was trapped in my body, in my house, in Melbourne. While I was cheerful enough during the day, I found the nights increasingly long and lonely because I was sporadically awake for much of them – nature's way of preparing us for the broken sleep to come. I started leaving the television on in our bedroom.

A couple of times during his tour, Greg made it back home. His schedule didn't allow for much longer than twenty-four hours, and the flight to and from Brisbane gobbled some of that up. But it was great when he came back because he could take me out somewhere – anywhere! He could help get me in and out of the shower and bed, and it was so good to not have to cope on my own. Above all, he was my best friend and we could share this amazing, incredible experience in person.

On one of these occasions, Greg took me for a walk along High Street in Armadale. By then I was enormous. I was wearing my trusty moccasins and the only maternity gear that would now fit me: a stretchy skirt and polo top, and they were at capacity. Greg and I noticed that people were responding to us differently than had previously been the case. A couple strolling along hand in hand, the woman pregnant, usually elicited smiles both knowing and kind, but now people tended to take a look and quickly avert their eyes. It made us laugh so much. Evidently, I was too huge to contemplate; I was unpleasantly, frighteningly big. So much so that the usual experience of warmth was replaced with panic: 'She's gunna blow! Run!'

It wasn't long before I really couldn't cope on my own anymore. I called Greg and asked him if he could pull out of the tour. Fortunately, the company had by then organised a replacement for Greg – someone who happened to be a close family friend of ours, Greg Saunders. The timing was right. I could no longer drive because my belly wouldn't fit behind the steering wheel, and if I adjusted the seat my feet couldn't touch the pedals and my hands couldn't reach the wheel. Plus they were still numb. That meant I wasn't able to get myself to the hospital or the supermarket, and I could only stand for short periods before my feet would swell and also go numb. I was short of breath and my lips were going blue.

In all this time, had I found out the sex of the babies, painted the nursery a certain colour and bought lots of clothes and playthings in line with their presumed gender? No. Other people talked about gender a lot, but it wasn't high on my list of priorities. My main goal was simply to have a safe birth. From thirty-four weeks is considered full term for twins, and there are all sorts of potential complications that might prevent a vaginal delivery, which I was hoping for. At any rate, as a woman carrying two babies, my responsibility was to bring them into this world, in collaboration with doctors and midwives, and I needed to be flexible about how that would happen.

During the last five weeks of my pregnancy, I was given weekly scans, so I had plenty of opportunities to find out what sex the babies were. The technician always asked and I always said, 'No, thank you.' Finding out seemed like cheating, like opening your presents before Christmas Day. Disclosure: one year, I did open all my presents before Christmas. There were raised eyebrows on Christmas morning when the tape lifted off remarkably easily on all my gifts, and I had to do a good job of feigning surprise. I've never done it again. And with my babies, I was resolute I wouldn't spoil the surprise.

I didn't have an instinct or a preference either way. Having grown up with sisters but no brothers, and having only ever gone to an all-girls school, I'd probably had more experience with girls. But tipping the scales the other way, I also had eight nephews and three nieces, and I loved playing with those kids when I got the chance, the boys and the girls. Adorable ragamuffins.

Having Greg home with me was such a relief. I'd been harbouring a tiny fear that I would go into labour while he was in Brisbane and he'd miss the birth. I had been quietly plagued by what-ifs, and now I didn't have to think about them anymore. Greg could also shop, take me to the hospital and take care of me when I could no longer do it myself. I started eating better because he could cook for me. Best of all was that we could go through this great big experience together.

We needed to buy a few essentials: bath, change table, baby rockers. The cot was the one I'd had as a baby, which had been handed down to my eldest sister, Cathy, for her two boys, Luke and Jack. I'd painted it a buttermilk colour and Greg's mum had made a Winnie-the-Pooh cot protector to go around the edge – not the Disney Pooh but the original drawings, so it was really beautiful. Most of the clothes we had were hand-me-downs from friends. My mum had knitted some beautiful cardigans, caps and booties. I had bought a few onesies and some sweet Bunnykins outfits that would suit a boy or girl. Oh, and four tiny soft toys of Pooh, Piglet, Tigger and Eeyore, plus a cot mobile. That was it.

Ollie had gone from acting weird to not coping at all. Piles of clothes started appearing that didn't smell like her people, and the sight of a cot set up with bedding and rockers ready to go pushed her over the edge. She peed and pooed over *everything*.

At thirty-seven weeks I was utterly exhausted, and at my weekly check-up I asked the obstetrician if there was any chance that, if I hadn't gone into labour within the week, I could be induced. I was numb in some places, in pain in others, not sleeping, and my skin, face and lips were pale and swollen. The skin on my belly was covered with a painful, agonisingly itchy rash from being stretched beyond capacity and all I could do was smother it in calamine lotion to cool the irritation. I felt that if I continued the pregnancy beyond thirty-eight weeks, I'd be too physically exhausted to attempt a vaginal delivery, let alone care for two babies afterwards. The obstetrician agreed, and I was booked in for one week's time. The certainty made life a little lighter, but I was convinced I'd go into labour before then. My cervix had already shortened and was dilating, so my body was primed.

The night before I was to be induced, towards the end of May 2000, I watched the Olympic swim team trials on TV. Hayley Lewis had stopped swimming to have a child and was making a comeback, hoping to make the Australian team. Even though my girth measured almost the same as my height, I imagined that surely I'd be able to make a physical recovery too, though not to an Olympic standard obviously.

That evening, I sat in the bath with a flannel over my belly to soothe the constant creep of stretching across my skin. I could feel my babies, pressing deep into my rib cage and pelvis, cramped and distinct in their movements. Twin 1, whose head was engaged, had slow, strong kicks. Twin 2, lying across my diaphragm, was fast, otter-like. All of us were ready to burst forth. Later that night, in a moment of joyful and excited optimism, I did my hardest to dance to some glam rock but the high kicks were underwhelming. It was strange to know that the next day I would see their faces, would hold them in my arms and to my breasts. We were packed. We had four names chosen in order of preference and combinations of sex. We were excited. We knew it was going to be a big day.

The drive to the hospital was slightly surreal. Two baby capsules fitted in the back of our car were a confident assertion that all would go well. There was no point in thinking otherwise.

On arrival, after having a final scan, we were taken to our birthing suite. Twin 1 was still engaged so it was safe to attempt a vaginal delivery; if they hadn't been in position I would have required a caesarean. The room was clinical but comfortable. Two cribs were lined up against the wall. One looked like a regular medical baby table and the other looked like a life-support system. That should have been a clue about how things often go with delivering twins. But it was time to get on with the show – no time to ruminate – and I was committed to giving this my all.

My regular obstetrician wasn't rostered on until later, so it was another doctor who broke my waters. It was an unusual experience to have someone not look me in the eye or say hello, but focus 'down there' on inserting a finger with a hook on the end to break Twin 1's amniotic sac. The midwives, bless them, had forewarned me he wasn't a talker so I was able to view his silence as quirky rather than downright rude. In short order, I was hooked up to two monitors, administered with induction drugs and had the epidural fitted ready to go if or when it was needed.

All was smooth and calm and contractions began slowly, despite the monitor suggesting they were relatively strong. Perhaps bizarrely, I fancied a cup of tea and a Cherry Ripe. No sooner had I put the cup to my lips than I was slammed by a huge and painful contraction. It was on.

With each contraction, it felt as though I was being ripped in two. Twin 1 was heading south and Twin 2 was being pushed north. Gradually, I went deeper and deeper into myself. The room became distant; the people in it, too. I heard everything they said, but I was no longer there. My world consisted of the pain and the babies. I was seized by the fullness of my body, the depth of the struggle, the focus on each changing moment within a contraction, and responded to the guidance of the midwives. I began to feel the urge to push but needed the epidural while delivering Twin 1 in readiness for Twin 2 to be born. In a flash, the room filled with nurses and doctors: two obstetricians, two paediatricians, one anaesthetist.

The epidural worked instantly. I came back into the room. It was as if I hadn't seen Greg all day. Outside it was dark already, but I had work to do. I could no longer feel how hard I was pushing.

'A crown!' someone announced. My hand was guided down to feel the top of the head, and that was all the encouragement I needed. As I pushed for dear life, slowly but surely emerged Twin 1: a boy! Greg cut the umbilical cord then brought the baby close to me. 'Hello, George,' he said. I was overjoyed.

The midwives pulled our attention back to the job at hand. We had another baby to deliver and it was showing signs of distress. An examination revealed that Twin 2's amniotic sac hadn't yet broken, and the baby, who apparently had been head-down until then, had scooted off in the opposite direction and needed to be manually brought down the birth canal. Various techniques were applied and at one point I wondered if I'd been poorly cast in an episode of *All Creatures Great and Small*. The obstetrician – my regular one, who was now on shift – had found a limb and was bringing this little one down for a breech delivery.

The midwives were urging me on. I heard the words, 'You have to get this baby out, now.' Twin 2 was getting stressed, and too long a delay would mean a trip up to theatre. By then I was indescribably tired, and I was scared because I couldn't feel how hard I was pushing or if I was pushing at all. Somehow, I delivered the bottom half of our second child.

'It's another boy!' the midwife said. With that I pushed and pushed so hard that I half-expected to pop an eyeball. The instant the baby was out, he was rushed to the waiting crib – the one that had all the bells and whistles. He lay there limp, and the specialists whipped an oxygen mask over his entire face; the atmosphere in the room was tense. I remember delivering two placentas and being stitched up, all the while watching my little baby boy struggling to find his breath.

Greg was standing there mutely, holding Georgie. Like him, I fixed my gaze on the activity around that crib. Our baby's tiny chest was heaving, and his little body was red. We were watching him like hawks.

When Greg and I later compared our reactions to this moment, he told me that as he stood there with Georgie, watching Harry struggle to come to life, he knew with absolute certainty that he'd do anything for this child. Should he need special care or have ongoing issues, he'd do everything in his power to give him a good life.

Meanwhile, I lay on the bed, a wreck. I was studying the body language of the doctors, catching glimpses of our little boy through the crowd of skilled and caring hands. They'd lift a tiny limb and let it fall, gently pat and tap him, waiting for him to grab his life.

Come on! Come on, my love.

The tension in the room continued to build. How far away I felt: I couldn't be near my baby. I hadn't even touched him.

Then, bam! His arms shot up and there came a cry. Quiet chatter immediately broke out and there was palpable relief. Everybody started moving again. The buzzing over me resumed and then someone brought my baby over. Harrison. He was held before me; I wasn't invited to hold him. He was grunting, red, tiny and breathless, and needed to go straight to the special care nursery. Within seconds he was bundled up and taken off. Greg handed Georgie to a midwife and followed Harry.

I began shivering violently and was covered in the warmest, loveliest blankets. Georgie was placed in my arms for our first cuddle. Unexpectedly, I found that the two of us were alone in the room apart from a woman who was quietly tidying up. I suddenly needed to vomit, as the medication that had been administered to prevent further blood loss had just kicked in. I asked for something to be sick into. Swiftly, the woman handed me a kidney bowl. In the suite next door, a mother-to-be was screaming blue murder. Good for her. In this state of altered reality, I sat there with one baby in my arms, with the other I had not yet held somewhere else in the building.

Utter exhaustion took hold as the warmth of the blankets entered every cell of my body. As soon as I stopped feeling sick, I was finally able to take in the face of my child. I registered the dark hair, the features, the serious expression. Oh, I recognised that face! There were reflections of family in that brow. Skin jaundiced but smooth. Beautiful long fingers. I knew this baby, this robust little person, my son George.

Greg returned from settling Harry in to the special care nursery and Georgie was placed in a crib. I needed Greg's help to shower. Moving gingerly, I was able to stand under that wonderfully warm water. When I glanced at my reflection in the bathroom mirror, I was shocked to see myself sheet-white – almost opaque – and my lips blue. I was barely able to walk. It was as though I'd spent the day being a punching bag for a heavyweight boxer. The belly that had that morning been full now hung down like an apron, a giant balloon deflated after the party ends. Blood was pouring out of me. I looked frightening and I felt overwhelmed. It was wonderful to put on fresh pyjamas, which made me feel slightly more myself. To ease the pain of the episiotomy, the nurses gave me a condom filled with ice, wrapped in a huge sanitary pad; it quickly became my favourite and only form of pain relief. I was put in a wheelchair, Georgie was placed in my arms and, accompanied by a midwife, Greg wheeled me to the ward, where I crawled into bed.

Georgie was taken to the nursery and put into a sun box for jaundice, and Greg headed home via the special care nursery. After devouring a packet of sandwiches and a cup of tea, I fell into a deep sleep that was broken intermittently by the ward buzzer going off just outside my door or my IV beeping and a nurse coming in to change it over. But then another sound broke through it all, rousing me fully. The sound of a baby crying. A forceful, determined yell. *Mum!* I knew it was my baby.

A nurse brought Georgie in for our first feed. I looked out the window, noticing that the wet night had turned into a grey and sunless morning. With my newborn snuffling and gurgling at my breast, I knew that nothing would ever be the same again. In the space of a day, I'd been transformed. I was the mother of twins. Two beautiful baby boys had been brought safely into the world and were relying on me. I'd better meet the challenge.

When I look back, I realise that Harry has always danced to his own tune. That should have been obvious to me when he came into the world feet-first, struggling for breath. It was as though birth had thrust him into the world before he'd finished packing. As though he'd had to run to catch the train.

The day after the birth, Greg wheeled me up to the special care nursery to feed him. Harry looked terribly fragile in the incubator and I felt intimidated by the monitors and attachments. There was nothing wrong with him, we were assured; he was just very tired from the birth and they were keeping an eye on his oxygen levels and temperature. We were told he could be with us soon. He was a kilo lighter than Georgie, with a staccato cry as opposed to his twin's deafening holler. Georgie has always had a powerful set of lungs! It was only their second day on this earth and already their distinct personalities had begun to manifest. I rarely referred to them as 'the twins'; they were always 'Harry' and 'Georgie'. Also, as they grew bigger, because of their size difference I would often be asked what the age gap was.

The third day after the babies were born was hard emotionally. Harry still hadn't been released from the special care nursery. It made me teary that he wasn't with Georgie and me all the time, and I was positive he'd thrive with us. I was beginning to get my strength back and my milk was coming in. I'd had the luxury of time with Georgie and now I yearned to have the same with Harry, to get to know him and bond with him.

At last Harry was moved to my room. The first thing I did was place my infants side by side on the bed and stare at them, my hands clasped to my chest. A wave of love surged through me, along with fear. How in heaven's name was I supposed to look after two babies? Harry promptly vomited. So began the journey of discovering and loving these new humans.

I was a proud mother. As I wheeled my twins around the ward or into the nursery, I felt awesome. I'd just pushed two little people out of my vagina. Some of the other new mums would steal glances at me as I arranged the pillows and loaded the twins up to feed them – I learned how to tandem-feed using what's known as the footy hold. Those women probably felt sorry for me. But I neither cared what they thought nor felt the slightest bit sorry for myself. I was really excited and couldn't wait to get home. Thankfully, on the glorious day of our discharge from hospital, Greg had finally figured out how to exit the hospital car park.

Caring for two babies at the same time is intense. I'd surrendered myself totally to their care and they were sleeping, feeding and growing as they should. I was learning their little quirks. For their part, they worked as a team to keep me on my toes.

When my mum came to stay about a month after the babies were born, she persuaded me not to be too worried when they cried. 'At their age, it's the only exercise they get,' she said. The most intense crying occurred at about 11 pm. With hope in my heart that they'd have a long sleep so I, too, could get to bed, I'd put them in the double pram and roll them back and forth or wheel them around the house, trying to get them to nod off. One of them would begin. If it was Georgie, we'd be in for a full-throttled tragedy in several parts. Harry would listen respectfully and quietly until, exhausted, Georgie fell silent. In the buzzing silence, like the one you get after a rock concert, my ears would tingle with relief until Harry, who'd been comforted by Georgie's crying, would begin his tale of woe in staccato notes, beginning tentatively then building to quite a thrilling crescendo. After perhaps a few more notes here and there from Georgie – it's hard for her to stay silent – a blissful hush would descend. Greg and I thought it was like trying to capture and sedate wild animals, so we referred to successful sleeping as 'two rhinos down'.

*

It was lovely having Mum with me for support. She'd brought five babies into this world and was an incredibly pragmatic and capable woman. Mum had me when she was forty, so Georgie and Harry were some years behind her other grandchildren and she was happy to be around babies again.

Mum gave me a lot of confidence in myself and helped me not to feel so overwhelmed by it all. But I noticed a change in her. She wasn't able to problem-solve as well as she had previously. Making a cup of tea in a strange environment wasn't easy for her, for example. And while our conversation flowed as it always had, somehow she wasn't herself. I found myself worrying about Mum.

When Greg's mum and dad, Jenny and Roy, visited us two weeks later, we had a feeling of deja vu. Roy's state of cognitive health was worsening. He'd been showing significant signs of decline the previous year, at our wedding. It turned out that Mum and Roy were both struggling with dementia. This period marked the beginning of the long goodbye for both of them; our two families experienced simultaneously the deep sadness that comes when a loved one struggles with this illness.

The days with Harry and Georgie all rolled into one. I was thoroughly enjoying myself, even though it's the hardest physical work I've ever done. There were at least ten nappy changes a day as well as baths, playtime, walks and sleeps. In the evening, when Greg came home from work, it was fun to share a meal and do the evening routine together. Breastfeeding was the most demanding part of my new role as a mother:

I'd find myself on the couch for at least eight hours a day, as each feed would be close to an hour long. As the babies grew heavier and bigger it was no longer possible to feed them at the same time. My lap wasn't big enough to accommodate two babies at once, even in the football hold, and feeding involved a lot of lifting, manoeuvring into position and readjusting. Hard when you're on your own. My hands were no longer numb but I had the most shocking pain in my wrists if I lifted anything even slightly heavy, and the pain would shoot up to both elbows and weaken my grip. For years afterwards, these joints would swell up when I exercised.

Breastfeeding can be the nexus of anxiety for mothers: a one-stop trip to Guiltsville for some and a status symbol of successful mothering for others. I wasn't so much anxious about it as simply trying to find a way to look after my own wellbeing. Keeping up with the demands was full on. I'd joined a twin club – a group of mothers who provided me with handy hints – and had been reading up on how mothers of twins were able to feed for a year. How the hell did they manage that? Turns out they have a pretty solid support team around them, with plenty of family on hand to cook meals and help out according to rosters and rotations. Greg and I didn't have that. Almost all of our family lived interstate, and my sister Jessie lived in England.

With or without support, I needed to begin venturing out into the world again. I'd been house-bound for months and months, even before the babies were born, and the occasional walk around the neighbourhood with the double pram wasn't making much of a dent in my unmet social needs. Unlike mothers of single babies,

I couldn't pop down to the local café with a baby papoose to read the paper. It was a military operation even to get out the front door. By the time I got to where I was going, I was usually stuffed, and if the babies needed a quick top-up in public, I needed pillows and props to position them both.

I spoke to the maternal health-care nurse and decided that perhaps it was time to introduce supplementary feeding, which meant that Greg or whoever else was around could bottle-feed one baby while I breastfed the other. If I was on my own, I could breastfeed one and bottle-feed the other at the same time. Bonza! Straightaway, I felt less trapped at home and everyone was a bit happier.

Your own babies can be mesmerising. For someone like me, who wasn't especially kid-oriented before I had my own, this was a revelation. Though I'd loved goofing around with my nephews and nieces, I'd been happy to hand them back, thank you. Having my own was a different story. I was completely and unashamedly besotted.

When Georgie and Harry were only months old, I began reading to them. At bathtime we'd read together from the little plastic bath books that had no words, just pictures, and often a squeaky button or some sensory aspect to them. Of the many things parenthood potentially offered in terms of activities, reading to my children was at the top of my list. Being an actor, I was able to bring the characters to life. Soft toys would become puppets that interacted with Georgie and Harry, and songs were a chance to move their little bodies around, causing ripples of giggles. They particularly liked songs from *Play School* such as 'A Frog Went Walking on a Summer's Day', 'Up in the Air I Fly' and 'Open, Shut Them'. All the hits! This ritual of reading was to continue as the years went by. Every evening after their meal and bath, we'd snuggle on the couch. There'd be a child on either side of me, nuzzling under my wings, and we'd enter a story together. For me, this was the most precious time. Occasionally, I'd read with one eye open, yawning at every second line, but a story would still be read.

Though they both adored storytime and were equally trans-fixed, from the outset Georgie and Harry responded to most other things differently. Georgie is, was and always will be talk-ative. While breastfeeding her, I got a running commentary, with loud gulps, sighs, eye contact and vocalisations letting me know how it was all going. Harry would fall asleep on the job and I had to tickle his cheek to get him moving again. Georgie liked to be close to me, and once she was on her feet at twelve months, she followed me everywhere. She'd pull every last pot out of my kitchen cupboard, spread toys extrava-gantly across the floor and always have some item of clothing draped across her person. She was a busybody, always wanting to know what was going on. Harry was a lot more laidback. He was the cutest baby, with soft, dark brown eyes that twinkled with mischief, and luscious lashes, a dimpled smile and an easygoing nature.

When the babies were born, Greg was reading a Haruki Murakami book. Subsequently, Harry was often called Haruki, which then evolved into the somewhat lengthy Haruki Kook Mook Dook, later shortened to just Mook.

Harry's extraordinary concentration became evident when at around the age of twelve months he discovered the buckle on his highchair. He'd play with that buckle for hours, brow furrowed, trying to work it out. He then developed a love for cars or, more precisely, the way the wheels rolled along, and would move them forward and back, forward and back, looking very closely at the movement of the wheels. It was fascinating to watch.

It was also fascinating to watch an amazing sibling relationship emerge between Harry and Georgie. From eight weeks old, they were cracking each other up on their floor rug. Their push-up exercise really gave them the giggles, and I don't know for sure, of course, but it looked to me as though they thought it was hilarious when one lost control of their head and toppled to the side. When they were about a year old they got into a new habit: they'd wake up ridiculously early, pull themselves to standing in their cots and sing what sounded like old Irish drinking songs, then fall about laughing.

Life trundled on, a mixture of good days, bad days, days on end when everyone was sick, days when it felt as if we'd been awake for millennia. Sleep was a major topic of conversation; in fact, it almost became a currency. Something to barter or bargain with.

One morning, when we were living in Williamstown, I popped the kids in the pram and we went to the bakery, where I bought a sausage roll to share and a coffee for me. We were sitting out the front of the bakery and I was feeling well pleased with myself for making it out the door by nine. I'd even had a shower! Out of the corner of my eye, I spotted a woman approaching, a knowing smile on her face. This wasn't unusual when wheeling around twins, as I'd discovered. You get stopped by everybody.

People would stand in front of the pram in the supermarket, peer in and pronounce, 'One's awake and one's asleep!' Or they might offer a thoughtful line like, 'Rather you than me,' or perhaps this original number: 'Double trouble!' At which I'd return serve with, 'Twice as nice!' In hindsight, assumptions made by strangers that one was a boy and one a girl seem prescient, but at the time I thought them presumptuous. Still do, in fact. But on this particular morning, I was feeling on top of things and ready for whatever was thrown at me. Or so I thought. The woman got closer, veered towards me and said with compassion, 'I've got twins, too. Older. It gets better.' I must have looked like something the cat dragged in! I could see the funny side, but it was still a little deflating.

I was at home while Greg was working. His hours tended to vary. Sometimes he was busy at night performing; at other times, there'd be rehearsals during the day. When the kids were almost a year old, I got back into massaging one or two days a week, depending on bookings. I also decided it might be time to get back to treading the boards again. Acting was a skill I had, and if I could land a job or two, the money would be helpful.

Aside from the odd cold, I had two healthy, happy kids. All the age-related milestones Harry and Georgie either met months ahead or took their own sweet time to achieve. Harry didn't walk until he was fifteen months old, perfectly content scooting about on his knees, but then he'd crawled long before Georgie, who could only go backwards once she first got mobile. Often, she'd get stuck under the couch and let out a cry of frustration.

At no point during this time was I concerned about the gender expression of my two children. It simply wasn't on the radar. My main concern was not losing them at the park once they learned how hilarious it was to run in opposite directions.

3

Toy Story

Much is said about toys and children, and the countless conversations I've had over the years have convinced me that we really need to revise some of our assumptions on this subject. Greg and I weren't wealthy and we didn't have the spare money – or indeed the inclination – to buy lots of toys, let alone fancy ones. Many of Harry and Georgie's toys were second-hand, and they got a good workout from the young Stones, let me assure you! Our family friend Joanie, an opera singer, had gifted a couple of Winnie-the-Pooh four-wheeled bikes, and the kids happily spent hours on those in the backyard. From the toy library we frequented, we'd choose blocks and Duplo, dinosaurs and puzzles, cars and farms for toy animals. From the *Trading Post*, Greg purchased a small slippery dip, which was a hit.

But as for all small kids, set Georgie and Harry up with a cardboard box, a few pots and pans and wooden spoons, and you'd have them entertained for hours. Sometimes, I used to put them to work 'painting' the house by giving them two buckets of water and two big paintbrushes. They'd be out the back for ages, slopping water all over the bricks.

At about two-and-a-half to three years old, their preferences began to show. Harry loved to dress up, but spent much of his time with his Matchbox cars and action figures. He loved them. If she could, Georgie would make a beeline for the dress-up corner and the princess dresses. She was drawn to anything that was pretty, frilly, sparkly or had a skirt that could swirl. Her preference didn't particularly concern me, but it was pronounced.

I loved discovering the world through their eyes. I loved the wonder and joy, the hugs and the laughs. The nude running around the house, the walks in the park, and the colourful baths that I would make for the kids.

'What colour bath would you like tonight, my darlings?'

'Purple!'

So we'd mix a little blue and red food colouring together then add bubbles. Bathtime was lovely fun. Georgie and Harry sat at either end, playing and chatting away merrily to one another. I sat on a stool beside the bath and we'd talk and laugh, sing silly songs. Their innocence was so divine.

'Shall we have some watermelon for dessert? Georgie, can you say "watermelon"?'

Georgie looked at me and valiantly made an attempt by wiggling her tongue around her mouth. I almost fell off my chair laughing. 'Say "watermelon" again, Georgie,' I said, tears in my eyes from laughing so hard. Again, her tongue wiggled out a sound with the same rhythm as 'watermelon' but with not a single vowel or consonant to rub together.

'Harry, can you say "watermelon"?'

He gave me a look and said, 'No.' This made me laugh even harder. Harry had such great comic timing.

It was during a bathtime just like this that Georgie first told me about her gender identity. Before that, she'd just been a really beautiful and expressive little person. A gentle little boy who enjoyed all things, but with a marked preference for what is seen as stereotypically female. As Georgie and Harry were edging close to three years old, bathtime was a good opportunity to talk about things like body parts and learning the correct name for each. We went through the whole body from top to bottom, including genitals. It was important, I thought, for a child to know about their body and be able talk about themself without embarrassment.

Harry was already dry and had run nude to the bedroom to put his pyjamas on. I was patting Georgie dry with a towel, those blue eyes looking into me deeply as they often did. We locked eyes. 'Mummy,' she said with cheery confidence, 'I don't want a penis, I want a vagina. I should be a girl.'

I was taken aback. 'But, darling, you're a beautiful little boy,' I countered. I finished drying her off and sent her on her way to get ready for bed, but there was something about the certainty with which she'd said those words that made me replay the scene in my mind. It was almost as though she'd put me on notice.

In the years that I've been supporting families, I've realised how common this experience is and that even the most progressive people, when their child shares something like this with them, can be floored. You might be the most 'woke' person in the world, but when it's your kid, statements like these can challenge everything you thought you were okay with. I really didn't know what to do or think or say about it, and I confided in Greg about what had happened. Was this something we should be alarmed about? Greg didn't appear overly perturbed: just leave it, it's probably nothing, he said. I agreed. Probably nothing. But I couldn't shake the feeling that it actually was something. The look in Georgie's eyes stayed with me.

Georgie and Harry's familiarity with anatomy was a useful education for them, and provided us with more classic comedic moments. Georgie, for reasons that are now obvious, had a fondness for the word 'vagina' and she wasn't afraid to use it in conversation.

One day, the four of us took a picnic to the beach. Greg and I sat on a blanket relaxing while we watched the kids running around on the sand not too far away. Walking towards them were a couple, a man and a woman who was heavily pregnant. We watched our two children greet them enthusiastically. We couldn't hear the conversation but could see the smiles of the adults. All of a sudden, they both looked slightly aghast. 'Ooh,' I said to Greg, 'you'd better check out what's going on there.'

Greg wandered over and asked if everything was okay. I heard them all laughing and when Greg returned he had a smile on his face.

'What happened?' I asked.

'Well, apparently Georgie pointed out to the lady that she had a baby in her tummy.'

'Good call,' I said.

'Yeah,' he said. 'She also told her that the baby was going to come out of her vagina. She warned her, "I think it's going to hurt."'

The two of us had a good laugh about it and were both quietly proud. Out of the mouths of babes.

Things continued to go swimmingly. Greg and I adored our little family; life was simple and full of love. We were alert but not alarmed, to use the vernacular of the day, about Georgie's expression of herself.

When Georgie was at the toy library she wanted to choose a Sleeping Beauty costume with a crown, and I was at a loss to explain to her why she couldn't have it. So I didn't bother. It's strange how I was already bracing for judgement from others. As we stood at the counter to check out our toy and dress-up choices, I was aware of my own discomfort at feeling I'd have to justify them. Georgie had been consistently choosing fairy wings and an old tutu from our dress-up collection, which consisted of costumes passed on from other family and friends, and had also commandeered a pair of tap shoes that were too big. Like a sylph, she'd dance around the house, a will-o'-the-wisp flitting from kitchen to bedroom and back again. None of this was on display, however, when she felt unsafe with new people or anyone she was unsure of. Even at a very young age, she instinctively recognised safe people and places in which to dress up.

On rainy days, we'd sometimes go to one of those large indoor play centres. Our favourite one had a dress-up corner. Georgie always headed straight for it and would rummage through the feral collection of grubby fabric to find her favourite item, a blue A-line skirt. She'd risk the friction burn on the back of her legs going down the big blow-up slide just to have that skirt on. On one occasion, she realised some kids were laughing at her for being a boy in a skirt, and from then on she rarely dressed up at that place – only if we went early in the day and there were few people there.

You know that phrase 'Let kids be kids'? Well, I caution you against taking it at face value. Beneath those deceptively simple words lies a world of judgement about gender roles, gender stereotypes and gender identity. Many would see comments like these as simple common sense: 'Boys are boys, and girls are girls, and that's the way it is, was and always will be.' But they don't work for everybody. For those who experience intersex conditions, wherein their physical sex characteristics don't fit the medical and social norms for male or female bodies, or for those who are transgender, non-binary or gender diverse, those rules simply don't apply. Rigid gender roles hurt us all.

Perhaps I'd agree with the phrase 'Let kids be kids' if people meant it literally – as a call to allow children the freedom to be themselves and to play and express themselves as they choose, safe in their own homes and schools from being sanctioned for the things that give them joy. Instead, the phrase is often used as a neurotic pushback against what is characterised as political correctness gone mad, a de facto 'warning' that there's an evil plan afoot to force us all to be genderless.

In terms of socialising with other children, Georgie and Harry started gently, by going to family daycare with only two other children. Occasionally, they received a hit of major social interaction. Over the years, Greg and I had built up a reputation for hosting legendary barbecues with our friendship group, and these had become an opportunity to gather our offspring for a big playdate. Still, it was a steep learning curve when the kids started preschool in 2005 and experienced other children en masse on a regular basis. They quickly worked out who they liked hanging out with and what games everyone liked to play.

Initially, Georgie would gravitate towards the dolls and 'feminine' dress-ups. But, again, she soon ascertained that it wasn't well received when she did this outside our home. I don't believe there was an incident; she just picked up a vibe. She'd race home afterwards to pop on her favourite skirt and spend the rest of the day in it. Her range of feminine dress-ups was limited only to what had been handed down to us. We didn't purchase anything for her; she made do with what was available.

I did buy two Buzz Lightyear costumes. Buzz was the 'Space Ranger' from *Toy Story*, and the kids loved the movie. The minute I gave Georgie her costume, she added a skirt to it and became Buzz's copilot, Mira Nova, a female Space Ranger and the Princess of Tangea. Mira Nova herself didn't wear a skirt but she did have long hair, which Georgie would make out of lengths of fabric, in addition to long, flowing trains out of towels or sheets.

And this was how it went. Anything Georgie had that she perceived as masculine or intended for a boy, she feminised. A truck, for instance, became a girl truck with a girl's name. She was attracted to all the female heroines in stories and in the media. One favourite was Atomic Betty, 'Galactic Guardian and Defender of the Cosmos!' from the animated series of the same name.

Like any kid, Georgie enjoyed all kinds of play. She loved cars and trucks, she loved Lego, she loved adventurous games and she and Harry both enjoyed hours in the sandpit or out in the garden digging around. Sometimes during a downpour, the three of us would put on gumboots and go out and feel the rain on our faces. The two of them would splash about in the drains, and half the time they'd pull their clothes off and run around in the nude. Moments like these ingrained in me the belief that we as a community get way too strung up about toys and clothes. Toys are toys; to ascribe a gender to them is ridiculous. Clothes are clothes; to ascribe a gender to them is limiting.

To me, Georgie was Georgie. We thought perhaps our son might grow up to be gay, and to Greg and me that was absolutely a non-issue. I recognise that many gay people still experience discrimination daily and that vigilance is called for; there's a need to address this. But we'd have embraced a gay child without question. Not that we were jumping to conclusions; it was more that we were ready to accept our children for who they were, and were open-minded. Obviously, not every child who dresses up in clothing usually worn by one sex or the other is transgender or gender diverse. As parents, we knew that kids like to dress up, play-act and pretend, which is another reason that for so long we thought nothing of the way Georgie was expressing herself. However, Georgie kept telling me she was a girl. In this she was absolutely unwavering.

My family's experience is our own. In no way does what I'm describing reflect the range of possibilities for when a person will feel comfortable or ready to share their understanding of themself. For many young gender-diverse people, it takes a long time to identify feelings of unease or difference, and to articulate their source. For others, that process takes longer still. Some people keep this truth hidden in their hearts until they reach breaking point.

Georgie, as a young person, was always upfront about herself, sometimes to comic effect. One day, Greg was driving somewhere with the kids, who were three or four at the time. Georgie had quite a nasty cold, and was snuffling and snotty in the back seat. Greg, feeling sorry for her, said, 'Oh, you poor little bugger.'

'I'm not a bugger,' she sniffed. 'I'm Cinderella!'

As Harry grew older, two things became clear: he was hilarious and he was an original. By preschool, he was creating amazing dioramas featuring all our toys – Lego, dragons, figurines, superheroes. Detailed stories emerged from these worlds he created, which would be spread all over the playroom floor. Each character or prop was perfectly placed in relationship to the others. It was mind-blowing.

For Christmas, we bought the kids some Madeline dolls – from the character created by children's author Ludwig Bemelmans – and furniture to kit out a cardboard doll's house I'd purchased at IKEA. Georgie and Harry both enjoyed watching *Madeline* on television. The stories were set in a boarding school in Paris and were really sweet. Madeline had two special friends: Pepito, who was the Spanish ambassador's son from next door, and Genevieve, the dog who had rescued Madeline from the Seine. Harry spent hours poring over the details of that little house – the pictures on the wall, the tiny books and candlestick – to arrange it all in a perfect tableau. He was excellent at entertaining himself. Independent, imaginative and inventive.

Harry was also extremely sensitive, easily frustrated and had trouble managing his temper. Around the age of five, when I started playing board games with the kids, Harry couldn't handle the randomness of the roll of the dice or a slide down a ladder back to the beginning. He'd get mad, want to give up, and if he lost or came last, he would never want to play that game again. None of our efforts to educate him out of this – including telling him sternly to pull his socks up – worked. Greg mentioned he had displayed similar traits as a boy and had grown out of them, so we weren't overly worried. We loved our idiosyncratic little Mook, our nutty professor. He loved gathering food from the kitchen – flour, sugar, food colouring and so on – to concoct potions and 'scientific experiments'. Greg helped him set up a laboratory in a shed in the backyard, just beyond the cubby. Grandma bought him a lab coat with his name embroidered on it, and we bought him a microscope with real-life slides of blood, animal tissue, hair and wood.

The start of school approached, and there was mounting excitement in our house. Both the kids were looking forward to it despite the nerves. They were hungry for more stimulation, more activities, more social interaction, more of everything. School was just the place.

Preschool had been fun, but Georgie and Harry wanted to learn to read and write, venture out and expand their horizons that bit more. They were both ready. So were Greg and I.

4

Welcome to school

In 2006 the kids began school with their year of prep. A good friend of mine, Lou, had twins at the same school and we met in the playground at drop-off time. She sidled up to me and said, 'How are you feeling?'

'Great,' I replied. 'I can't wait. We're so ready.'

It felt somehow traitorous to be saying those words. All around us were parents shedding tears as they watched their little ones toddle into school, swimming in huge uniforms and giant backpacks.

'I know!' said Lou. 'It's bloody fantastic. You want to go for a coffee?'

This was an exciting day. It gave me extra confidence knowing that Georgie and Harry had each other, even though Greg and I had asked for them to be placed in different classes. We wanted them to develop in their own way and with a sense of independence.

So it began: the daily routine of packing lunch boxes, checking the plethora of school notes and being there for pick-up.

Knowing what I know now, I might have chosen a different school. I might have chosen a different kind of educational model. Back then, Greg and I assumed that our kids – like any new students – would go through a period of adjustment to their new environment. What I now suspect is that both of them were 'learning' that, somehow, there was something wrong with them.

Within the first few weeks, Georgie encountered problems. She came home one day insisting she needed to get a very short haircut. This piqued my attention as she'd always liked to wear her hair slightly on the longer side, not shoulder length but certainly longer than her brother's. Now she wanted it off?

When I asked her why the change of heart, she told me a boy in her class had been teasing her because, according to him, long hair made Georgie look like a girl.

'Do you want to have short hair?'

'No, but he'll stop teasing me if I get it cut.'

'I'll do whatever you want me to do, Georgie, but if you get your hair cut it needs to be because you want it short, not because he does.'

'I want it short.'

So we went and got her hair cut short, and I could see something in her shrink. Something in me shrank, too.

Then, another day, a kid – possibly the same one – teased Georgie about the colour of her water bottle. It was pink with a purple lid. 'That's a girl's bottle,' the child declared.

In prep, the children had their lunch indoors under the

supervision of their teacher, who had overheard and at this point intervened. 'Georgie has Georgie's drink bottle. It's not a girl's drink bottle, it's Georgie's,' she said.

Incidents such as these continued for the three-and-a-half years Georgie was at the school. Although it didn't happen every day, and it presented in subtle as well as overt ways, Georgie's expression of herself was constantly questioned. Older kids were the main problem for her, and she tried to avoid them. What was amazing was how she continued to be outgoing and formed strong friendships, even while constantly honing her ability to identify who was safe and who wasn't. Georgie was open with her friends about who she was and how she felt about herself. There was no secrecy or shame, and she often played a girl in their make-believe games. I was so proud of her courage though so scared for her at the same time.

One of her friends – let's call him Phil – a beautiful little fellow with a Christopher Robin countenance, came from a Christian background. He showed no sign of being in any way perplexed by Georgie. Her expression was perfectly natural to him, so he explained to himself not that Georgie was a mistake but that God had made a mistake: He had accidentally given her a boy's body when she had a girl's heart and mind.

One Saturday morning I encountered a despondent Georgie. She had a cold and was a bit out of sorts, and I asked if there was anything else the matter.

She replied, 'Phil told me God will answer my prayers, and that it only takes two minutes for a prayer to reach heaven. I prayed so much last night and I've still got a cold and I've still got a boy's body!'

When she was four she'd asked me when the good fairy was going to turn her into a real girl. God, fairies, adults – all were letting her down.

Meanwhile, Harry wasn't having the smoothest ride at school, either. He's always been a person of few words until he has something to say. This is fundamental to his nature. Harry doesn't do small talk, and if you chat about something he's not interested in, he'll quietly tune out. From a tender age, he could also be remarkably direct – not with any malice or forethought, but his words could seem abrupt, especially when they came from one so young.

Gradually, I was realising that the skills of social interaction were emerging as an issue for Harry. Things like how to relate to people when no two were alike. How to master the sometimes complex conventions of human interaction: where honesty was valued but only under certain conditions; where being yourself was always encouraged but rarely rewarded; where difference could be tolerated but was sometimes punished. It was a confusing mix for him. It's a confusing mix for most of us!

At the same time as Harry was painfully sensitive to his surroundings and experiences, he was also struggling to navigate or process them. Once he hit upon a subject that fascinated him, though, he was off, and it was delightful to hear his voice. He was very articulate, often using adult phrasing and words with complex meanings, which were chosen precisely and delivered in a posh way that amazed those who were lucky enough to hear him when he was on a roll.

Harry was always ever so slightly lost in a school environment. He preferred the friendship of one or two close people rather than a big group, he was small and you could describe him as a little socially awkward. These factors conspired to isolate him at some point every year and made it easy for bullies to target him, which they did. But Harry has never wanted to change himself to 'fit in', and never wanted to hang out with people he didn't connect with. For this reason alone, he is one of the bravest people I know, someone with a lot of integrity. If Harry Stone is hanging out with you, he means it.

At school, finding a friend who was like him was difficult for Harry. He loathed anything competitive, and finding activities that he could enjoy was my yearly challenge. We tried ballet, swimming, karate, Little Athletics, circus skills, chess, Minecraft workshops, gaming workshops, piano and drama classes. These final two were the longest-lasting activities, the ones that reflect his preferences and talents.

But nothing came or has come close to Harry's love of writing or his incredible talent for it, as we were to see in the years to follow.

Towards the end of 2006, tension between Greg and me was beginning to build around Georgie's insistence that she was female. There was a silence hanging in the air between us. It was loudest when we lay beside one another in bed. In the past this had been a time when we'd talk about the day's events or share some small question or vulnerability that might have been plaguing us. The intimacy was now frozen, and I could almost feel my breath rising to the ceiling to form stalactites of unspoken words. To break the silence would mean bringing everything crashing down on top of us. So I lay in the dark, tense, resentful, scared and feeling alone, wondering how I could navigate this.

The discord was evident in Greg's off-the-cuff remarks or carefully worded admonishments. I got the sense that he felt somehow, something I was doing to Georgie was making his son confused. I was deeply hurt and felt abandoned at a time when I really needed him. To show Greg my anger and disappoint-ment would, I felt, have been counterproductive, and I didn't want Georgie to hear or witness any conflict concerning her. I did understand his fears and I shared them, but I didn't understand how he felt that I was the cause of Georgie's experience. Greg had witnessed Georgie's preferences from the very beginning, so his resistance seemed to me to be more than mere fear or confusion but a red flag indicating some deeper resentment towards me. It felt like there was more to it: a stand-off between his parent-ing style and mine. It was true that we had different approaches, but we almost always agreed on the outcome we wanted. Perhaps he resisted because Georgie had never articulated to him her feelings in the same way she had to me. I regularly tried to talk about it to Greg, but he deflected. I became the bearer of unwel-come news, speaking the truth but feared and disbelieved. I was his Cassandra.

As Christmas approached and the warmer evenings began to invite us into languid nights, I took evening walks on my own. I had a strong sense of something huge impending as I walked the streets of my neighbourhood.

Christmas is a particularly happy time in our household. All of us love the Christmas trees, the decorations and the little bit of magic around that time of year. In the past, I'd often taken the kids to see Santa at Myer and David Jones. Every year, even now, we each find a new decoration to put on the tree. It was at Myer in 2004, while waiting in the queue to see Santa, that Georgie had stepped out of line to watch a gorgeous little girl walking towards us, happy and excited from seeing Santa and now leaving Santaland. Georgie's eyes scanned that child from top to toe, and as she passed, Georgie said appreciatively, 'Nice shoes.' Georgie's love affair with Mary-Janes had been going on for some time, and was now given voice. I bet she wished Santa would bring her some for Christmas.

But this Christmas was different for a number of reasons. One of our dear friends was very ill, with no hope of recovery, and we were teetering on the precipice of life without him. Richard and Lisa had been friends of Greg's for many, many years, and were a central part of our lives. Our children, of similar ages, had brought our circle even closer together. Motor neurone disease is about as bad a diagnosis as you can get. Richard's was fast in robbing him of almost everything. Certainly not his wit, his intelligence and his gallows humour; nor was he robbed of the people who loved him so dearly. But it took everything else.

When I recall this phase of post-dinner walking, what vividly comes back to me is the narrative running in my head, this sense of a suspension of time, waiting, questioning, perched in readiness for the next pendulum swing that would alter our course. As dusk settled and homes lit up from within, I'd ponder the extraordinary lives squirrelled away in suburban homes. I saw glimpses of people moving around their houses, passing from one room to another, and caught snippets of conversations floating on the night air. I saw homes where the Christmas tree was in the window, flashing and shimmering, a lighthouse to guide loved ones safely home, or maybe a message to those already departed: 'I miss you.' I wondered what trials these people were dealing with, what dramatic and unexpected change of course had befallen them, what heaviness lay in the depths of their hearts. What bell was tolling for them? Did anyone in those homes know someone like Georgie?

I cannot say all that introspection made me happy, but I felt comforted by the thought that we all suffer. Somewhere, sometime, life will blow your mind with its ruthless gutting of all you know and maybe of all you dreamed of. All people want to avoid pain. None of us welcomes it. I was soothed by the Christmas lights blinking out their own erratic Morse code: 'Go home and hug your family.'

Days before Christmas, the phone rang very early one morning. Normally, I wouldn't have answered it; I'd have let it go through to the answering machine. But I knew in my heart who it was. 'Beck, he's gone.'

The day Richard died, the skies opened after a long, long drought and the world softened. Our hearts broke, and tears flowed. There was so much love between our friendship group in the days that followed, and that love flowed through to everything.

At Richard's memorial service, Paul Kelly sang 'Meet Me in the Middle of the Air', and the song resonated deeply within me. I realised that floating in the air, among the stalactites and unspoken words, the resentments, the frozen intimacy and the loss, could be found a meeting place of grace and acceptance. Perhaps Greg and I could be okay.

5

Our turning point

2007 began with a visit from my sister Jessie, her husband Kevin and daughter Priya from England. They rented a holiday home on the Mornington Peninsula and a few family members converged on the house. It was wonderful. Georgie was able to be in Priya's dress-ups all day every day, and that was about as good as it got for her. If she could have, Georgie would have worn them horseriding and to the beach. We all gave one another massages and reflexology treatments, swam, talked and laughed and reconnected after a few years apart.

When the school year recommenced, Georgie and Harry were looking forward to starting Year 1 with new teachers. Around the same time, I began rehearsing *All My Sons* with the Melbourne Theatre Company and Greg took on a show. This was a juggle. I'd make the kids dinner, greet the babysitter, and head out the door around 6 pm, struggling with the guilt over not tucking them in and reading them their story. I missed our time-honoured evening trajectory: dinner, bath, stories, cuddling and tucking in. Six nights a week for six weeks, there were sad eyes as I left the house: 'How much longer will you be in the play, Mumma?'

No matter how much I enjoyed it once I was at the theatre, it was always a relief for a show to be over. By the beginning of May it was, and I resumed my full-time duties as mum and massage therapist, inviting my happy clients back to their regular treatments. I basked in the simplicity of our unfolding days: picking up Harry and Georgie from school, having afternoon tea, and our much-loved evening rituals. But all was not well.

Increasingly, Georgie was coming home from school distressed and angry from being hassled. She became frustrated with us, with me. I was her mum and I was supposed to have this in hand. I was supposed to be able to sort this kind of thing out. The anguish in her face was heartbreaking and terrifying at once.

'You don't understand! I wish I was dead!' When you hear those words from your child's mouth, it feels like a body blow. Sometimes she'd come home from school and sob quietly. 'It's so hard, trying to be a boy,' she'd say, or 'I go to school disguised as a boy.' She stopped using the boys' toilets at school and would hold on all day until she got home.

It was the language Georgie used that conveyed to me the depth and sincerity of her plight: the way she described being labelled a boy as a pretence. For her, it was confusing that others couldn't see for themselves her truth, rendering her invisible in her own skin.

It was impossible for Georgie to understand why we didn't help her, and it was difficult to explain that to her without causing her more pain. Tensions were never far from the surface in the discussions Greg and I had. I'd raise the subject, wanting to address Georgie's pain; he'd again deflect, avoid eye contact and say, 'Well, I'm not going to encourage it.' If Georgie brought it up at dinner, which she always did as it was her primary subject for conversation, silence would hang over the table for a second and her eyes would dart to me to see if everything was okay. I'd make some lame statement along the lines of, 'Dad and I have been talking about it, and we just need to talk some more.'

But that wouldn't cut it much longer, and in July 2007 a watershed moment occurred.

Georgie was displaying a deep love for music, which was forging a wonderful bond between her and her dad. In a short break between gigs, Greg decided to take Georgie to *The Phantom of the Opera*. Of course Georgie loved Christine, the leading lady of *Phantom*, and she was really excited to be going.

The day arrived and I sent Georgie to her room to get changed into something smart. She was gone for some time. Curious as to why she hadn't come bounding out ready to go, I went to investigate. Georgie was standing by the full-length mirror in the kids' bedroom in her knickers with clothes strewn all around her. Her good pants, nice shirts – almost every item of clothing she owned – lay dumped on the floor like old skin, and she was in tears, giant beads falling silently. She turned to me and said, 'I've got nothing to wear.'

I knew exactly what she was getting at. 'What would you like to wear, darling?'

'A ball dress! We're going to *Phantom of the Opera* and it's opening night and I should be wearing a ball dress!'

My brain was racing, as was my heart. This was absolutely the moment that everything was going to change, I sensed, because Greg was there to witness it.

I said that we didn't have a ball dress and that her princess dress-ups were too tatty to wear, but there might be something else in the dress-up box I could find. I beckoned Greg and told him what was happening. Instantly, he could see how upset she was. Georgie wasn't just a little kid cracking a hissy fit. Her response was genuine and profound.

I put together a little outfit of pink bootleg pants some friends of ours had passed on for dress-ups and a plain black jumper Georgie owned, which I jazzed up with a sparkly love-heart necklace of mine. As I was dressing her, I promised that we were going to find some help and that the next day we'd go to Target and buy her some clothes from the girls' section.

Georgie went off feeling much better, thoroughly enjoyed the show and the next day we did indeed buy some 'girl' clothes from Target. I came into her room later to find she had cleaned out all of her 'boy' clothes and put them in Harry's drawers. Folded carefully in her chest of drawers was the small selection of new clothes we had purchased that day.

Greg took Georgie to a shop down the road and bought her a dress she'd been admiring in the window. She proudly put it on and modelled it for Harry, Greg and me. My heart swelled. 'That,' I thought, 'is what's known as a breakthrough.'

Immediately, I set about trying to find some help. Where to go? Who could guide us? In 2007 there was nothing on the internet about children with this experience in Australia. What do I google? 'Boy who wears dresses'? 'My son wants to be a girl'? 'Transsexualism'? All these searches took me to places on the internet I didn't wish to go. In the process, they fed my fears and reinforced all the stereotypes I had about what Georgie's future would look like: marginalised, drug-addicted, homeless; a life of sex work, mental illness and premature death – either murdered or by her own hand.

Images kept flashing through my mind of the girls working on William Street leading up to Kings Cross in Sydney. Before I had children, I viewed the transgender working girls as a curiosity, a colourful yet tragic taste of what Kings Cross had to offer. Something about their presence was so defiant that it was unsettling. I'd look away, trying to imagine their lives.

How entirely ignorant I was. Driving along the same road in 2012, with my perception utterly transformed by our understanding of Georgie, I wanted to leap out of the car and say hello to these women. My heart was full of respect. These days, I am honoured to know so many transgender adults and children. Having heard firsthand their stories of struggle, courage and beauty – so much beauty – what I now saw were human beings, in a community. I saluted them as I drove by.

After my many, many frustrating and upsetting hours of googling, I decided to telephone the Gender Clinic for adults at the Monash Medical Centre in Melbourne. I told the woman at reception about our situation and asked whether she knew of anybody in Australia who worked with children experiencing this kind of thing. In all honesty, I didn't even know what to call it. 'Transsexualism' seemed too big a word for such a small child. The term was too loaded, too linked with preconceptions of the kind of life Georgie might have to endure. It's not that Greg and I couldn't accept Georgie being trans, it was that the future for a trans person was a daunting, frightening prospect. What doctors then were calling 'gender identity disorder' entailed dreadful mental health outcomes and barriers to social inclusion. Greg and I didn't want this for our child. I was so bone-shatteringly scared for her. And yet I knew in my heart this was her experience. I knew Georgie wasn't gay. She knew she wasn't gay. 'That's not how I am, Mum,' she said firmly.

The receptionist spoke with exceptional kindness. She seemed to be able to tell I was in distress. Her manner made me a little less desperate. 'Let me just check,' she said. 'I think there's one doctor at the Royal Children's Hospital.'

I heard a hand cover the receiver and a muffled question to a colleague, then the sound of a ring dragging across the mouthpiece as she brought the phone back to her ear and spoke to me again. Seconds later, I wrote down the name Associate Professor Campbell Paul.

A number! A person! I dialled straightaway but there was no answer. Then, in what I would recognise over the following years as one of my greatest strengths, I persisted. Every day, I dialled this number again until I heard back. Perhaps a week later, the phone rang and I found myself speaking with Doctor Paul. If only I could've squeezed through the telephone line, I would have hugged him.

The dam burst, and I poured out all my anxieties and fears to the poor fellow. 'What do you think? Is it something we should be worried about? What do we do? Are we doing the right thing? When are you free? Book us in, yes!'

At that time there were no long waiting lists. Georgie was the
third child to present at the RCH with this experience, and an
appointment was available within weeks. But the stars weren't
fully aligned in our favour. As bad timing would have it, Greg was
about to go away on tour, leaving shortly before the first available appointment, and that meant we would need to wait for three
months. But I was determined not to jeopardise family unity.
All four of us were going to start this journey together; it was
important nobody was left behind.

The next step was procedural: I needed to get a referral to
Doctor Paul from our local GP. This man had been our doctor for
a number of years. He enjoyed the arts as well, so I was confident
that he would be more open-minded than some other doctors.
More worldly. Georgie came in with me and the consultation
began with a cheery greeting and a 'What can I do for you?'

I told the doctor as much as I could and the reasons for
wanting a referral. When I asked Georgie to say in her own
words what she'd been experiencing, she was very shy. By then,
the doctor's demeanour had changed considerably. Not that he
said anything; I found myself filling the silence. The atmosphere
became beyond awkward, so I asked Georgie to pop out into the
waiting room for only a minute or two. Still nothing from
the GP. Not a question from him. From my handbag, I fished
out the information needed to complete the paperwork and
showed it to him. He printed out a referral and folded it up, then
slid it into an envelope and pushed it across the table towards me.

I considered whether to say any more but thought better of it.
I had the referral; I didn't need this individual's approval. 'Right!'
I said as I got up. We never went back to him again.

Since that awkward and disconcerting day, I've learned that many families report similarly unpleasant experiences with their GP. When asking for a referral for support around gender identity, often they encounter rudeness, ignorance, disbelief or, as in our case, total silence. Some doctors have refused to write a referral altogether, forcing the young person to seek out another doctor and have to explain over and over again their situation.

Until recently, medical students received scant or no training in gender identity or gender dysphoria. But thank goodness that's beginning to change. In 2018, Isabelle Langley, an adolescent trans girl from Victoria, was invited to speak at the University of Melbourne MD Student Conference. An accomplished and articulate young person, Isabelle provided many of those in attendance with their first experience of hearing a young trans person's perspective. It was a golden opportunity to learn from her how to be better doctors, and her speech was well received.

The long wait to see Campbell Paul was proving to be hard on Georgie. Again life was in suspended animation for those three months, and I appreciated just how patient that kid was. For many trans or gender-diverse children, I later learned, waiting to see a specialist becomes a dangerous period for their mental health. Many experience severe levels of depression and anxiety in the lead-up to the first appointment. It was just the three of us at home and we muddled on, taking it gently, chatting about what we thought might happen, not promising anything. I was mindful that Greg was away and wasn't privy to these conversations.

It was valuable for Harry to explore his feelings, too. Although he's always accepted Georgie as herself, he expressed his fears around the adjustment that was likely to happen. One bathtime when we were chatting I asked Harry how he was feeling and he said with real concern, 'I don't want a sister. I love my brother.'

'But I'm not going anywhere, Harry,' Georgie said.

I hastened to reassure him. 'It's a bit scary, isn't it, because things might be a little different to how they have been. I'm a bit scared, too, Harry, and a bit looking forward to learning what we need to do to help Georgie be happier. Georgie will always be your twin and will be the same fun and annoying person she's always been. But she might start wearing more girl clothes out and about, and we might start saying "she" instead of "he". Nobody's going anywhere.'

Greg was living with his mum while doing the show in Perth. I planned to come over with Georgie and Harry for a few days soon after he opened, so I suggested he talk with his mum and let her know what was going on. I hoped a pre-emptive conversation would help limit any surprise when Georgie arrived looking much more like a girl than the little boy Grandma had last seen.

The visit was tense from the start. It was plain that if there had been a discussion, it hadn't been a very long one. We were going on a trip to Rottnest Island when Greg had a few days off and Georgie was begging me to let her buy a pair of one-piece bathers she had seen in one of the chain stores. I asked Greg about it and we agreed that it was okay, so off we went the next day and bought them. Nothing special, but Georgie was thrilled, and I purchased a little swimming skirt to wear over the top for modesty. Back at home, she tried them on to show Greg. But on seeing Georgie in her new bathers, Grandma got a shock. In response, Georgie ran off and hid under the bed.

It took some time for Grandma to really understand what was going on. That day I explained that we were going to see someone as soon as Greg got back to Melbourne, that nobody knows why some people identify differently from the gender they're assigned at birth, but it's who Georgie is and she needs our love. In small degrees over time, Grandma came to understand. It can be hard for family who don't live near you to fully grasp the depth of this experience, or to know how to react to it. But Grandma is totally on board now and is a very proud grandmother of Georgie and all her other grandkids. She genuinely tried hard to understand, and is so loved and respected because of it.

Don't let an initial difficult response convince you it will never be any different. Grandma needed more than educational material. She needed to understand Georgie by spending time with her. And that's what happened.

By the time Greg returned to Melbourne, for Georgie the anticipation and the build-up to this visit to Dr Paul had grown out of proportion. I suspected that in her mind, this visit was going to solve all her problems in one go. Managing expectations is a massive part of the role we play as parents. It's a delicate balance between providing enough information to satisfy curiosity, especially in younger children, and helping them to manage fear of the unknown and their great hopes for what might be possible. Parents worry about striking this balance. Some fear that even going to an appointment or accessing a service to discuss gender identity is somehow endorsing a particular course of action. It most certainly is not; what it is endorsing is a willingness to seek the best information possible to make the most informed decisions. Being trans, non-binary or gender diverse isn't a choice and not everyone takes a medical pathway to affirm who they are, but there are potentially some important choices to make if you seek a medical pathway to affirm your gender, and these need serious consideration.

From some quarters there's a fear that gender diversity is a new trend, as if gender is a switch that can be flipped on and off at whim, like taking on an avatar in a game. I hope our story will disavow anyone of that notion. Georgie has had years and years of therapy; professionals from many areas of medical discipline have filled folder upon folder with meticulous documentation about her. Kids don't want this as a fad. They usually like fun activities that can be shared with friends. Fidget spinners, skateboarding, rollerskating – hell, *Pokémon GO* was a fad! Having to deal with discrimination, judgement, bullying and rejection isn't fun. Having to attend endless appointments for years on end isn't the blast you might imagine it to be. Having to constantly justify your existence is exhausting; it's isolating and it's hard graft. And though critics say the child is begging for attention, the kind of attention you get if you're trans isn't particularly enjoyable.

The night before her first appointment with Doctor Paul, as I was tucking Georgie in, I asked, 'So, what do you think is going to happen at the appointment tomorrow?'

'Well, I think they might have a tablet or something that will make my vagina grow and the penis disappear.'

'They don't have tablets like that, darling. This doctor is a talking doctor. You can tell him how you feel about everything in your life, not just how you feel about yourself being a girl, and he's going to help us all find the best way to help you.'

I don't actually remember much from that first appointment with the man who'd become affectionately known in our house as Doc Paul. I do know that we were there not to change Georgie or 'fix' her, but to learn how to best support her. We went to see him privately, as he practised from home on Mondays. Greg, Harry, Georgie and I all shuffled into his office. It was full of books, toys of various kinds, pencils and paper: traditional, certainly not clinical, and if anything slightly dusty and chaotic.

Doc Paul has a shock of silver-white hair and dresses as you'd imagine any professor would. Yes, the thick corduroy slacks are a thing, but nobody could have predicted the tartan trousers we would encounter on a later visit! Nor could any of us have predicted the profoundly positive presence he became in our lives.

The dominant impression I have of that day is the deep relief that Georgie appeared to be feeling. It was as though a crushing weight had been lifted from her shoulders. Doc Paul was someone who wasn't family, who didn't treat her as though she was weird, and he told her that, yes, some people felt the same way she did. But they should talk some more. Would next week be okay?

Georgie started making weekly visits. Sometimes we were all invited along; other times the sessions were just for her. I'd sit in the waiting room of Doc Paul's home, and though ABC Classic FM was playing quietly in the background, I could pick out the cadence of Georgie's voice rising and falling as she regaled him with what I assumed was her life story. Georgie has never been shy of a good chat, and I have to say sometimes Doc Paul would emerge looking somewhat dazed. I'm sure he heard more than he cared to about Hannah Montana!

Other parents have expressed to me their concern about not knowing what is being discussed in those sessions. I admit that, at first, I was cautious about my child being alone with a doctor and mightily curious about what they discussed. But I was determined that Georgie should have all the space she needed, and I was confident that she'd tell me anything when she was ready or inclined. I know this must be a worry for those who have kids who are not as communicative as Georgie.

After about two months, Doc Paul called Greg and me back in to see him to discuss his findings. Georgie's experience, he told us, was typical of someone with gender identity disorder (transsexual type), as it was known then. The wording of the 'diagnosis' has now been revised to gender dysphoria, as have the diagnostic criteria. The language around gender diversity is constantly and rapidly evolving, and heading thankfully to a less pathologising tone. But gender identity disorder was the label that was matched to Georgie's experience back in 2007 and transsexualism, rather than transgender or gender diversity, was the term we were introduced to.

The diagnostic criteria for gender identity disorder were written in the *Diagnostic and Statistical Manual IV* (*DSM-IV*) as a 'strong and persistent cross-gender identification (not merely a desire for any perceived cultural advantages of being the other sex)'; that this cross-gender identification across a number of key areas was persistent and insistent; that the experience not be concurrent with a physical intersex condition; and that the person be clinically experiencing significant distress or impairment in social, occupational or other important areas of functioning. Another important factor in this 'diagnosis' is ruling out any other possible diagnoses.

In the *DSM-5*, released in 2013, the updated description of what the manual now calls gender dysphoria outlines the discomfort and distress experienced because a person feels an incongruence between their gender identity and their physical body, the sex they were assigned at birth. The *DSM-5* no longer sees a person's gender identity as itself being pathological; rather, the distress that gender dysphoria causes is the problem requiring support and treatment. The World Professional Association for Transgender Health first published consensus guidelines for the treatment and care of transgender individuals in 1979, and the seventh version was published in 2011. In May 2019, the World Health Organization (WHO) announced it would amend its health guidelines by no longer categorising being transgender as a 'mental disorder'. Being transgender, gender diverse or non-binary is no longer seen by the WHO as a mental disorder, in the same way that being gay is no longer considered a mental disorder. It appals me to even write those words. Imagine living with the day-to-day consequences of the world you live in being structured to label you as dysfunctional simply because of who you love or your gender identity. Discrimination flows from those attitudes like poison.

This is the world that many LGBTQI+ people still live in today. What's more, they have to hear complaints from some small sections of our wider community about the growing positive visibility of LGBTQI+ people; they have to listen to these critics purposely stumbling over the acronym as though it's just all too absurd, calling for a 'Straight Pride March' and wondering why queer people have to 'flaunt' themselves for one day of the year. One day! There's a reason straight, cisgender people don't have a march all to themselves. They are privileged for their gender and sexual identities for the other 364 days of the year. Though they may of course be subject to other forms of discrimination, they don't get kicked out of their homes or schools for being cisgender. They don't lose their jobs or opportunities to reach their full potential for being straight. They aren't excluded from an expression of their faith by their religious leaders. They don't search the media to find positive representation of their lives and experiences. Everything – from movies, to fashion, to the highest seats of power in every land on earth – preferences and celebrates being straight and being cisgender.

Significantly, straight, cis people are not subjected to the ineffective, cruel torture of conversion therapy. At Victoria's Midsumma Festival Pride March in February 2019, the Andrews Labor Government announced a ban on conversion therapy. It's mind-boggling to realise that this kind of quackery is still practised in our country and around the world today. If you have never heard of conversion therapy before, it is the practice of attempting to reprogram an individual from being gay, transgender or gender diverse through various unscientific means. The 'therapy' attempts to 'cure' a person, as though they have a disease that needs to be expelled, and the experience of those individuals subjected to it is one of torture and erasure, pure and simple. For the intersex community, surgical interventions on minors without consent forms a really disturbing aspect of this form of erasure. Far from achieving its truly insidious goal, conversion therapy instead leaves people scarred and broken, shamed and hurt.

The LGBTQI+ community deserve their visibility. They deserve the acceptance of their existence that grows every year. They deserve to learn at school that they're just fine, thank you very much. They deserve to be welcomed into every single organisation and endeavour our country has to offer. And they deserve, more than anything, the love and support of their families. That is exactly what we wanted to give our Georgie.

Doc Paul had already given Greg and me a lot of reading material so by the time we got the news that Georgie had 'gender identity disorder', it had ceased to be the outcome we feared most. Confirmation was a relief, but more importantly, now we could start to learn how to support our daughter better.

I had oodles of questions. There was so much more to learn and get our heads around. But what I needed now, more than anything, was to not feel so alone. I needed to talk to another mum.

'Do you know any other parents I can speak to?'

6

Transitioning

When Georgie and Harry were seven years old, in Year 1, both of them found aspects of school tough going. The nub of the problem seemed to be that much about school life was presented as black and white, but neither of them bought into that. Harry's particular struggle was that he didn't fit the ultra-masculine criteria for a boy that age. Although active, he wasn't sporty, and he found the rigid gender stereotyping claustrophobic and soul-destroying.

It was hard to find a buddy as gentle and imaginative as Harry was, and there was one boy in his class who was truly toxic. This kid told outright lies about Harry, whispering them to Harry's closest friend to drive a wedge between them. In an effort to placate and befriend the troublemaker, Harry gave this kid his password to Club Penguin – an online game – even though he knew he shouldn't. The next time Harry logged on, his password had changed. When he finally got back in, the penguin world he'd created had been trashed. Harry was incandescent with rage. After that incident, and now having lost his friend, Harry didn't bounce back fully. The troublemaking kid also targeted Georgie, but she was buffered by her good friends Alex and Leah, who stood up for her. In turn, she stood up for Harry.

Georgie hadn't transitioned either at school or at home. We were all still getting our heads around what was happening and what we needed to do. And we still hadn't met anyone in our situation. At that point in time it was unheard of, at least in Australia, for a child as young as seven to transition or be supported in a schooling environment. There was no government school policy for transgender kids and no initiatives like the Safe Schools program that was to come later.

In 2007, Jazz Jennings, a trans girl from the USA who was only a few months younger than Harry and Georgie, would burst onto our screens, interviewed by Barbara Walters on the US television program *20/20*. The only other place I'd occasionally seen trans stories was on the TV shows hosted by Oprah Winfrey or Jerry Springer. Nothing at all came out of the UK, Canada or Australia. It wasn't until 2011, when trans advocate and writer Janet Mock came out publicly as a trans woman in an issue of *Marie Claire* magazine, that Georgie was able to see a positive representation of herself and a glimpse into her potential future. Almost always in media coverage of trans people there was a detractor or critic interviewed; it was so rare to see, as in Mock's interview, a trans person speaking in their own words and being portrayed in a positive and affirming way. Janet had a career, close friendships, a boyfriend. All the things Georgie hoped would be possible for her in adulthood.

Though I knew that we were doing the right thing in supporting Georgie, I longed to feel less isolated; it was incredibly lonely.
There was still precious little in print, so I was constantly on
the lookout for information, and spent hours researching and
reading all that was available. Everything I read made me fearful.
Whenever Georgie and I discussed her life, there was no doubt
in my mind – and certainly none in hers – that her future was as
a woman. It's difficult to convey the firmness of her conviction.
She was patient and kind with everyone who struggled to understand. Knowing how little understanding and validation we were
experiencing from the wider world as her parents, it broke my
heart to think about how isolating it all was for her. If only we
could find other families.

At a session with Doc Paul I gave him my phone number
and said, 'You have my permission to give this to any family who
wants to connect.' Pretty soon after that I got a call from Jane.

Jane and her child, Vanessa, were from interstate, but had
been travelling to Melbourne to the RCH. Our daughters were
the same age. That first time we spoke, we were on the phone for
two hours. Since then, there have been many more conversations.
The voice I heard on the other end of the line was clear and sweet
and tentative. Jane was a warm-hearted, thoughtful woman and –
like me – was tormented by fear and racked with guilt over her
child's suffering, and desperately needed to vent.

Our conversation was a massive unravelling, with both of us
speaking in a language the other understood and finding that our
stories were astonishingly similar: how Vanessa and Georgie had
both told us they were girls at bathtime; the words they used to
describe their feelings; the things they were afraid of, like growing

a beard and having a deep voice. We talked about everything we'd discovered, about our other children, our extended families and our husbands. From the start, I trusted Jane completely, and more than a decade on, she's still the first person I reach out to for solace and advice. Over the years we've developed a short-hand – in some conversations, this consists of swearing a lot. Our swearing conversations are brilliant, and usually we end up laughing pretty hard.

One of the main difficulties we'd both been encountering was that, as the parents of transgender children – at that time especially – we were under constant scrutiny, both with and without our consent. We were placed under the microscope with the detailed and meticulous assessments of our doctors, along with the judgement of teachers, principals, fellow parents and students, in addition to friends, family members and casual acquaintances – and then, down the track, the lawyers and judges of the Family Court. Facebook also became a source of discomfort; we were hyper-mindful of the interest our children were attracting. We were also expected to have the answers to every question and, not only that, we were expected to convince those who were never going to accept our children's gender diversity as a fact of life. Adding to our crippling worry and exhaustion, Jane and I agreed, was the effort to educate all those around us, often to no avail. Expletive-rich phone calls provided a much-needed antidote to having to be perfect and magnanimous when all you really wanted to say was, 'Mind your own goddamn business!' Jane was and always will be my darling travel buddy on what was a long and lonely road, and that first phone call brought together not only us but our two beautiful daughters as well.

Around this time, Georgie wanted to give up ballet. She'd been dancing since she was three years old, always joining in the end-of-year concerts dressed in the male costume. Performing had been exciting, and she'd always seemed cheery on stage, but there was a melancholy there, too, as she watched the tutu-clad girls with flowers in their hair getting ready. Following the big concert in 2007, Georgie announced that she wouldn't dance again until she could dance as a girl. The ballet shoes were put away. It was so sad because she'd loved dancing so much.

Georgie also wanted to play sport, but not in the boys' team. As a consequence she wasn't able to enjoy this aspect of her education. Yet again, I felt guilty that I couldn't change the world fast enough or make it safe and inclusive for her when she needed it most. In order to survive she was forced to become less than herself, but I wanted her to be able to eat life up like every other kid.

2008 was a highly creative year for all of us. Georgie discovered Pink and started songwriting, and Harry began writing his hilarious cartoon series, *Funny Monsters*. That year the kids also really got into filmmaking. They'd invite friends over to play different characters and often throw me a choice role as well. Some of my best work is in those movies! There was my Old Lady with Shopping Trolley and the much-underrated performance of Evil Snake, in which I climbed into a sleeping bag and writhed around on the floor hissing. Yes, it was genius. What *Hannah Montana* (junior remake) movie could do without its Evil Snake character, right?

Greg spent hours and hours filming and editing with the kids, which he enjoyed immensely. He had another busy year of theatre lined up, including a tour to Perth again for several months. Meanwhile, I was playing Mae Gooper in *Cat on a Hot Tin Roof* at the Melbourne Theatre Company, directed by Gale Edwards. Tennessee Williams is a favourite of mine and this play – made famous by the movie with Elizabeth Taylor and Paul Newman – had everything going for it. With a star-studded cast and creative team, it was one of the highlights of that season. Despite this, the play didn't quite hit the mark, but I had enormous fun as the fecund, ambitious and brittle Mae.

Meanwhile, Mum's cognitive ability had been gradually worsening. Over the phone she was full of life, still able to have good conversations. But caring for Mum on the hobby farm where they lived had become increasingly difficult for Dad, and he'd reached the end of his tether. My sister Fe, the only remaining daughter in Tasmania, put the word out to ask if any of us could give Dad some respite.

Mum stayed with Fe for a spell then flew from Launceston to Melbourne, where I met her at the terminal gate and took her home. It was May, and she'd be with us for the kids' birthday and a concert at school. It was lovely to have her with us all to ourselves. But Mum was markedly changed. You wouldn't pick it to chat to her casually; she could hold a most interesting conversation with you, adding salient points of her own. But later she'd forget the entire thing. She could look after herself and was still beautifully groomed, but I was frightened she'd escape the house and become lost. She'd wandered off on Dad and had been found walking along a country road near their property. Luckily, that time she'd been brought home. But what about next time? It was so dangerous.

Curiously, Mum had no recollection of Georgie's gender, and I'd never discussed Georgie's gender identity with Mum or Dad before. It would only have worried Mum and confused Dad, and I didn't want to add to their cares at their stage in life; nor did I want to add to our family's stress level with possible conflict about what was happening. Dad was a man of his generation, and I think he'd have struggled with it. Because they lived in Tasmania they weren't in our day-to-day lives, so I decided not to broach it with them. Mum, whom we checked in on by phone every week, was no longer on the ball with things like ringing her grandchildren for their birthdays. That type of communication was over, which was sad. But the beautiful thing was that when she arrived in Melbourne to stay with us she accepted Georgie at face value as a delightful little girl, along with her twin brother, Harry.

One of the ways the dementia manifested in Mum was nocturnal wakefulness. One night, I woke up to the sound of the front door lock being turned. When I rushed down, there in the hallway was Mum, fully dressed, handbag held firmly at her side.

'Where's Dad?' she asked.

'Dad's back home in Tassie, Mum. Come back to bed.' I led her to her room. She was quite agitated and I asked her what was wrong.

'I've got to get up now or I'll miss the parade.'

I wasn't sure what she was talking about, but just rolled with it. 'You won't miss the parade, Mum.' In an attempt to soothe her, I carefully helped her remove her hat and set aside her handbag, and we sat on the bed together. 'Besides, it's too early. It's still dark, nobody will be there yet. Hop back into bed and I'll make sure we get there on time in the morning and if we're a bit late, we can take the car. So don't worry.'

'You've got a car!' came the wide-eyed response. 'Nobody's got a car!'

Then it clicked. She was reliving a moment in which she was a little girl and the dad she was asking for was her own – not mine. She was giddy with excitement, so I put her back to bed and promised once more that she'd get to the parade right on time. I went back to bed heartbroken.

Very soon after this, Mum had to go into full-time care. Four of her five daughters lived a long way away. Fe, who was wonderful in the last years of Mum's and Dad's lives, took on the carer role. It fell to her to take Mum to her new home, and the day she did was probably one of the hardest of Fe's life. I don't think I'll ever fully appreciate how that must have felt.

Greg's dad, Roy, had been in a home for some time, and when we went to visit our Perth family we went to see him too. Dear Roy had become frail and could no longer communicate. Determined to do the best we could to engage in some way with Roy, we played music for him and the kids sang to him by his bedside. He did respond, which was beautiful. Harry and Georgie held and patted his hands, and from his facial expression we knew he could feel the love.

Roy had been a gregarious man and music devotee. It was he who'd instilled in his three kids a love of music, which had become the cultural foundation of the family. After Greg and I got together, the first tune he always played on Christmas Day was 'Feliz Navidad' by José Feliciano. This was a family tradition created by Roy, and it continues to this day. Christmas just isn't Christmas without 'Feliz Navidad'.

Dementia and Alzheimer's are hideous diseases. Sufferers don't just forget minor details but can lose memory of entire relationships, connections, shared joys, the ability to communicate. Even the personality of the sufferer can change beyond recognition, leaving them and their families with an aching silence. But somewhere deep, the person remains. You can sometimes get through the fog in fleeting moments of recognition. Love still shines through.

During the primary school years, the TV cartoon series *Scooby-Doo* was on high rotation in our house. The theme song, I think you could say, was the soundtrack to those years. Both kids loved it, Harry especially. He'd collected many of the comics, games and some of the toys, and knew all the episodes back to front, so it was with enormous excitement that we went on holiday that year to the Gold Coast to 'do the parks'.

At Movie World, Harry met the characters Scooby-Doo and Shaggy, had his photo taken with them and purchased his very own Scooby-Doo dress-up. He was in heaven. Hilariously, he decided to put it on straightaway and walk around the park in it. People around us were delighted by this mini-Scooby wandering around, waving at passers-by, doing little dances. My heart almost burst with joy. Harry was so sweetly and innocently happy.

This was the first holiday we went on where Georgie was able to dress all the time as her affirmed self. Her hair wasn't very long at this point but was long enough to gather into a ponytail, and we were using female pronouns for her because to do otherwise would have 'outed' her, exposing her to unwanted attention and questions. She was undoubtedly a happy, excited little girl; it was, I suppose, a 'test run' before any decision to socially transition at school. This time to be herself was precious and Georgie revelled in it. Her big thrill was to buy a wand from the Harry Potter shop. It was Hermione Granger's, ten and three-quarter inches long, made of vine wood with a core of dragon heartstring.

While we felt like we were edging closer towards Georgie's eventual transition, the downside was that she was living two lives, one at home and one at school. If we were parenting now, we almost certainly would be doing things differently, but we were terribly afraid; we had no roadmap and very limited support. We were already right out there on a limb. The tension between Georgie's need to be herself and our responsibility as parents to understand those needs and their implications, to anticipate any issues and educate others before we placed her in new or even current situations, was endlessly complex and shatteringly exhausting. There were so many minuscule decisions to make.

Running into people who knew my kids but didn't know the story was tricky. It's surprising that a question like 'How are the boys?' can make your heart race. Many times I've had to decide on the spot if the person needed an in-depth answer to their semiautomatic enquiry. My brain would flick between pros and cons. Is this person going to have an ongoing relationship with my kids? Are they trustworthy? Do we have time for this conversation in the street? Countless times I walked away having simply said, 'They're fine. And your little ones?' But when I took a deep breath and gave them a brief but straightforward update, people were often fascinated. They seemed almost greedy to hear more details. I found that disconcerting.

While on one hand it was good for me to let it out, on the other hand I realised that many of those intensely interested people seemed to feed off the drama, shared more than they should with others and got the information wrong. And because it was obvious that Georgie was gradually presenting as a girl, I began to share with some of the mums from school more strategically. I chose women who were smart and whose parenting I admired. They had fabulous kids who you could see already had humanitarian or leadership qualities. I knew for sure these mums would share with others what I'd told them, but I figured they'd pride themselves on getting the information as correct as possible. And I hoped they'd model positive behaviour to their children. This proved to be an effective approach because these mums would come to be staunch allies when everything went to shit the following year.

Greg and I were still learning ourselves, still tentative, polite and grateful to anyone who listened or provided an opportunity for Georgie to express herself safely – or, on an even more basic level, anyone who would not reject her outright. We took considerable pains to share and explain our situation, most especially with the school leadership. We were patient, open and pragmatic; calm, polite and positive. But it was relentlessly difficult. You'd catch the flash of judgement or panic behind people's eyes or in their voices. You could see them eyeing Georgie off, gawking. Walking through the playground with her at pick-up, I'd often notice, especially in the older students, a look of disdain on their faces. But my daughter wasn't deterred.

No amount of bullying, exclusion, persuasion, coercion or conversion therapy is going to force someone to change their gender. Countless times I've been asked whether I'd 'just told Georgie that he was a boy', the implication being that a parent had only to take this firm approach and that would put an end to this gender 'confusion'. Well, the answer is yes. It didn't work. All that approach does is make a person better at hiding; all a child understands from that parental stance is that they are shameful, unnatural, perverse and wrong.

I have no regrets about supporting Georgie, but I do have regrets about not affirming her gender sooner. In hindsight, Greg and I took it slowly and cautiously, which was understandable given the context of the time, but it's the delay in seeking help when Georgie was five and six years old that I feel guilty about. She had to survive not being fully understood or supported by two fearful parents. What Georgie saw wasn't caution, but her mum and dad not having the situation in hand. The effect on her was to internalise shame about who she was, to begin to hate herself, believe she was a freak, a mythical being who didn't belong in this world, utterly powerless to change her situation in any way. I regret that with all my heart.

The use of the word 'transition' to describe the process by which a person affirms their gender identity can be misleading, as it can create a perception of a shift from one state to another. For Georgie and our family, transition was the process by which we, as her family, grew to understand who Georgie had always been. Georgie's self was the solid, central point. She had not transitioned; she had affirmed. We had to grow as parents and people to support her in the way that protected her integrity, her dignity and her rights as a human being.

Harry became the 'Pronoun Police', stating when he thought it was time everybody got on board and correcting anyone who slipped. It was amazing to see his active love for Georgie, which is deeper than anyone can ever really understand, I think. Harry and Georgie have always been a formidable pair. Many people expressed genuine concern about how Harry was dealing with these big changes. We certainly kept him involved with what was going on with Georgie; there were no secrets.

One summer's day, we were driving to the beach in a hot car with our blow-up dinghy shoved into the boot. En route, Harry threw his arms out as wide as they could go and declared with immense love and happiness, 'I've got a sister!' Then he wrapped his arms around Georgie and gave her a giant hug and kiss.

That boy kills me.

During childhood, trans kids are forced to think about their lives in ways no one would expect of their peers. Often, they're keenly aware of what they want their future to look like and who they want to be within that future. A simple conversation about an utterly prosaic thing can turn into an exploration of the ways the world works: perceptions, privacy, secrets, bodies and autonomy. One such conversation springs to mind.

Georgie and I happened to both be sitting at the dining room table, where I was working at my computer. Georgie was playing with one of her Barbies. She was a well-established Pink fan by this stage, and had cut her Barbie's hair short and drawn replicas of Pink's tattoos over the body. Georgie was telling me that when she grew up she wanted tattoos just like Pink. I have a small tattoo myself, on my ankle, so I'm not against them, but I had pang of resistance nonetheless.

I said to Georgie, 'You have to be really certain that you'll always like what you want to tattoo onto your body, because they're really hard to get rid of and your skin will never be the same.'

'But you've got one, Mum,' she said.

'I know,' I said, then recounted to Georgie what my mum said when I'd showed her my tiny bit of body art. She'd looked at it exasperated and exclaimed, 'Oh, Becky! I spent nine months making that skin perfect.' By then, I was twenty-seven years of age and had been taken aback to realise she still felt protective of the body she created. My body. There was still a sense for her of, if not ownership, then stewardship to maintain its integrity and, I suppose, the perfection she felt she was responsible for.

'It really took me by surprise,' I told Georgie, 'but I under-stood her love for me differently. And in this moment now with you, I understand it even more. You're perfect to me, Georgie. You don't need to add anything to yourself to make yourself more beautiful.'

'Well, I don't want to have a boy's body. When I grow up I'm going to be a girl.'

For a long time, Georgie had been saying some confront-ing things about wanting to get rid of her penis, including that she wanted to cut it off with scissors. At times she was disgusted by her anatomy. She didn't like looking at or acknowledging her body at all, let alone talking about it. I was worried that at some point she would really hurt herself. How do you as a parent alleviate this kind of pain? I knew that as an adult Georgie could have surgery if she chose to. But was it appropriate that I tell her that now? She needed hope.

'When you're an adult, you might be able to change your body.'

'How?' she demanded. 'Is there an operation?'

She held my gaze determined to understand, sensing a revelation was in the offing.

'Yes, there's an operation. It's very big and not easy, but special doctors can create a vagina with what you already have. So look after yourself, sweetie. Look after your body. You have to be a grown-up, though; you can't be a kid.'

Without skipping a beat and still looking me in the eyes, she said, 'So, when I'm eighteen, I can have an operation?'

'Yes.'

'Okay. That's what I'm going to do.'

From that moment onwards, Georgie never threatened to hurt herself again. She called a truce with her body, which instead of a source of shame or disgust became a means for her salvation. A reason to take care of herself, love herself even.

In consultation with Doc Paul, we made the decision that Georgie would make a social transition into her school at the start of Year 3 in 2009. A social transition simply entails using the pronouns, name, clothing and bathroom facilities of the gender the child identifies with. A social transition has nothing to do with hormones or surgery, but simply affirms the child's gender identity, which may be male, female, non-binary or in any way gender diverse. Georgie wanted to be known as a girl and use the girls' bathroom. She was quite happy to wear shorts or bootleg pants as most of her friends wore these anyway.

We spoke to the principal and Georgie's teacher about how she might be supported, and provided a written report from Doc Paul assuring them that this was an appropriate and positive course of action for Georgie. I'd already apprised the principal of Georgie's circumstances when she began seeing Doc Paul; I felt I had to, as Georgie was missing school every Monday in order to attend her appointments. The school agreed to Georgie's social transition, but with reservations. As the saying goes, the devil is in the detail. Allowing Georgie to use the girls' bathroom was a sticking point. Rather than let it stop her from transitioning at school at the beginning of the year, we agreed – against our instincts and without a viable alternative – to Georgie using the disabled toilet. We could see that her transitioning was difficult for our school to accommodate. Beneath the general reticence, I got the feeling that we were seen as difficult, troublesome parents.

As for Georgie, she didn't want a fuss made. The last thing she wanted was for us to have a battle over the bathrooms; she didn't want to 'cause any trouble'.

Nevertheless, this was a massive step forward. It was decided that the teacher would tell the students in class time, and we discussed what should be said. My suggestion was to avoid complication, and stick to the basics. Something like this: *When Georgie was born, the doctors thought that she was a boy. But*

Georgie's always said she's really a girl and now the doctors agree with her. So we're calling Georgie 'she' and 'her' now. Apart from that, nothing has changed.

When I picked the kids up that afternoon, I asked how it all went. Georgie said it was fine; that her teacher had told the class and they had gone on to do their reading.

Even though it was out of my control, I wondered about all the discussions taking place over dinner that night in the homes of her classmates.

The following day, as usual, I stood in the playground waiting to pick the kids up. This was often when parents would organise playdates or chat about school life. Although I appeared calm, I was hyper-alert to the vibes I was getting. Some parents wouldn't meet my eyes; others came up and shared with me what their kid had said about the announcement about Georgie. One mum – in fact, she was one of the mums I'd originally told, a beautiful woman who had the most divine son – came up and said, 'I have to tell you what Jack said last night. He said, "Mum, today our teacher told us that Georgie is really a girl. I don't know why she said it because we already knew that!"'

A few of the other mums waved hello and I was comforted to feel they were still open, even if they didn't quite know how to respond.

Then the fallout began. One mother, who was a devout Catholic, started making waves. This woman had earlier objected to the school fete being held on a Sunday to accommodate the large Jewish community at the school, or at least that was her assumption. The fact that many folks were also busy with extra-curricular activities on a Saturday must have eluded her.

I often mingled with a group of parents, mostly mothers, who'd hear the children do their reading every day. We'd set up chairs in the hallway outside the classroom and a child would bring their reader out and read it to a parent. I loved doing this. It was so exciting to hear these little minds shape new words and concepts all from the pages of a book. The activity also helped me to get to know the kids in Georgie's and Harry's classes.

One such day, I had an uncomfortable encounter with this particular mother. The energy that came from her was vicious. By turns she'd ignore me or glare at me. Once she'd gone, I turned to my friend Anne and asked what the hell that had been about. Anne told me that 'Griselda' – for that is what I wish to call her – had been complaining bitterly about Georgie's transition to the other parent volunteers during reading time earlier in the week, in front of the children. She was accusing me of abusing my child and of twisting the mind of her own precious daughter. Well, her own daughter didn't care and actually was quite kind to Georgie, but this woman insisted it was disgusting. 'What kind of a mother does that to her son?'

Griselda had chosen the wrong time to holy-roller. Rostered on that day was a mum whose youngest was in Georgie's class and in whom I'd confided. This woman was both active and visible in the school. She had serious school cred and years of history as a solid community member. She went toe to toe with Griselda, telling her it was none of her damned business; that Georgie's wellbeing was the most important thing, and if this meant she could be happy and learn at school, then that was all right with her. She had no problem with her daughter supporting Georgie and learning to be kind. Then she stood up for me, too, saying that none of the other parents knew how hard this decision was, and that I wasn't a child abuser.

I'll always be grateful to that mum for what she said that day.

From that moment on, there emerged a division between those who supported us and those who didn't. Those who supported still sent birthday party and sleepover invitations, and those who didn't shut up shop. The divide didn't immediately affect Georgie, as she had good friends and nothing changed. But once the older children at the school began to discover more about her situation, the bullying began in earnest.

Every recess and lunchtime Georgie would be confronted by someone demanding to know if she was a boy or a girl. Usually they'd ask over and over, a broken record. 'I'm a girl,' she'd say.

'No, you're not. You're a boy. You can't be a girl.'

Frequently, I was worried about her going to school. Harry also. He was bullied by association and was often placed in the position of defending his twin. To be honest, I didn't know the extent of the bullying. Georgie kept a lot of it from me, again to minimise the fuss around her. A fuss in her books was saying anything at all, drawing any attention to herself. She was frightened that talking about her situation would make it worse. Georgie just wanted to get on with life, but her circumstances and the people around her weren't allowing that to happen.

7

Learning to swim

Swimming lessons are at the epicentre of discomfort and trauma for many trans and gender-diverse school students. More than almost any other Australian school requisite, this one strikes fear into the hearts of gender-diverse kids and their parents alike. In previous years Georgie had worn board shorts to swim, but Year 3 was different. She now had one-piece bathers and a pair of 'girls' board shorts to wear. Her hair was shoulder length and often tied back in a ponytail or bunches. She was unmistakably a lovely little girl, so I assumed that common sense around bathrooms would prevail. How shockingly wrong I was.

In the lead-up to swimming lessons, I contacted the school to reassure them I had a plan for maintaining Georgie's privacy and discretion, and the privacy and discretion of the other girls. I'd already confirmed with the swimming pool that there were no family bathrooms to use or disabled toilets that were unisex. The only options were male or female and, as it was a public pool,

the children were sharing these facilities with adults not associated with the school. My suggestion was that I would escort
Georgie into the girls' room and help her change in a cubicle.

No, I was told. That wasn't acceptable. Georgie would have to
use the male toilet.

'But she's female,' I protested.

The reply was that it was non-negotiable.

'What if I was to change her in the grounds with a towel
wrapped around her? So many parents do this at swimming
pools.'

'No, it must be the male change room.'

I was flummoxed. I couldn't believe it. I said I'd have to think
about what to do and would ask Georgie, too.

When she came home later that day, I told her what had transpired. 'How do you feel about that, Georgie? They aren't going
to let you into the girls' change rooms. How would you feel using
the boys' toilets?'

'I don't know. I don't want to . . . I guess I could use a cubicle.'

I didn't want Georgie to miss out on swimming lessons so I
wanted to find a way to make it work. It's unthinkable now that
I would have been so compliant or accommodating. I wasn't
brave, and we were out on a really precarious limb. Georgie didn't
want to cause problems; I didn't want to cause problems for her.
But Georgie and I were changed forever that day.

The pool was walking distance from school, and it was a
glorious February day. The children walked two by two, chatting,
silly, bags swinging from shoulders. I'd already dressed Georgie
in her bathers underneath her school uniform, so there was no
need for her to go into the change room first up. Harry's class was

coming to the pool for a different session so he wasn't there that day. When Georgie started easing her way into the water, I saw staff and parents looking at me then at her.

The vice-principal came up and spoke to me, reiterating that Georgie was not to use the girls' facilities; then, separately, Georgie's teacher came up and told me the opposite, that she could. When I relayed to her what the principal and the vice had both told me – that Georgie wasn't to use the ladies' – she shook her head, shrugged and walked away.

Once the class was over, the kids ran to the change rooms. I stood by the entrance to the men's as Georgie went in. I still replay this moment so often. I wish I'd stopped her. She was a girl going into the men's room of a public swimming pool! If only I could reach back through time and hold her and say, 'You don't have to. Don't go in.' But that's not how it happened. Georgie went in, and I couldn't follow. I couldn't protect her. The screams and shouts that came instantly from that bathroom could have lifted the roof.

What the school had failed to tell me was that also in there were the Year 5 and 6 boys, many of whom were responsible for some of the worst bullying Georgie had been experiencing. They were outraged that a girl was in their bathroom. Her classmates, wanting to protect Georgie, spoke up. Sadly, the only defence they offered was that she was really a boy. They were doing their best to help her – and Georgie to this day is fully aware of that – but the message crushed her nonetheless.

Weeping and weeping, she tried to dress in the cubicle as quickly as possible, with the cacophony intensifying around her.

When I recall this moment, I think about how hard it is to dress wet skin quickly.

Outside, I was loathing myself for my impotence and for my acquiescence. Every shouted word pierced me. I felt sick to my stomach, anxious beyond words, utterly powerless to do anything until Georgie emerged from that change room. Anger surged within me, sharp and focusing.

Totally humiliated, head bowed, body slumped into a protective stoop, Georgie emerged from the change room, mostly dressed but dishevelled. She'd managed to pull on her shorts and shirt, gather up her wet things and escape. After she fell into my arms, I led her away from the exit of the men's room, with its terrible din. Then I dropped to my knees and held her tight as she sobbed into my neck. 'I'm sorry, darling. I'm sorry. I'm so sorry.'

Some of Georgie's friends came up to her, terribly concerned, willing her to be all right. The teachers kept their distance. The mothers watched on. Some had no idea what was going on. Nobody helped us.

I guided my daughter back to school, holding her close to me. She was utterly devastated. One of her friends accompanied us, walking by her side with his hand supportively on her back. As we walked, I swore to Georgie that this would never happen to her again. I was going to speak to the principal immediately and I'd sort it out. When we reached the school, I hugged her, reassured her and let her friend walk her back to class. Then I went directly to the principal's office.

From the start, the principal was defensive. It's no wonder, because I was white hot with fury, and my efforts to remain calm merely concentrated it. I wasn't there to hear excuses or be patronised; I was there to deliver an unequivocal message. I explained what had transpired that morning. That it was a predictable outcome, one I'd tried to avoid by putting forward other strategies, all of which had been refused.

She tried to deny it, to gaslight me about what had been said to me, but I didn't buy it. I told the principal she'd failed to protect my daughter and had prevented me from protecting her. And I assured her that for the rest of Georgie's life, she'd never again set foot in another male bathroom or be forced to endure the indignity and humiliation she'd just endured. What's more, I told her, my daughter wasn't going to be disadvantaged by not attending swimming lessons. I would not put her through another traumatic event by demanding that she go into the girls' change rooms – the experience was too raw – but I would be helping her get changed in a quiet corner of the pool grounds.

There was more. Calmly, I asked that the principal speak to the boys involved. To explain diversity, to help them understand. But the request fell on deaf ears, and on this issue I was never able to extract any action from her.

As far as I was concerned, as the school leader, it was the principal's responsibility to model desirable behaviour, but instead she kept saying she had to think of the other children. As though my daughter was a disease she had to quarantine.

For the students, the unspoken message was that it's okay to bully and shame people you don't understand. Sure enough, the bullying escalated, the principal took no further action to educate the students, and in turn Georgie took from all those experiences the message that she wasn't worth caring for.

My eyes had been opened. That day at the pool was the first real taste of the discrimination I'd foreseen and been terrified of, and I knew I had to rise to meet the challenge. I had to be a better advocate and ally than I had been. Never again would I leave my daughter unprotected and exposed in that way. And I knew now that as long as she remained at that school, she was never going to be able to thrive.

The clincher came when Georgie asked me one day, 'Am I disabled?'

'No, my love, you're not disabled. There's nothing wrong with having a disability though. You have different challenges. Some people don't understand those either. Has anyone said anything to you?'

'No, but I don't want to use the disabled bathroom. It's never unlocked anyway and I have to go to the office to ask for the key, and I don't want to do that because I get funny looks and it makes me different to the other girls.'

It was time to move on.

At the time of the swimming lesson incident, Safe Schools wasn't established and available as a resource and there was no Victorian Government school policy around gender diversity. There was nobody but Doc Paul to offer us support. This experience is a clear example of why education around gender diversity is needed by staff and students – yes, that means primary schools too – and why schools and public spaces need to provide accessible and safe bathroom options.

It also demonstrates why whipping up fear around transgender people in bathrooms makes absolutely no sense. The harm that's done when a transgender person is forced to use a bathroom that doesn't align with their gender identity is to the transgender person only. Those boys were confused by the presence of a girl in their bathroom; that confusion heightened Georgie's anxiety and made her unsafe. If common sense and compassion rather than reactive fear had prevailed, or had there been just one family or all-gender change room at this swimming pool, Georgie wouldn't have gone through the ordeal she endured that day. Better still, if she'd been able to use a cubicle in the girls' bathroom, she would have felt just fine and, I suspect, so would everybody else.

I do understand that for schools at that time, this situation was completely alien to them and they weren't part of a broader community dialogue about it, let alone a policy framework to guide them. Today, there should be no such excuse.

My next step was to ring around new schools and give each principal I spoke to a brief outline of our story: twins, one is transgender, both experiencing exclusion at school; these are our needs. Georgie must be able to wear the girls' uniform, use the female-only spaces like bathrooms and change rooms; she needs to be included in the girls' dorm on camp and to be able to learn in peace.

The responses were telling. One principal with a tiny, high-pitched voice shovelled platitudes all over me. 'Oh, you're such a good mother, what an incredible story! Your child is so lucky to have you! I'll certainly speak to our council about it and see what we can come up with.' Bullshitter: immediately crossed off the list. Others had nothing to offer; they simply didn't quite know what to say. *Click.* Another – I imagined her to be related to Griselda – spoke in authoritative tones that harked back to a generation of sensible women and no-nonsense educators. With about as much warmth as Margaret Thatcher after being knifed by her own party, she said, 'I'll have to speak to the department about this.' She took my number and promptly hung up. I never heard back.

This problem was vexing me because we couldn't remain where we were, stuck in a school where neither of my kids could make the most of their education. Once this questioning mindset takes hold, you start to notice all the negatives that previously you hadn't reacted to: unimaginative projects, staff who should have retired ten years ago, the daily drag on the spirit of your kids. Why was there so little garden? Couldn't they improve the dry, patchy grass? We needed badly to get out of there, and soon.

One day, I was telling one of my massage clients our dilemma. I knew she was in admin but didn't really know where. 'Come to our school,' she said. 'There's an open day coming up soon and the principal is lovely.'

The primary school had once been one of the most run-down schools in our area, but many of its ugly buildings had recently been torn down and beautiful new 'learning pods' had replaced them. We arrived at the open day and what we saw was astonishing. The community was buzzing. There were families milling about, stalls had been set up and there was the obligatory sausage sizzle. Strikingly, the grounds and the people exuded optimism, a healthy confidence and a *pride* in their school.

It was exciting to imagine our kids coming every day to this place, with its brand-new learning facilities. The staff also looked like they were modelling a positivity that I realised I hadn't seen for a while. It looked like learning was going to be possible for the kids, and maybe even . . . creativity! We were pretty impressed by it all, though both Georgie and Harry did have reservations: Georgie would miss her friends and Harry was just unsure.

The following week I rang the principal. I talked her through our situation, told her what had happened with swimming lessons, described Harry's needs and what we hoped for. I told her that many trans students are too distracted by their circumstances to properly focus on their studies, and that I wanted Georgie not to experience the bullying and shaming she had been subjected to thus far so she could learn.

The principal listened.

'Can you accommodate us in your school?' I asked hopefully.

'It's my job to educate children, Rebekah, not my role to judge who they are. Of course we can accommodate you. Pop in and we'll work through a plan for Georgie.'

There was so much in her reply that I found comfort in. She was honest. She was forward-looking. She was certain of her role. Done deal.

While the clock was running down on our time at what we quickly dubbed the 'old school', I attended our final parent-teacher meeting. Georgie's teacher took me to task about moving schools. They had, according to her, bent over backwards to accommodate Georgie. She suggested that some people might perceive our leaving as a criticism of the school.

I said, 'I don't care how people perceive it. We're leaving because we've found somewhere that can give our kids the education and environment they deserve.'

I do want to say this: the parents and children who were kind to us at the 'old school' – and there were many – will always have a special place in our hearts. If you're reading this, please know that we very much appreciated the support you and your children gave us.

And I want to share this final story of a boy in Georgie's class, Bert, who was one of the smartest kids in the year. He was on the highest level of reader and had loads of after-school activities to stimulate his young mind. He was clearly curious about many things. One day when I was reading with the kids, Bert came out to read with me. Often the kids would put the book into my hands and awkwardly twist their shirt in their fingers, twirl long hair or wipe a fist across a snotty nose. But Bert was always bright in demeanour.

'Hello, Beck,' he said.

'Hi, Bert. How are you today?'

'Good thanks. I've been meaning to ask you a question. Georgie's a girl, right? But she has a boy's body? But she feels like a girl. How does that happen?' In his brown eyes I saw so much sincerity. He was a friend of Georgie's and the question was completely reasonable. He wanted to understand.

'Bert, that's a really good question, but it's a complicated question. The truth is that at this point people don't know how this happens, but there have been people like Georgie all through history. In some places and times, they've been accepted and in others they haven't. I want Georgie to be accepted, because – yes – this is a real thing and Georgie really is a girl. She's not hurting anyone and she's a nice person. All we need to do is be kind and be a good friend to her.'

'That's what I thought,' he said, and proceeded to read his book.

Sadly, Greg's dad Roy passed away. It happened while Greg was performing in Tim Finn's musical *Poor Boy*, and he had to leave the show and fly to Perth immediately. A few days later, the kids and I flew over for the service, and to be with Greg and the family.

Roy's was a beautiful send-off, with a crowd of family and friends, fabulous music and lots of love. Together we sang 'Will the Circle Be Unbroken?', an old Christian hymn of longing to be reunited.

For many in the Perth clan, it was the first time they'd seen Georgie after her social transition. It was actually the perfect time, because the focus wasn't on her at all. There was nothing but love and welcome for her, and she and Harry could flit about getting to know cousins and run around on the bowling green outside.

On our return to Melbourne, Greg went straight back to work for a few short weeks. After that, we could take off for a much-anticipated and much-needed family holiday to Bali, then the pace of our life would pick up dramatically: Greg was scheduled to fly to Sydney for the tour of *Poor Boy* and I was to begin work on *August: Osage County* by Tracy Letts for the Melbourne Theatre Company. It was to be one of the most wonderful plays and productions I've ever had the pleasure of working on and would later earn me a Green Room Award for Best Supporting Actress.

*

Georgie was keen on the idea that at her new school nobody should know she was transgender. She wanted to be taken at face value and was fearful of being bullied again. The plan with the school was that only the principal and Georgie's class teacher would know her story. When she went on camp, there had to be at least one staff member who knew, and to whom Georgie could go if there were any issues. This satisfied all of us.

Few people appreciate that transgender kids are extremely private. Many struggle with their relationship with their bodies, so the last thing they would want is to be placed in a position where they'll be exposed, let alone deliberately put themselves in danger of that possibility and the conflict or embarrassment that might result. I always took pains to look into the layout of the change rooms for swimming and camp. Did they have lockable cubicles for Georgie to change in? I turned up to every swimming lesson until I was fully confident that she was going to be okay.

At the new school, I was relieved to discover two things. First, lots of the girls wore their board shorts to swimming lessons. Second, many of them used the cubicles so they could dress in privacy. This meant Georgie wasn't standing out. She was just one of the girls.

This new start was brilliant in every way. The sense of dread that school life had held for us previously was gone, and suddenly we could breathe again. Both Georgie and Harry had great teachers. Harry had a fantastic male teacher, which is just what he needed, and he instantly responded well. His imagination was allowed to take flight, was valued and encouraged. For the first time in Harry's schooling, someone got him. It was wonderful.

Georgie, too, was finding her balance and learning to trust again. She found some girls to hang out with and seemed to really like her teacher.

I did have a private meeting with her teacher in the first days of term. Georgie had appeared to be an average student, but I suspected she could do a lot better. I was determined that she reach the potential she was capable of. I asked the teacher to have high expectations of my child. By the end of that school year, Georgie was beginning to make massive leaps in her learning and to show signs she was a natural leader, the direct result of being able to live and grow as her true self and not be bullied for it. Even in the way Georgie dressed, there was no longer a need to overstate her femininity by wearing the most sparkly thing she could find. At the age of almost ten, she was moving out of the dress-up stage, which had continued for longer than it might have otherwise, a means to release the stress of not being able to fully embrace herself.

Georgie's love for music, singing and songwriting was growing by the day and would stay with her all through her tweens and teenage years. It offered many things – comfort, solace, inspiration and creative outlet – and it was a key part of her relationship with her dad. Greg loved introducing her to new artists and they shared a love for show tunes.

We hadn't as yet changed any of Georgie's documentation. By law, it wasn't possible in Victoria for an individual to change the sex marker on their birth certificate without undergoing surgery to affirm their gender. As of the time of writing, this is still the case. Sadly for Georgie, the lack of documentation made for some uncomfortable moments.

This disjunct was problematic at appointments both within the hospital and outside it. The name that appeared on Georgie's birth certificate and Medicare card was often called out across crowded waiting rooms as she was summoned in to an appointment. She'd feel exposed and embarrassed as she walked up to the counter with me. This usually happened outside the relative safety of the endocrinology department at the RCH, in places she wasn't known. When questioned by a staff member calling out for and expecting George, a boy, I'd quietly say, 'Please read the reason for our being here on the referral.' They'd take another look and the penny would drop. But by then the damage would have been done.

We learned to remain vigilant and anticipate problems ahead of time. I felt like a landmine detector sweeping the terrain ahead of Georgie, making sure each step she took was on safe ground.

It was always a shock to step outside our little bubble and see how isolated we really were, even within the hospital system. Very few people working at the RCH really knew about or understood this emerging area of medicine. We were a tiny part of a bigger machine, a handful of kids who figured in the budgets of a few departments. Soon, we asked that Georgie's preferred name be used on her file and from then our visits to the RCH were a much easier experience.

As far as the kids were concerned, we'd hit upon an even keel.

8

Puberty looms

In so many ways, Greg and I were living quite different lives. We each had our roles to play, but I was no longer convinced that either of us was all that happy within them. More than anything, it was our teamwork that had deteriorated. Greg was often on tour or working nights, and as a result had a built-in social life. On a daily basis, he could talk with interesting adults about art, books and politics, and I missed that. He'd go to bed hours after his show finished at night and I'd rise early, so we were ships that passed in the mid-morning. This was simply how it had always been. It wasn't workable anymore for us to transport the family so we could all be together when Greg was on tour. Often it would be term time when he was away and it wasn't fair to pull Georgie and Harry out of school, so Greg missed a lot of family life.

My life was a highly domestic one, given my top priorities were Georgie and Harry. I felt the need to be as present as possible for them after the tough time both of them had experienced in their early years at school. Another priority was supporting the family financially. We didn't have much of a buffer. While I'd enjoyed building up my humble little massage business, and loved the fact that I could flex the hours as required, it wasn't all that lucrative. The need to find other options exercised my mind.

Voice acting or voice-over work was an area I really wanted to break into. Television and radio commercials, book or video narrations, or even being a character voice for an animation or video game was something I really wanted to do. The working hours were perfect (no nights out), the work was done in short, intense blocks of time and you didn't need to spend hours learning your lines. And the money was excellent.

Voice-over work is highly competitive. Even though I had a dedicated voice-over agent and a great demo that showcased my range, for a while I knocked on doors in vain. Slowly but surely, however, over the space of two or three years I managed to get a foothold and by the end of 2011 I'd landed a big account. Professionally, things started looking up.

I began to understand how extraordinarily lucky we were to live in Melbourne. Nowhere else in Australia would Georgie have had the support she was now getting at the RCH. The new school had proven to be as supportive as we'd hoped it would be. In turn, Georgie was doing better academically and socially. Harry was too, and he'd found some friends to hang out with. We'd been through a lot to be settled in this way and none of us took it for granted.

Once I was breathing easier, the realisation sneaked up on me that something fundamental had been shifting in me. I'd begun to see more clearly my own qualities, needs and aspirations. I also began to see my vulnerabilities. All of these realisations were a mess in my head and I needed to tease them out. I decided to see a counsellor to help find out which were genuine, which were personal mythology; what I needed to act upon, what I shouldn't.

The consequences of those enquiries felt catastrophic and overwhelming. Responsibility weighed heavily on me; I felt responsible for everyone's happiness, wellbeing, safety and relationships. As for the wellbeing of Rebekah Robertson, I felt totally inadequate, guilty, a failure, alone and frightened. It was confronting to recognise the parts of me that were dead, dying or redundant. I'd been too busy or distracted to see them before, and as soon as I did they started hurting like hell. Sometimes, while the kids were at school, I'd cry all day.

One evening, as I was sitting in the backyard alone, I found myself staring up into the canopy of the huge peppercorn tree where Harry had spent hours swinging on a rope in his Spiderman costume and thinking that I would never be happy, truly happy, and carefree again. I wished I could go back to simpler times and I grieved for them. There was no sense of optimism for me and my life. I saw it as a long, slow, unhappy road. A slog.

In that anxious state, I took up smoking again. Again I was frustrated with myself, given that at that point I'd been cigarette-free since I'd extinguished my last one at the Ngurah Rai airport in Denpasar in 1997.

My usual sunny disposition drained away. I walked around on automatic pilot, and it was only when the kids were home that I cheered up. Partly, I was putting on a bright face for them, but in reality they've always brought me great joy. They were my reason for putting one foot in front of the other.

*

Georgie and I used to have long conversations about the difference between privacy and secrecy. According to the Oxford
English Dictionary, the noun 'privacy' denotes 'a state in which
one is not observed or disturbed by other people. The state
of being free from public attention.' That sounded lovely for
her, like an oasis. By contrast, a secret is defined as something
that's actively 'kept or meant to be kept unknown or unseen
by others'. Our position was that Georgie's gender identity
was private; it was nobody else's business; it didn't affect other
people and therefore had nothing to do with them. Having a
secret felt sad and a little shameful, and Georgie was neither sad
nor shameful about herself; she just didn't trust other people.
This distinction may well seem like semantics, but choosing to
think of Georgie's gender identity as private gave her and us a
positive outlook.

While she'd chosen not to share her experiences with her
new schoolmates, and there was comfort in the circuit-breaker
of changing schools, we weren't complacent. It stood to reason
that there could be problems maintaining that privacy in the long
term, and we were mindful we might have to address an issue
related to this at some point. For now, we remained hopeful that
maybe Georgie could get to experience life without intrusions
into her privacy having such an impact on her.

Georgie had made a couple of good friends at her new school,
but she also began to appreciate more her longer-term friends
from the old school who knew and didn't care. She was able to see
how valuable they were and I think she wanted to be able to have
that trust with her new friends. One day she came home with the
news that she'd confided in two of her new friends and was now

regretting it a bit. Straightaway, I felt myself go back on alert. We'd worked hard to create this safety for her, but I understood that she wanted her new friends to really know her, to understand something important about her.

I felt so sorry that Georgie had these tensions in her life. I felt them, too. It was a constant balancing act between authenticity and safety, difficult to navigate but without an alternative.

'It's okay, Mum. They said they wouldn't tell anyone else.'

'Darling, they need some support. You can't ask them to keep a confidence without their parents knowing and being able to help them understand. I'll speak to their folks.'

I organised a time to have a cuppa with the two mums and carefully explained our situation. What I wanted to convey was that we didn't want the girls to feel they had to keep a secret from them or try to understand things in isolation. We hoped they'd encourage the girls to be kind and help Georgie maintain her privacy at school as she was scared of being bullied again and had told the girls because she trusted them.

The two women were wonderful, very understanding and generous. It was no surprise that those girls always supported Georgie and never gossiped about her. They had quality parenting.

Since 2007, Georgie had been seeing Doc Paul regularly. In 2008 he'd referred us to Dr Z,* an endocrinologist at the RCH. The appointment had been a routine examination to see if there may

* Name changed to protect privacy.

be any other causes for Georgie identifying as female. Doc Paul's role was to ascertain if there was a psychiatric basis involved; Dr Z's was to discover if there was a physiological basis, such as an intersex variation. In both cases, nothing was discovered that would indicate there was any other reason for Georgie's experience of herself as female.

The RCH's endocrinology clinic was always full to overflowing with children of varying ages and different endocrine needs. Plans were afoot to build a new hospital; frankly, this place was gloomy and depressing. But our endocrinologist, Dr Z, was not. A charming older man, he was always kind and gentle whenever we saw him.

Throughout the following year, 2010, we increased our visits to Dr Z. Puberty was looming for Georgie, and we needed to monitor the situation, to know when her body would start to change. Both Greg and I had gone through puberty early, and Georgie very much did not want to experience male puberty. The doctors agreed with Greg and me that it would cause Georgie severe distress; that it would usher in changes that held dire consequences for her. To date, the blood tests and physical examinations revealed puberty was still a way off, so we strictly maintained our vigilance with the tests and used the time to get our heads around what we would need to do to obtain medication.

My friend Jane and I were in the same boat. We'd discovered that in order to access puberty-blocking medication for our trans kids, we'd have to file an application to the Family Court of Australia seeking their permission. It turned out that Australia was the only jurisdiction in the world to have such a law.

We couldn't kid ourselves that getting puberty blockers in order to prevent our girls from falling into a black hole was going to be straightforward. At that stage, few Australian families had been through court trying to access the treatment. According to our research, the whole process was costly and time-consuming. Also, getting the timing right for the maximum clinical benefit was going to be challenging, as we needed to make sure we were granted treatment orders before irreversible physical changes occurred. We didn't want to miss the once-in-a-lifetime opportunity for our daughters to live comfortably as themselves.

Georgie had pleaded with me to help her prevent masculini-sation. I was acutely aware of how much she feared developing an Adam's apple and deep voice. She and Vanessa had already had to manage a lot of serious and hurtful things at a young age; now there was this mountain ahead of them, and it appeared they had no choice but to climb it. It broke my heart that their childhood should be so complicated.

I ploughed on with my reading, immersing myself in the findings of previous cases, trying to wrap my head around the legalities, the language and the basis on which the court had reached its decisions. There was little cause for optimism.

Jane and I also joined an online group for parents of children experiencing 'transsexualism' (the term that was still being used at that time). It was not run by other parents but by people with lived experience, which was useful and informative, but I felt unable to let my guard down and share what was happening for our family. It was like we were always failing the parenting test. We'd get pulled up abruptly for getting the language wrong or not understanding fully things that were new to us. The parents themselves were amazing and generous. But the vibe of the group seemed rigid, and the free-flowing conversations I'd hoped would occur seemed few and far between. Parents could feel unwelcome if their child was gender-questioning and didn't have a binary identity. The word 'transgender' was practically banned.

It was in this group that some divides within the trans community became apparent to me. Like Georgie, I too was having trouble finding people I could trust. Each time I logged on, my anxiety would ramp up. So I avoided it and just called Jane instead.

I discovered that we needed to seek pro bono representation by a trained family law specialist, otherwise we'd be looking at up to $30,000 in court fees. This, to a family like ours, was a ludicrous sum of money. Greg and I had no assets and no savings. As jobbing actors, we lived a hand-to-mouth existence. But this time I didn't want to let Georgie down by not being as prepared as possible.

We learned to live with a level of anxiety and exhaustion that became almost like white noise. It was undetectable, even to ourselves at times. We pretended that things were okay. Normal.

'Normal' is a word I've come to actively dislike, despite the expectation it ought to provide comfort and reassurance. To me it's a value judgement, a cudgel used to belittle those who are deemed to have fallen outside its bounds. A taunt that forces us all to spend our lives proving to ourselves and others that we're somehow standard and uniform, trying to be perfect rather than allowing ourselves to be as extraordinarily authentic as we could be.

One of my mother's favourite sayings was, 'Dare to be different.' I'd taken that to heart and been the only one of Mum's five daughters to pursue the arts after school. Three of my sisters were nurses and one a science and maths teacher who moved into the biotech industry. Being an actor or an artist of any kind often entails living life on the margins. We're observers of human nature, including our own, storytellers for whom there's no job security. As a young woman I took some menial jobs to stay afloat, and when I look back on those experiences, I appreciate how they rounded me out as a person. One of them was as a domestic cleaner for a company that serviced the wealthier areas of Melbourne. The experience was an eye-opener. I'd come from a pretty privileged background, but I'd never been exposed to wealth like this before.

There were a few lessons I learned in that time. The first was that having a ton of money cannot buy you taste or class. Second, that in our leafier suburbs there are a lot of extremely lonely people holed up in homes with too many bathrooms. Third, I discovered I loved pickled walnuts. A lovely lady introduced me to them. She was a widow and I actually spent a lot of my three hours a week in her house chatting with her. The two of us would stand pressed to the kitchen counter, a fork in our hands, wolfing down pickled walnuts. I also learned that when a person is talked about while they're present but are not invited to participate in that conversation, it feels demeaning. It feels like you don't matter at all. This is what it's like to live on the margins or in a minority, or what it's like to be a child.

The final lesson was delivered in the opulent home of my wealthiest clients, who featured in Australia's richest top-fifty list in *The Bulletin*. I'd begun cleaning for them during the so-called recession we had to have in 1990. At the time I was living in Fitzroy and I could see every day the impact the recession was having on that community. But my clients' house was huge, brand new, with a tennis court, pool and all the trimmings. An au pair was employed to look after the couple's three children – and they appeared to be running rings around her.

Just before the Spring Racing Carnival that year, there was a lot of entertaining action and I was booked to clean for them three days a week for four hours at a time. One day, the lady of the house was having some tennis friends over for a game, followed by lunch. I was finishing up in the living room when they bustled in, already well into a conversation about how lazy people were and how much people had been complaining about the recession. Someone commented, 'And if they don't like it, they should just get on and change their circumstances . . . Look at *her*.' The woman pointed at me. 'She clearly has some pluck and is trying to make the best of it!'

The effect of her words was immediate: I was hot with anger and embarrassment. On Brunswick Street, there were people who had no chance of making the best of it. What embarrassed me was that after my secure and well-provided-for upbringing, had I chosen a more conventional path in life I might have been saying the same things. And that thought horrified me.

During my early twenties, I woke up to harsh realities to which I'd previously had little exposure. The consequences of inequity, sexism, racism and intergenerational trauma were right before my eyes, and once you know something you can't unknow it. The world wasn't as I'd been taught it was. This was the start of an ongoing process of redefining what I believed and what I stood for, and led me to join Amnesty International. I read stories of people jailed for their beliefs, their sexuality, their politics, their religion, their bodies. I also became aware of countries that still carried out the death penalty. It shocked me to know that a country like the USA carried out this barbaric form of punishment.

I'd seen on commercial television the lead-up to an execution in California in 1992, which played out like ghoulish entertainment. It was the first execution in California for twenty-five years and took place at San Quentin State Prison. I couldn't see why this was getting coverage in Australia, a country that had abolished the death penalty. What I saw on TV really disturbed me.

A short time after, I was reading an Amnesty newsletter and spotted a call-out for pen pals for death row prisoners around the world. I made some enquiries about who I might be writing to, what I should talk about. It made me very nervous, but I decided to go ahead.

Soon I was put in touch with Carl, and thereby given a window into a world I'd never imagined. A world so alien to me, so harsh, that I could barely comprehend its reality. Carl was on death row at Ellis Unit One, in Huntsville, Texas.

When I sent my first letter to this man, I had no information other than his name and where he was incarcerated. Briefly, I explained who I was, how I had come by his details, and I offered to write to him if he felt that would be of benefit to him. It was a guarded letter. I didn't ask Carl what his crime was. I think my old cat Lily featured heavily. I posted the letter and wondered if I would even get a reply. Eventually I did. Carl's letter arrived in a crisp envelope, addressed with the neatest handwriting I'd ever seen. In the top corner the sender had drawn, with utmost care, a butterfly and cat paw prints. I turned the letter over in my hands for minutes before I carefully opened it. I know a letter can't hurt you, but I didn't know how to feel about this experience. I was scared he'd be a monster, a manipulator, needy or broken. How was I going to relate to this person who'd taken a life, maybe more than one?

I read that Carl had been on death row since 1984, the year I'd left school. Straightaway, I thought about all the things I'd been able to do in those seven years since. My life as a young adult, full of dreams and aspirations, was the antithesis of his, in his tiny cell with a limited view of the sky.

Carl's tone was friendly and respectful, and so it continued over the next two years. Never once did he ask for a single thing, or make inappropriate suggestions. Never once did he attempt any form of manipulation. He wasn't sure who'd put his name forward, he explained, as he'd never asked for a pen pal. Nonetheless, he appreciated the opportunity and was happy to write to me. He described his surroundings and how his days were spent, and reflected on how mischievous my cat seemed.

Carl was a skilled artist, despite only having black ink or pencil at his disposal. He sent me pictures he'd drawn. Some expressed his feelings about the death penalty, offering bleak insights into his world; others were more whimsical. He once drew me a picture of a stork eating a frog. The frog was headfirst down the stork's throat, but had its own sticky front feet wrapped around the stork's throat to prevent it from swallowing. The caption read, 'Never give up.'

I learned a lot about the American judicial system, and why the death penalty is such a poor form of justice. Bit by bit, I discovered Carl had been convicted of an armed robbery in a bar in Houston and a man had been shot dead. He always professed his innocence; I don't know if that's true or not, but his criminal history didn't help him convince a jury they might have had the wrong man. Prior to this conviction he'd been convicted of seventeen felonies, which included eight aggravated robberies, two robberies by assault and three burglaries. In all, he'd been sentenced to a total of 223 years in prison, which he'd served concurrently over three separate prison terms. He had spent most of his youth in prison.

My pen pal activities attracted comment. Not everybody agreed with what I was doing and I don't deny their logic. Carl's life choices caused so much pain to so many, and I make no excuse nor have any desire to minimise that. But writing to him gave me a particular insight into how the justice system can fail the most vulnerable. How it guarantees, in fact, that those who are least able to defend themselves will get tougher sentences than those who can afford a defence.

In his final statement before being executed in 1994, Carl said, 'My record looks like I'm John Dillinger or Al Capone, but I never was in that bar.'

A message from Carl arrived in the post shortly after his execution. It was a pencil sketch he'd drawn of me from a photo

I'd sent him. The caption on the back read, 'To Beck, Australia's Fineness!! [*sic*] With faithful emotions and pure pleasure, I send grand wishes, genuine inspiration and endless music . . . from, death row Texas, a World of Concrete and steel. Yours Evermore, Carl.'

The death penalty is a stark example of how entrenched institutional inequity demands its pound of flesh if you cannot pay for justice. That concept is integral to my understanding of the difference between the law and justice, and in the times ahead, fighting for my child, it informed my thinking and drove me on. My daughter's body would not be collateral in the Family Court system.

It was time for action: time to prepare for court and apply for puberty-blocking medication for Georgie. I set about contacting legal firms asking if anyone would consider taking on our case on a pro bono basis. It was reminiscent of my search for a new school – days went by when I was having no luck at all. Again, it was massage that paved the way to a solution: a barrister client offered to ask his colleagues for advice. Heartened, but keeping my expectations in check, I waited to see what would happen.

At that stage, the idea of mounting a big legal challenge to the Family Court's involvement in this process hadn't entered my head. All we wanted was for Georgie to be able to access the medical treatment that was appropriate for her, and in good time, so her health outcomes would be protected. I knew that the court process could be lengthy, but also that applications for treatment for gender dysphoria fell under the legal category of 'special medical procedures'. With luck, our case would be given some priority because special medical procedures are usually – but not always – relatively urgent.

Ahead lay a process with many moving parts: accessing lawyers, booking in and having Georgie undergo assessments by second-opinion doctors and court writers, the writing of affidavits, collecting reports from doctors and any intervenors, and, once all that was done, securing a court date. Apparently, getting a matter to be heard in the Family Court could take up to twelve months. My heart sank when I learned that. The issue of timeliness was a major source of stress from the start. It was difficult to ask lawyers to commit to representing us pro bono when I had no idea when they'd be required. But for my own peace of mind, I needed to know who we could call on when the moment arrived.

The energy changed for the better as soon as my barrister client called me back. A colleague of his who worked in the Family Court had recommended a Queen's Counsel who was expecting my call. A QC! I wasn't sure how it all worked and I didn't know if I had to ask him directly to represent us for free. I was completely out of my depth. I took a deep breath and phoned.

We had a long discussion about Georgie's history and about what we needed to do. To my massive relief, the QC was a straight shooter and made it plain that he and his junior barrister would act for us pro bono. By way of clarification, he explained that the expression 'pro bono' means 'for the public good', and that our case met that criteria.

'Save your money,' he elaborated. 'I've made a good living from my work. Put yours towards your children.'

I was so grateful, and thanked him profusely.

In addition to senior counsel, however, we still needed family law specialists. Our QC gave me the number of some solicitors and asked me to phone them, which I duly did. I'd assumed they were also offering their services on a pro bono basis. As I was winding up one call by offering my thanks, I was asked, 'What's been discussed with you on that matter?'

Apparently, I'd need to make an application for pro bono legal representation. The application process proved to be simple and straightforward; so, too, was the answer. But I had to divulge the embarrassing details of our parlous financial situation: I had $100 in my purse and there was $80 in our bank account. We had no shares or assets. Nothing to sell or mortgage. We were broke.

Our application was accepted.

9

Court orders

Late in 2010, Georgie's blood tests showed that she was beginning to edge closer towards puberty. Although puberty wasn't imminent, it was definitely time to keep a closer eye on things through more regular visits to the hospital, physical examinations and blood tests. Around this time, we also learned more about the treatment options available and the benefits and consequences of those treatments. Georgie was counselled about what any future medical interventions could be for her – none were surgical – and was given plenty of opportunity to ask questions.

We were about to discover a whole lot about the different phases of puberty, a broad term that covers the appearance of external primary and secondary sex characteristics. We were introduced to a measurement system called the Tanner scale, which identifies pubertal growth not by a person's chronological age but by visible signs. In those assigned male at birth, for example, one measurement is testicular volume, a pronounced increase of which indicates that puberty has started. For those assigned female at birth, doctors can track breast growth. The growth of pubic hair is also an obvious physical sign.

The Tanner scale ranges from 1 to 5, where 1 is pre-pubertal and 5 is the most advanced stage of puberty. Puberty-blocking medication for transgender adolescents is ideally administered when the young person is between Tanner 2 and 3. It shouldn't be administered only at a specific age – say twelve years, for example – because for some young people the ship would already have sailed. Medication cannot reverse secondary sex characteristics once they've developed. The pitch of a broken voice cannot be made higher; breasts or an Adam's Apple won't disappear; and so on.

Our education was about much more than puberty, however. What we call puberty blockers – more accurately called gonadotropin-releasing hormone (GnRH) agonists – are the first of two stages of medical interventions for transgender adolescents. In Stage 1, the development of secondary sex characteristics is delayed with puberty blockers. In Stage 2 of treatment, by taking gender-affirming hormones, the young person begins developing the sex characteristics of their affirmed gender. For Georgie, this would mean developing breasts. In 2010, when Georgie was receiving counselling around these treatments, the minimum age at which gender-affirming hormones were administered was sixteen years. There wasn't a skerrick of doubt in her mind that she wanted this treatment. Nevertheless, she still listened intently to the advice she was given and the alternatives offered.

As with every medical intervention, we wanted to be sure about the physical implications under every circumstance. What reassured me on that score is that puberty blockers have been widely used for a long time to treat children undergoing precocious puberty, a condition that can occur in children as young as two years of age whereby they develop secondary sex characteristics way before they're developmentally ready for them. The same medication is used to treat prostate cancer in adults, so it has been carefully studied. The medication is safe, and if or when it's no longer required, the regular processes of the body resume without issue.

For transgender adolescents, there are several benefits to delaying the onset of puberty. For someone like Georgie, whose physical attributes were already distressing to her, the treatment would spare her the further distress of developing a masculine appearance – including an Adam's apple and facial hair – and the thing she feared most of all, her voice breaking. Blocking puberty also allows the young person more time to consider their options or explore their identity, if that is of benefit to them.

Fertility counselling was also provided. In order to have a biological child, Georgie would have to go through enough male puberty to produce viable sperm, which could be stored cryogenically for future use. But this option didn't appeal to her. It meant she'd have to develop secondary male characteristics. All the features she was trying so hard to avoid developing would be permanently etched on her body, requiring greater surgical intervention when she was an adult. And some – like broad shoulders, for example – couldn't be altered at all. To Georgie, this was a terrifying prospect.

Georgie definitely wanted to have children. She imagined a life for herself in the future in which getting married and having children were a natural progression. After the fertility counselling, she told us that she expected she'd adopt.

These are major conversations to be having with a ten-year-old, but Georgie had been thinking about such things already for many years. For her, being able to live comfortably as a girl was her first priority. Having children in the future was incredibly important to her, but she stated very clearly that if she had to forgo having biological children in order to live her life safely and feel comfortable in her own skin, then that is what she would do. This position was not arrived at flippantly or quickly. She considered all possibilities, and her conclusion caused her to grieve for the possibility of having her own babies. Sagely, she put her own wellbeing first.

For many, Georgie among them, these medical interventions are literally life-saving. Her distress and anxiety at the thought of not being able to access this treatment was painfully apparent when she was asked in the lead-up to her court case how she would feel if the court denied it.

'I really, really desperately need that treatment because without it I wouldn't be who I feel myself to be . . . and that would just be terrible . . . because for the rest of my life I couldn't be who I feel myself to be . . . and that would just be devastating . . . For me, it would be an incomplete life, and I wouldn't feel good.'[1]

In 2014, when interviewed for a *Four Corners* episode called 'Being Me', her reply was much more blunt when asked what her life would be like if she couldn't be who she is.

'Very dark, very bleak and very short,' she answered.

'Short?' the reporter asked, probingly.

'Yeah. Very short,' she said.[2]

In mid-2010, we organised a meeting with our full legal team in chambers to prepare our application to court to grant Georgie Stage 1 and Stage 2 treatment. Once again, so that everyone present was on the same page, we recounted our story from the beginning. At that point, we still believed we had plenty of time. There was a sense of comfort in having these skilled people supporting us, as this new world we were immersing ourselves in was fascinating yet daunting. The process also gave my mind a focus and purpose that helped me deal with the sense of power-lessness I'd long been holding in my chest.

The more I understood what we were up against legally, however, the angrier I became. A special medical procedure is brought before the court when medical treatment falls outside the ambit of parental responsibility. To put this another way: as parents, we were deemed *incapable* of making a decision on our child's behalf or in her best interests. Effectively, the court was taking over our responsibility as parent. This made me furious. Here we were, two parents in full agreement with our child's clinicians and Georgie herself, willing to take full responsibility for the decisions made, understanding the benefits, impacts and consequences of the treatment. Yet we were legally unable to do so. The depth of that unfairness sank into my bones.

I swallowed that bitter pill and focused instead on getting my head around all the background knowledge required.

The definition of a special medical procedure, I discovered, hangs on the distinction between treatment that's deemed to be therapeutic and treatment that's deemed to be non-therapeutic. Therapeutic treatment would be to treat a 'disease or malfunction of the body', which would still fall within the bounds of parental responsibility. Non-therapeutic would be anything that did not treat a 'disease or malfunction' and had potential benefits for those other than the child themself.

Then there were the three cases I kept hearing about: *Re: Marion*, *Re: Alex* and *Gillick v West Norfolk and Wisbech Area Health Authority* (from the United Kingdom). It was essential for me to understand each of these cases because they would directly influence our case.

Re: Marion was a complex and emotionally charged case that went before the High Court of Australia and was decided in 1992. It centred on 'Marion' – the name assigned to the subject of the application; everything is anonymised with these cases – an adolescent girl with significant physical and intellectual disabilities. Her parents had sought from the Family Court an order giving them authority to proceed with two surgical interventions, a hysterectomy and an ovariectomy, which would cause her permanent infertility. The parents were concerned that Marion was unable to comprehend sexuality, pregnancy or motherhood, and that she wasn't able to look after herself physically. But Marion was also unable to understand or consent to the operation to remove her ovaries and uterus, and would most likely never reach a point where she could.

The rights of the parents, the rights of the child, the child's bodily integrity and human rights, the child's best interests, the permanence of the procedure, the risk of making a wrong decision and the authority of the court were all under consideration. Should the surgical procedures be carried out, they would render Marion sterile, which was one of the desired outcomes for her parents. The question was, did it impinge on her human rights? In *Re: Marion*, the High Court found that the scope of parental authority did not extend to special medical procedures resulting in sterilisation.

Gillick was a 1985 English case that centred on mother and Catholic activist Victoria Gillick. She was campaigning against the Department of Health and Social Security, which had produced some material about contraceptive prescription for minors, notably minors under the age of sixteen, without the consent or veto of parents. The matter was ventilated in the House of Lords and focused more on whether a minor was able to understand and consent to treatment than the rights of the parents to veto.

Ultimately, it was found that if a minor displayed sufficient maturity and understanding of the treatment, its benefits and its side effects, they were able to consent to medical treatment without the responsibility shifting to their parents. This standard of medical law was applied in Australia in *Re: Marion*.

Re: Alex was the first case in Australia centring on a transgender minor, and both *Re: Marion* and *Gillick* featured in the 2004 decision, which became a legal precedent for those who came after and created a legal nightmare for families like mine. Alex was a thirteen-year-old ward of the state in Victoria. The question in this case was over who should have responsibility for Alex's care and welfare.

Professor Fiona Kelly of La Trobe University explains the decision succinctly:

> When the question of whether parents can consent to medical treatment for gender dysphoria first came before the Family Court in 2004 in *Re: Alex* (hormonal treatment for gender dysphoria), Nicholson CJ concluded that treatment for Stages 1 and 2, which he considered 'part of a single package', required court authorisation. The decision turned on Nicholson CJ's assertion that the treatment was non-therapeutic and therefore fell within the ambit of Marion's case. Nicholson CJ's conclusion flowed from the distinction made by the High Court between treatment that is in response to a 'bodily malfunction or disease' (therapeutic) and all other forms of medical treatment (non-therapeutic). Not wishing to pathologize those experiencing gender dysphoria by labelling it a 'disease' or 'bodily malfunction', Nicholson CJ felt that the only option open to him was to conclude that the treatment was non-therapeutic. Subsequent case law adopted this conclusion.[3]

To put it in perspective, our fate had been sealed by these disparate precedents.

As we headed into summer, and as Georgie was starting to undergo regular testing to track her pubertal development, we worked with our lawyers to put together an application for both Stage 1 and Stage 2 of a single treatment plan. It wasn't unprecedented to apply for puberty blockers (Stage 1) and gender-affirming hormones (Stage 2) in one application. They were solving the same issue, and would cover Georgie's needs from now until the age of eighteen. In special medical procedures of this kind, the Family Court had routinely ordered both at the same time and we hoped that they would do the same for Georgie.

Then came a bombshell: during a routine examination, our endocrinologist discovered Georgie was developing at a hugely accelerated rate. Her testosterone levels had jumped much higher and a physical examination revealed she was at Tanner Stage 4. Georgie, at the age of ten, was experiencing the pubertal growth of an average fourteen-year-old boy. Getting those puberty blockers for her had become urgent.

Georgie's endocrinologist, Dr Z, phoned our lawyers to explain that time was of the essence and asked if there was any way they could expedite the process. Georgie was now in real danger of permanent masculinisation. Everything we'd tried so hard to avoid was happening.

This sudden and rapid progression through puberty was a perfect example of why the court process was harmful to children. Had a court process not been an obstacle for Georgie, the endocrinologist would simply have consulted the team treating her and decided between them the correct course of action. And they would have been able to deliver relief almost immediately. But instead we went into a panic-fuelled nightmare of applications, obtaining second opinions, and hashing and rehashing our story to different strangers. All the while, we were hoping that Georgie's voice wouldn't start breaking. The point of all these efforts was for her to live comfortably

as female for the rest of her life. We could see the door to that
future starting to swing shut because of Australia's lumbering
legal system.

Now we encountered another phenomenon that frustrated
us: the Christmas divorce rush. It turns out the new year is the
busiest time in the Family Court because unhappy couples look
at the calendar and decide they can't face another year of being
married to one another. Consequently, the court was at this
time suddenly overloaded with proceedings, parenting orders
and a myriad of applications full of misery. It also turned out
there weren't enough judges to cope with the load, the Family
Court was groaning under the pressure, and the judge assigned
to our case was about to go on holiday so we'd have to wait for
her return.

It was almost too much to bear. Greg and I tried to protect
Georgie and Harry from the stress we were under and never let on
to Georgie how precarious her situation was. All we wanted was for
everything to move as quickly as possible. There wasn't a moment
to consider anything that could hinder a fast decision in her case.

We submitted our application. Immediately, up sprang our
next big hurdle: securing an actual court date. Even though our
matter was critically urgent, the court list was jam-packed. We
tried everything to have our hearing brought forward.

With the clock ticking, in February 2011 we took the extraordinary step of turning up to the Family Court with our lawyers
and specialists, and sitting in the back of the court waiting for the
listed cases to be dealt with so we could jump in. It was so stress-
ful, taking our chances in this way, but we had to. There simply
was no other way.

As I sat there on that long and awful day, I had plenty of time to take in my surroundings. The Family Court, I concluded – with its courtroom after courtroom, each cheek by jowl with bland conference rooms and floor upon floor of forbidding admin rooms – isn't designed for good times. Even though from the outside the place looks sleek and clean, it's a purpose-built container for the management of grief, greed and sadness, and, invariably, it's children who bear the brunt of the decisions of the adults who pass through the doors. I found so much about that place alienating. Upon entry, your belongings are scanned airport-style by security. Court regulars proceed through, not even pausing conversations, hauling carry-on luggage-sized bags full of court documents onto the conveyor belt, expertly whisking them off at the other end and bounding purposefully to one of the many courts operating. It's their world. We were there, beggars at the table. *Give us what we so desperately need and we'll quickly be gone.*

All around us we could hear the language of the court being used. Terms like 'procedural hearing', 'trial', 'evidence', 'your matter' all created the impression that you and your child were on trial and were going to be judged. It wasn't a mere feeling, of course; for us, that is actually what was happening.

It was hard not to dwell on the possibility that our application could be refused. At ten years old, Georgie was by far the youngest child to have sought orders of this kind. Would the judge baulk at her age? Or at our audacity in showing up when we weren't on her list for that day? It was all very, very scary.

But our persistence paid off. An opportunity arose, and our lawyers asked leave to set a trial date, given the urgent and precarious situation Georgie was in. I am eternally grateful that we had these highly skilled professionals on our team – it's hard to imagine anyone else could have made this happen. A directions hearing date was made for 16 March, the earliest available opportunity.

While this was genuine progress, everything was still balanced on a knife's edge. Every hint of delay made me flinch. Every day that went by was one less day Georgie was protected from permanent masculinisation.

The purpose of a directions hearing is for the judge to work out how they want to run the trial and if they need to include intervenors who may provide them with valuable alternative points of view. At our directions hearing, the court appointed a lawyer to represent Georgie's best interests, and a court writer whose role was to interview Georgie and the family. A court writer is a psychologist or psychiatrist who can give the court advice on what may be the child's wishes, the family dynamic and whether they believe the orders being sought are appropriate in a given context.

The court writer assigned to us had no experience with transgender children and this compounded my growing anxiety that those making the decisions for our child had no understanding themselves. It was like there were several different languages being spoken in the court at once: the legal, the medical and the almost imperceptible voice of a child begging to be heard and understood. We, as her parents and advocates, had no more power in this situation than Georgie did. It was agony to watch it unfold; even once a trial date was set, my inner tension was extreme.

Our lives were put on hold. Greg and I had to withdraw from good jobs in order to meet all the requirements leading up to our court date. Greg had a role in *The Wild Duck* at Belvoir St Theatre in Sydney that he had to pull out of. I was rehearsing *The Laramie Project* at Red Stitch Actors Theatre and had to leave the production. It hurt when I had to relinquish a terrific role in the television series *The Slap*, which was filming the week of Georgie's court case. Between us, we had to forgo around $30,000 in wages and some promising opportunities. Of course, this was simply what had to happen, but there was no hiding the fact that this was affecting us as a family in every imaginable way. Fortunately, I was doing a lot of commercial voice-over work and that put bread on the table.

Our court date was set for Monday 28 March 2011. Less than a week beforehand, Georgie's follow-up tests showed that her testosterone was at adult levels. It really was critical that we get an order, and fast.

The same day we received those test results, we attended our appointment with the court writer whose job it was to assess us as a family. She seemed a perfectly pleasant woman, asked the usual things, and we pretty much recounted our entire story again. Next, she interviewed Georgie and Harry separately from one another and us. When Greg and I sat down with her, she questioned us on Georgie's imagination and her style of play; then the questioning began to stick in my guts. Did we think Georgie was acting, pretending to be a girl because both her parents were actors? Staggered, I quipped that nobody was that good an actor.

I added that I didn't believe a pretence as elaborate as this could be imagined by a two-and-a-half-year-old and sustained until she was ten for fun or attention. I was incredulous that the court writer had entertained the thought that a kid could, let alone would, endure what Georgie had thus far – bullying, exclusion, humiliation, hours and hours of therapy over several years – for a lark. My anger after that session was stratospheric.

With Georgie's recent testosterone results being so extremely elevated, her endocrinologist was trying to arrange an MRI for her before the court date the following Monday. Dr Z wanted to rule out any other pathology or possible reason for the rapid spike. To get an appointment at late notice in a busy public hospital seemed nigh on impossible, but late on the Thursday afternoon we received a call asking us how quickly we could get to the hospital; there'd been a cancellation. We made it across the city to Parkville by five o'clock.

I detest driving through the city at that time of day, but needs must. Georgie and I had taken that hospital route on countless occasions and had amassed a selection of her favourite upbeat music to listen to on the trip. It was a playlist packed to the hilt with Beyoncé, Lady Gaga, Pink, Taylor Swift and Delta Goodrem, to name only a handful. Keen to minimise Georgie's fears about why we were going, we stuck to our routine. My anxiety was through the roof, but I kept it under wraps. On my mind was Dr Z's answer when I'd asked him over the phone what else might possibly be elevating Georgie's hormone levels. A malfunctioning pituitary gland, he'd said, or it could be a brain tumour. Also, I'd been told MRIs are deeply unpleasant and I didn't want Georgie to be anxious. All I said to Georgie was that the doctors wanted to check everything before the court date, just in case they were asked.

At the RCH, I looked on as the purple dye was injected into her veins. Georgie was positioned inside the MRI, her head held in place, and she was asked to stay really still. Loud bangs and whirring sounds crashed through the confined space; she said afterwards that it was scary. The following day the result came back: no malfunctioning pituitary gland, no brain tumour. I hit the wall emotionally and wept solidly for an entire day.

It was becoming too much – for all of us – but by Sunday afternoon I just had to pick myself up and carry on. There was no other way.

Monday came around. Georgie and Harry were heading off on foot to school that morning, sunny and bright. 'Good luck, Mum and Dad,' Georgie called over her shoulder. 'Get my treatment!'

Greg and I smiled and waved, hoping too that we wouldn't let her down. We then drove into the city, where we were meeting our legal team at their offices. Together we all walked along William Street. It was a bustling Melbourne morning. Commuters competed for space on the pavement with the legal types weaving expertly through the crush, wheeling cases that presumably held within them the destiny of their clients. Through the law district we went – past chambers, past the Magistrates Court, the County Court – and arrived at the Family Court in good time. I observed the faces of smokers near the entrance. Some had a practised air – not their first time here, perhaps – as they cast aside their

butt and strode straight through the literally rotating doors of
the legal system. We joined that tide of humanity in which pain
was etched in furrowed brows and worry weighed down already-
heavy footfalls.

As we entered the courtroom, my internal monologue
sounded something like this: *We're going to court because our child
is transgender. Nothing's gone wrong. Nobody's in disagreement.
The only controversy is that our child's transgender and she's seeking
relief just to be herself. Not more or less than anyone, and certainly
not singled out for special attention. Why does this have to be
so adversarial?*

As parents, our only role that day was to be in attendance.
I'd written a detailed affidavit, and Greg and I had submitted to
all kinds of formal scrutiny. Georgie, too. As a family, we'd been
assessed by two separate psychiatrists and the court writer; then
Georgie had gone through it all as an individual. This court case
had been casting Georgie in a role as an 'other', and she didn't
deserve that. None of the kids who went through the Family
Court did.

But it was no use feeling sorry for ourselves, and once we
took our seats I turned my mind to what lay ahead. Apart from
Greg and myself, our legal team and a few interested parties
who were granted leave to stay, also settling in for the hearing
were the Independent Children's Lawyer (ICL) – there to
ensure Georgie's best interests were taken into account – the
court writer and some medical specialists. Aside from that, the
court was closed.

Greg and I sat mutely and waited for it all to unfold. Already,
it was excruciating. As I've said many times in my role as an

advocate, the court process for transgender adolescents and their families was the very definition of powerlessness. Georgie had no agency over her body. As her parents, we had no power either. Strangers were about to make life-changing decisions for her that day, and I wasn't confident she was going to receive the justice she deserved.

The formality of court proceedings is at once a comfort and a barrier. Everyone rose and bowed when the judge entered the court. She wore robes but not her wig; her manner was efficient and relaxed; pleasantries were exchanged but there was an unspoken instruction: 'Let's crack on with this.'

All court cases are written up and those reports go on the public record. In Family Court cases involving minors, enormous care goes into ensuring the parties concerned cannot be identified. Georgie was to be given the pseudonym of 'Jamie'. Everybody else involved was anonymised, too.

To this day, revealing exactly what transpired in that courtroom is impossible without an order granting leave to do so. I can, however, quote from the publicly available 'Reasons for Judgment' dated 6 April 2011. When I read the transcript of our day in court, despite the impersonal tone the bristling urgency is apparent in every exchange.

What shines out in my memory is the expert and compassionate evidence given by the medical specialists. Their advocacy for Georgie's best interests was something I will always remember with gratitude. It was an intimidating situation. They both took turns standing in a dock being cross-examined.

So Georgie knows how hard they fought for her, I've read her passages from the court transcripts that record these doctors defending her eloquently, putting forward her case. Our legal team, too, was absolutely relentless in arguing that both Stage 1 and Stage 2 should be seen as two parts of the same treatment plan for the same 'diagnosis' of gender dysphoria. Not divided into two, requiring separate orders for both.

As the day wore on, the court wanted more detail about how the administration of Stage 1 GnRH agonist medication for blocking puberty would work; Stage 2 was yet to be considered. Georgie would receive a subcutaneous implant of the slow-releasing GnRH agonist Zoladex, which would stop in its tracks any further pubertal development. Another medication, cyproterone acetate, would have to be used alongside it because while Zoladex is starting to take effect it can cause a spike in testosterone. With Georgie already at Tanner Stage 4, the slightest rise in testosterone at this point could have been disastrous for her. Cyproterone acetate is an anti-androgen and would protect her from the effects of testosterone on her body: there could be testosterone in her system, but her body wouldn't react to it. She would need to be on this medication for a month only, but the Zoladex would be regularly administered until around the age of sixteen, when oestrogen would be introduced.

Was there an alternative to the treatment being proposed, the ICL wanted to know. It was explained that there were only two alternatives: to administer Zoladex and cyproterone acetate, or to withhold treatment. The implications of Georgie having no treatment were further elaborated by the doctor: 'Paradoxically for Jamie, this would be experienced as quite "invasive" in itself as the unwanted masculinisation of her body will be experienced as an increasingly distressing perturbation and disruption of her sense of self.'[4]

Questioned on Georgie's capacity to understand, the response was:

So in the sense that Jamie is aware of the exquisite predicament of the conflict between her experienced gender identity and biological gender, and of the options for treatment with Zoladex and later oestrogen, or of no medical treatment, I believe she is able to make an informed decision to commence treatment. Jamie has excellent cognitive and reasoning skills, and I believe that at a later stage, around the age of sixteen years, she will be able to clearly understand the range of treatments available, in particular commencing female hormone treatment. I believe she also has the intellectual and emotional capacity to change her mind and inform her parents and carers to cease treatment at a later stage, should that be her desire.[5]

Everything was pointing in one direction: that it was in Georgie's best interests to consent to Stage 1 treatment. All the evidence supported that course of action. But our desire to have both stages granted that day was looking increasingly unlikely. The obstacle was her age and, to put it bluntly, the fact she wasn't trying to kill herself. How bittersweet it was to hear that because she had such good family support and was subsequently a happy, well-adjusted child, the court had concluded that it wasn't a pressing need to make orders for Stage 2 treatment now or even to allow us as parents to make that decision if it was required closer to age sixteen. The logic was that much could happen between now, at ten years, and the age of sixteen. Among the obstacles the court imagined might be at play were bullying, or that Georgie's somewhat 'rosy' view of life might get a reality check. To me, their presumptions only indicated that they didn't understand her fully. They presumed that Georgie might change her mind about treatment not of her own volition but because shame or bullying might be a 'reality check' on her potential future.

How ironic, then, that the decision in this case and the subsequent appeal was the one and only cause of significant distress Georgie was to feel in the subsequent years. Her sunny, positive outlook was a blessing; her ability to make friends and contribute to her community went on unhindered; but the fact that she had no control or agency over decisions made about her own body came very near to destroying her.

Nevertheless, it was with an enormous sense of relief – and no small amount of gratitude to Her Honour, Justice Dessau, for granting a speedy decision – that an order for Stage 1 was given that afternoon. By then, we were beyond exhausted. The fierce concentration and the emotional load had both taken their toll. Mercifully, it was decided that rather than drive across the city and back again that day, I'd bring Georgie to the RCH before clinic began the following morning for her first shot of Zoladex.

We were already discussing an appeal.

When we arrived home, Greg and I shared with Georgie and Harry the news that we had indeed got her treatment – as per her jaunty parting words of that morning. You could see Georgie's shoulders soften. 'Good,' she said, 'so I don't have to worry about that anymore?'

'Well, they gave you Stage 1, so you're safe now, but they decided not to give you Stage 2 until you're older. So at this point, we will have to go back to court then,' I said.

She looked at me, perplexed. 'Why?' she said. 'That doesn't make sense. I'm still going to be a girl.'

Exactly.

The following morning, with music blaring, Georgie and I drove to the RCH through the morning peak hour. There was no way we were about be bothered by the slow traffic. It was a happy day with a new horizon. Georgie was excited, but also wondering how much it was going to hurt. She knew she was to receive an implant and that the needle to be used was thicker than most. Dr Z assured her a local anaesthetic would make it much easier, but that meant two injections. Yow!

'It's all for a good cause,' she said, shrugging philosophically.

The traffic eased and we swung into Parkville with a growing sense of certainty that, from here on, everything was going to be all right.

That day, I began a new tradition: for every injection of puberty blockers Georgie received, I'd add a charm to her charm bracelet. In a few years' time, she'd begin oestrogen, which is when I imagined we'd be done with these painful implants. Little did I know how many shots she'd have, and over what period of time. Eventually we'd rename it her 'bum bracelet'. Weighed down with charms, it was a tangible reminder of all the jabs Georgie had in her poor bottom – right up until she was eighteen years of age.

10

The appeal

It was a sliding doors moment. We could have taken Georgie's court order granting only Stage 1 treatment, been grateful, accepted that the Australian system was a stinker and that we'd need to go back in six years' time to go through an identical application hell all over again to procure Stage 2 treatment. But that wasn't really an option we were considering, not with the anger that had crept into my bones over this process.

Straightaway, we started discussions with our lawyers to ascertain the potential of an appeal in our case. What did we hope to achieve? One of two outcomes: to remove the law altogether or, if we weren't able to, to at least be granted an order for Stage 2 so we didn't have to return to court around Georgie's sixteenth birthday. Several things needed to align if we were to go ahead with an appeal. There had to be a decent chance we'd win, plus a strong likelihood the Full Court would hear the appeal given we hadn't ventilated the issue of the jurisdiction of the Family Court in the first instance. Once we worked through those scenarios, if we decided to appeal we were to file an application within twenty-eight days of the date of judgment in our case.

It was an ambitious undertaking to attempt to change a law. It called for the right people, the right time, the right arguments. But by god I wanted a crack at it. I was horrified by what Georgie had been through and what we had been through as her family to keep her safe and well. I didn't want anyone else to endure that and I didn't want us to have to go through it again either. I had no idea how long the challenge would take or where the attempt might lead us, but I recognised that opportunities to change a law like this would be few and far between.

All the ducks lined up, with our legal team advising us that they were keen to appeal and would again work on our case pro bono. It was indeed for the public good. The grounds for appeal would be that treatment for gender dysphoria was not a special medical procedure. This was going to be bigger and far more complex than our first case, as there would be less emphasis on Georgie's personal circumstances and far more about points of law. Accordingly, 2011 was gearing up to be almost exclusively a year of directions hearings, applications, and formulating cogent and convincing arguments in order to weave a new pathway through the legal minefield that had been created.

Once word got around that we were planning to appeal, all sorts of people came forward wanting a piece of the action. There were those who wanted to frame the argument, those who were absolutely against law reform and those who wanted to 'piggy-back' on the case and simply tried to invite themselves. I burrowed into case law, trying to learn and understand as much as possible.

Some of it went right over my head, but my understanding about the implications of one decision or another grew, and I could see the direction our lawyers were taking the case.

One of the most significant hurdles was the *Diagnostic and Statistical Manual of Mental Disorders* (*DSM-IV*). The fact that the experience of being transgender still appeared in the Sexual and Identity Disorder section was distressing for the transgender community and for us. That label had been a huge contributor to the stigma, marginalisation and discrimination experienced by trans and gender-diverse people for decades, an immovable obstacle and a burden so heavy that many could not continue to carry it. It seems incredible that it took until October 1973 for the Australian and New Zealand College of Psychiatrists to declare that homosexuality wasn't an illness. In December that year, the American Psychiatric Association removed homosexuality from the *DSM-II*. But still, in 2011, the term 'gender identity disorder (transsexual type)' was applied to my sweet girl as a mental disorder. It was outrageous. Gender identity disorder appeared in the *DSM-IV* alongside some pretty challenging proclivities. I was personally offended that my daughter's experience of herself was being linked to things like transvestic fetishism, sadism, voyeurism and frotteurism. Was that an indication of how dirty this fight could get? Were we in right over our heads? The stakes were incredibly high.

The challenge for us, once again, was to parse the definition of a special medical procedure, which hung on the differentiation between treatment that was for a 'disease or malfunction of the body' and was therefore therapeutic, and treatment affecting an otherwise healthy body – say, donating an organ or bone marrow – for the benefit of another, which was seen as 'special' as it was not for a disease or malfunction. The treatment for gender dysphoria didn't fit neatly into either of these definitions. To further complicate matters, Stage 2 treatment, normally delivered around sixteen years of age, would require the consent of the young person. This is where the legal concept of 'Gillick competence', named for the UK case over the dissemination of information to adolescents about contraceptive medicine, really came into play. If a young person is competent, does the court have a role to play in their medical decisions; and, if not, who decides they are competent? Our argument would be that it was between the young person and their doctor to make that call.

It takes a long time to organise an appeal of this size, and over the following months we appeared in court another four or five times for directions hearings. By November 2011, we had nearly settled a court date for early 2012. Even by then, the adrenaline hadn't subsided. I was running on raw energy. Greg started calling me Erin Brockovich. I wasn't at peace; if anything, the trips to court had heightened all my fears about my daughter's capacity to survive the world in which she lived, and I had to remind myself constantly that at least her personal environment was safe. She was protected from the things that I was reading in the court papers and in the world at large.

Around this time, the anonymised findings of our original court case were released publicly. When the media got hold of the report, it was treated as juicy news. Subeditors went to town with hyperbole and shrill headlines such as, 'Boy, 10, the Youngest

Australian to Have Sex Change' and 'Jamie Wants to Be Janie'. Polls were run, outrage was whipped up. People I had fortunately never heard of before but can't now forget offered their 'balanced' opinion of our parenting or how screwed up our kid was.

The term 'trans-exclusionary radical feminists' – or TERFs – entered my vocabulary after an article was published by a proponent. TERFs reject the validity of the trans experience, and this person accused us of failing to accept our gay son. They compared our parenting to eugenics, the ideology Hitler espoused of 'improving' the genetic quality of humanity by excluding certain types considered undesirable. Essentially, the TERFs believed we didn't want our kid to be gay, so we'd turned her into a girl. Because that just makes so much sense, right, and seems like the easiest, simplest and most obvious option. All sarcasm aside, early on, we'd have been relieved to have a gay son, so great was our fear of what Georgie's life would be like as a trans female, but we supported her.

Right-wing commentators – you've probably heard their names many times – launched in for a good kick. Social media fired up. Satan! Abomination! A volley of now-familiar accu-sations of child abuse were directed at us as parents. Because I was the parent quoted in the court findings, I was singled out for some quite descriptive vitriol. Apparently I suffered from Munchausen syndrome by proxy, an accusation that would be repeated many, many times. Statements from this commen-tariat proclaimed that 'Jamie' was a poor boy brainwashed by a depraved mother, that 'it' – Georgie – should be put out of its misery and the parents thrown off a cliff. Even the seemingly more genteel mums' forums weighed in, rolling the 'facts' of

our case around in their mouths like gobstoppers. One thread
I read gave me a very poor review as a mother. The starting
point of this long discussion was how pushy I'd been to want
to put my child on hormones so early, but by the end of it I was
being criticised for not doing it soon enough, thereby causing
my child distress. This intense bagging made me want to hide
and I became extremely protective of my privacy and that of my
family. I could see plainly what Georgie already knew: that the
world wasn't safe for a kid like her.

Also around this time, I encountered a group of people I
named Drama Vampires. These were folks who *loved* to know
all the juicy details. Acquaintances, typically people I wouldn't
have heard from for ages. Out of the blue, they'd phone with all
the feels. Usually, it'd be at night, perhaps after a glass or two
of vino.

'Hi. How are you, Beck? You've been on my mind and
I thought I'd call. I was thinking of you the other day as I read an
article in the paper and it just reminded me so much of Georgie.
Are you all right?'

'Yes, yes we're all fine, thanks. Tiptop. How are you?'

'Yeah, great. So is that case you? Jamie, was it?'

The ones who rang up knowing full well it was us would want
to know all the gossip. 'You're so good,' they'd say. 'Georgie is so
lucky to have you.' You shouldn't need to be 'lucky' to be loved
and supported, I thought.

There was something strangely familiar about their manner,
their tone. It actually reminded me of the days of wheeling around
newborn twins, when strangers kept commenting, 'Rather you
than me.'

But what are my options as a mother? I have one and only one: to love my kids, however they came to me, whoever they are, without caveats, one hundred per cent. I made the decision to bring them into the world and it's my job to raise them, not abandon them because it's all too hard.

How about we try a shift in thinking on this. If ever a parent is struggling to accept their LGBTQI+ child, instead of expecting that parent to withhold their love and support for their kid as the low bar we set ourselves, how about we encourage the opposite: 'You know, you're really lucky to have that kid. Your love and support is going to make their lives so much better and your relationship so much stronger.' Sometimes it takes a shock for parents to wake up to their child's despair. Don't let that be you. Don't let that be your kid.

With close friends, we were open, and it was a relief to drop our guard. The empathetic ones listened and just said 'That's really fucked' when I related what we'd been going through. The gift of support can come in one pithy sentence. But the circle of people I confided in or shared my time with began to shrink.

The only people I felt totally comfortable with – because they understood our situation better than anyone – were the parents of other trans kids. Jane, Vanessa's mum – numero uno on my list – and I had gradually built up our network. Some of the people we were in contact with had been to court or were about to. These families were scattered across Australia, but many travelled regularly to Melbourne to attend the RCH clinic. All of us were gathering and banking information for when it might be needed. Vanessa had shown no signs of pubertal development, but with Georgie's experience, those in our circle with kids of a similar age were hyper-vigilant and were making sure their treating clinicians were also staying on top of things. Being privy to their experiences helped me to process mine. I knew that the force of Georgie's development was nobody's fault; it was just how biology works, not at the glacial pace the Family Court does. This is why the court process was such a hindrance to good decisions and good outcomes, not an asset. Nevertheless, having the support of these people made me more calmly determined than ever.

Soon after she started her Stage 1 treatment, it became evident that suppressing Georgie's testosterone levels was going to be harder than anticipated. Over the years to come, various tweaks were trialled. Intervals between treatment were changed; different medications with similar effects were tried; doses were increased; and so on. Throughout, Georgie was fine and her case was managed well.

It was noticeable how rapidly the hospital was evolving: the number of children presenting at the RCH seeking support in regards to their gender identity was steadily increasing, and the available staff were stretched. There was a period of time where we didn't know who'd be available to administer Georgie's treatment, as Dr Z retired and the only other endocrinologist went on maternity leave. This shortage of resources – the fact that nobody was available to manage Georgie's treatment – was a hoop we hadn't expected to have to jump through.

I was encouraged to communicate in writing my concerns to hospital management. At that stage, the Gender Service didn't exist at the RCH; the cost of providing care for our kids was shared across a number of departments, and money was tight. To their credit, they absolutely did their best. Now I was aware of the bigger picture: at hospital level, a plan for the future needed to be made, and fast. The RCH needed to provide a dedicated multidisciplinary service for trans and gender-diverse kids, and it needed to be funded somehow. Otherwise, I wasn't sure how Georgie and kids like her would get on.

When the opportunity arose in the future, I would return to that thought, but for the time being I had to attend to the appeal.

My research for the upcoming court case was making me feel depressed. I don't use that term flippantly. I wasn't diagnosed with depression, but I was aware I had some of the symptoms: cynicism; always feeling tired; having no sense of enjoying my normal activities; I'd go to bed in the middle of the day, isolating myself. Oh yes, headaches too. Work was my saving grace. Nobody at work knew anything about Georgie or what we had been going through, so in that environment I enjoyed the opportunity to feel totally free of it. My colleagues and I would banter, watch the latest movie trailers or some hilarious clip and be silly. The work itself got done, but it was fun. It was the best tonic. I think work might have saved me from going down a rabbit hole.

Meanwhile, the kids were thriving: playdates; learning; school camp, where Georgie could sleep in the girls' dorm and the only thing to complain about was the food. Swimming lessons were no longer an issue and I didn't have to go to every lesson to protect her. Her whole outlook had been transformed by not having to worry about male puberty, and by not having to deal with bullying and being able to be herself all the time at her new school. Among the impacts was Georgie's academic progress: she'd arrived as a C student but would finish that school as someone who routinely achieved As and Bs. She was also showing more interest in sport, she was dancing again, and was passionate about her singing and songwriting. Georgie was deeply involved in the life of the school. She had some nice friends and life was good for her. Without the tensions and fears that had initially consumed her childhood, she was like any other kid at school.

The only worry Georgie had were the days when interschool sport took place. What if they were to compete against her old primary school? Someone might say something and her protection from judgement and bullying would be over. It was an unpleasant possibility, but we had our plan and a hope that the other kids would be kind.

Harry, always taking his own path, was doing okay. Sport days were the definition of a living hell for him. The kudos that kids, mostly boys, received from performing well at sport left him cold. He'd cottoned on early that this affected how others perceived his masculinity. Not that he altered his behaviour to fit in. Moulding himself into a shape that others could relate to better wasn't for Harry. He wanted friends – to be understood, liked and loved – without pretence. To be this aware and determined from such a young age is testament to a strong mind and character. Because Harry would rather be in his own imagination than kicking a ball around a field, he frequently spent recess and lunchtime alone. It comforted me that he and Georgie still interacted a lot in the playground, so strong was their bond and friendship. And when the Pokémon phase hit, it was a boon for Harry. Suddenly play-times were about swapping cards and having conversations about characters and their different powers, and new friendship groups formed.

Whenever his teachers talked about Harry, their eyes would sparkle. His progress in literacy and creative writing was way beyond his peers'. Even though he wouldn't always seem to be listening, he was a sponge for information. He'd hear some-thing, process it and down the track it would appear in a plot. His instinct for storytelling was advanced: he had a gift for character, and his writing was tight – there was no fluff. He brought a lot of joy to people.

In my life, I've never had more fun than when hanging out with Georgie and Harry, my two favourite people. Our creative minds and sensibilities acted like a protective force field around our challenges. And our lives were not all about having or being a transgender child or sibling. It may have looked like that from the outside, but it wasn't how we wanted to live. At night, I still read to the kids, but would also ask Harry and Georgie to read their books. Harry liked to entertain us with excerpts from his beloved Captain Underpants series as well as anything by Andy Griffiths. Later, he'd have us in absolute stitches reading the Mr Gum books, then The Floods. There were times he simply couldn't get the words out, it was so hilarious. Georgie, sitting next to me, would also be paralysed with laughter.

Greg, too, was protected by his work life. It provided a complete and immersive experience – rehearsing, performing, touring – and lots of social interaction. Being creative and playful is so important.

All of us loved making plans to expand our horizons and see new things. With Greg often working over weekends, the kids and I sometimes headed off on the spur of the moment. We took trips to places like Phillip Island and Glenrowan, staying in cheap motels and taking in all the quirkiest tourist attractions we could find.

On our regular visits to Mum, we'd catch the *Spirit of Tasmania* and drive to her aged-care home in Burnie. If time permitted, we'd stop at the Ashgrove Cheese Shop, the Christmas Hills Raspberry Farm Café and the House of Anvers. At the latter, we discovered how deeply delicious a proper hot chocolate could be.

I wanted the kids to remember Mum in years to come. If they couldn't remember her before dementia, they could have memories of how we held her hand and took her for little walks around the courtyard and chatted away. My sister Fe, a highly experienced midwife, sometimes came with us. Fe could skilfully engage Mum in conversation. Even though Mum was much less able to communicate than she had been, she'd pick up on the tone of the conversation and would often laugh along with us. The sense that we were familiar to her, connected to her, meant a lot.

'Mum, who's this lovely girl?' Fe asked one day, indicating Georgie. Mum turned to study Georgie. She struggled to find and shape the words, but her face said it all. Love. 'She's families' was her eventual reply. And that exchange contained the essential Mum.

The fog in her brain might clear momentarily, and there would be my caring, perceptive mother. As we sat together on one occasion, I was chatting to her about our life in Melbourne, the kids' activities and school, when she turned and put her hand on my arm. 'Are you all right?' she asked.

My throat tightened and I looked into her lavender-coloured eyes. 'I'm all right, Mum.' My voice was on the cusp of breaking, and a wave of hot emotion was surging up and down my neck. Mum always used to be able to help me cry. 'Let it out,' she'd urge me.

'I'm okay,' I said.

'Are you and I all right?' she pressed.

'Oh, Mummy. We'll always be all right. You and I have nothing to sort out. You're my butterfly.'

'Yes,' she said, patting and rubbing my hand, 'we're all right.'

It was on these visits to Mum especially where I felt the beautiful piquancy and delicacy of love and loss, grief and laughter, which flowed naturally with no confusion. All feelings were possible at once, playing out on a canvas as big and as simple as the Tassie sky that Mum loved so much.

Fe and I were there another day when Mum wasn't great. I'd moved off to speak to another resident. 'Where's Becky?' I heard Mum say with some urgency, as though she'd lost me at the supermarket. It had been a long time since she'd spoken my name.

I spun around – 'I'm here, Mum!' – and hurtled back to her.

She'd never say my name again in her lifetime, but in that moment I realised something profound. Within one utterance were encapsulated thousands of ordinary days. Words, chores, calling at the back door, soothing conversations in the kitchen, frustrations, wonder and pride had worn the name smooth and round. Nobody else who said my name imbued it with so much of everything I am. When she died a few years later, I wept for my lovely Mumma, and I mourned, too, that nobody on earth would say 'Becky' with such complete, intricate and delicate threads of identity.

As I reflected afterwards, it struck me that parents of trans and gender-diverse children must be faced with this same sorrow when a change of name is necessary for the wellbeing of their child. With Georgie, I never experienced the grief and longing that I've heard parents express at this releasing of the past, but now I could imagine with more clarity the courage it sometimes takes to let go and embrace the present.

Preparations for the appeal gathered pace. Via court filing applications, we discovered which organisations the Full Court had invited to participate. It was confronting to know there would be detractors in that courtroom who were going to fight tooth and nail to prevent law reform. Each party had their legal counsel. What, I wondered, aside from their legal backgrounds, gave those people authority to speak on this issue? I researched them all.

A final directions hearing was set for 24 November 2011, which would determine what evidence could, would, should be included, and the date of the actual appeal. As I've mentioned before, when they call a directions hearing 'procedural', they're not joking. Its purpose is to cross t's and dot i's to make sure everything's in place, that all parties are in agreement on how to proceed and all submissions have been made. But at last we had our hearing date: 6 March 2012.

It was going to be adversarial, and it would hurt – I knew there was no escaping that. Already, I was finding it a struggle to give full respect to authority. I'd had to listen to some disgusting arguments in court. Not infrequently, my eyes rolled back in my head so far I gave myself a headache. To deal with it all, I'd hit on the strategy of viewing court as theatre. In my head, I cast all the players in a movie mashup, the sort of thing Harry and Georgie did for fun with their friends. The whole scenario was absurdly reminiscent of a Dickens novel. One intervenor I cast as Mr Bumble from *Oliver Twist*, another as Professor Umbridge from the Harry Potter series. I invented an original character for another: Pious Pete, a combination of Scrooge and the Crooked Man who walked a crooked mile, from the nursery rhyme. Then, swinging in on the sturdy ropes of justice, came Captain Jack Sparrow and his sidekick, Pirate #3. The latter had a non-speaking role. A character with no lines and no given name will usually be the first casualty in the hero's quest, but no harm came to Pirate #3 in the making of this story.

Diminishing their authority in my mind helped me handle my own anxiety. While the case wasn't exclusively about Georgie, many aspects were. Often I sat in court with my head bowed, fingers pressed together hard, trying to suppress the desire to roar. I was by turns enthralled and appalled by what was discussed, and how it sounded coming out of these people's mouths. It was curious. They were bouncing around ideas that were exquisitely important for kids like Georgie and families like ours, but the way they presented their arguments was so understated; they could have been reading the phonebook.

I didn't give our legal team characters. I left their authority intact in my mind. That was totally unconscious, by the way. I've only realised it now as I'm writing. But if I did, they'd need a badass trailer and voice-over: 'In a world where injustice is everywhere, this legal team is fighting back! One special medical procedure at a time.' (Cue slow-motion shot of legal team walking in formation towards camera, brows furrowed, foreheads sweaty, suits immaculate. Cue explosion of court documents. Cue face of a sad, innocent, beautiful child turning towards camera.) '*Re: Jamie*. In cinemas this summer.'

The day of the trial dawned hot. Greg had flown back from his current play in Sydney. Harry and Georgie were now in Year 6. Georgie had been made school vice-captain; her leadership qualities had been noticed and nurtured, and she was highly engaged with the role. Harry had been unsuccessful in his application to become the library monitor, which had hurt. At first, no library monitor was named at all; then the position was awarded to someone who hadn't asked to do it. Harry was cross about that. Sometimes grown-ups have no idea what they're doing.

Almost a full year after our scramble to access treatment for Georgie, we were challenging the law in its entirety. I was incredibly nervous. For families like mine, in some instances the outcome would literally determine whether their child would receive treatment or not. Several people I knew personally had made the excruciating decision to abandon the option of treatment rather than tackle the enormous barrier the court process presented.

People in regional and rural areas were most disadvantaged. I knew there were also kids whose parents didn't support them or who didn't have the means. That could have been us, if not for the kindness and sense of civic duty of our lawyers. Justice wasn't available to all. A family I'd become close with had remortgaged their home to pay the approximately $30,000 in court fees. We knew some families who had taken matters into their own hands, accessing hormones illegally.

I was conscious that the outcome of this appeal had profound consequences not just for my family but for so many who had become dear to me – and to even more whom I would never know. The Family Court had practically no concept of the tsunami of young people heading their way. Georgie was the tip of the iceberg, as we'd seen at the RCH. The Gender Service was experiencing an exponential growth in referrals and that pattern was repeated across the country.

The courtroom was in one of the upper levels of the Family Court building. Greg and I entered to find an unremarkable scene as the various parties milled around chatting. Captain Jack and Pirate #3 were having a conspiratorial laugh together. I envied the fact that this was impersonal to them. Tonight they'd go home, satisfied with a job well done, free to cast a forensic eye over the minutiae of our case and the cases that intersected with it at their leisure.

The court clerk entered and bade the room to rise for Their Honours: Chief Justice Bryant, Justice Strickland and Justice Finn were presiding. We all shuffled to attention. Such was the preparation and planning of an appeal of this nature that very little of what was said in court that day was a surprise to us. Our argument was clear: that treatment for gender dysphoria was not a special medical procedure requiring court oversight as it followed the internationally agreed guidelines of all medical bodies experienced in gender medicine; that parents consent to irreversible medical treatments for therapeutic reasons every single day, and treatment for gender dysphoria should be no different; and that the treatment being irreversible did not detract from its therapeutic nature.

The submission from the Australian Human Rights Commission (AHRC) aligned with our own for the question of Stage 1 treatment, but disappointingly diverged for Stage 2. They tackled each plank of the law in turn. First came a thorough-going argument for why aspects of the reliance on *Re: Marion* as a precedent were problematic when applied to the circumstances of transgender adolescents. They started with the ability to consent to treatment: Marion was never capable of doing so, but transgender children were. Further, there were no benefits to the parents if their child had treatment for gender dysphoria aside from having a much happier, healthier child, as opposed to the parents of Marion. Stage 1 treatment, the AHRC then argued, fell outside the jurisdiction of the court and within the bounds of parental consent, as the treatment was fully reversible and therefore there was no risk of making a wrong decision with permanent consequences. They did opine, however, that because Stage 2 treatment was partially irreversible in nature and the consequences of a wrong decision were grave, it should still be within the ambit of the court to review each case. The final piece of this puzzle was Gillick competence. The AHRC considered that the Gillick measurement was still appropriate to use and that the wishes of the young person should be central to any decision, but the court should decide if a young person was Gillick competent.

This was a surprising caveat. Who normally assesses a young person's Gillick competence? The medical practitioner responsible for administering the treatment. The AHRC proposal continued to make treatment for transgender adolescents 'special' by not allowing them to consent to their own treatment without court oversight. This was totally different from the rights of their peers in the general population.

When there was no more to discuss and all parties had given their arguments, the long day drew to a close. I wasn't sure how it had all gone. The judges were inscrutable, as you'd expect them to be. Chief Justice Bryant acknowledged that the speedy resolution of this appeal would be of material benefit to those families who would soon be making court applications for their children.

After a year of wall-to-wall submissions applications and court appearances, overnight all activity on the appeal halted. A thick silence descended and the business of living continued while the judges – well, what? Presumably they went off and followed their mysterious protocols to decide the case. There was no sense of how long it might take. But I was unable to flick a switch and get on with business as usual; I was changed forever by our encounter with the Family Court.

Waiting, waiting, waiting. It was hell. Jane was my sounding-board and the receiver of many phone calls while I tried to come to terms with the situation. When alone, I'd ruminate for hours

over the details of the case. Slowly, I began to process the traumatic events of the previous twelve months. My faith in some
organisations, like the AHRC, was shattered; I was still shocked
that they'd argued against law reform for Stage 2.

But I tried to remain hopeful. I wanted to believe that our
arguments were more persuasive, that the treatment for 'gender
identity disorder', as it was still then called, was therapeutic and
therefore not within the jurisdiction of the court.

While we waited for a decision to be handed down, many
families close to me headed to court. It was like watching people
I love being forced to drink a terrible poison to save their child.
All I could do was explain what I knew, help them connect with
lawyers, guide them through the process, and offer a shoulder
to cry on if it was needed. The trauma for these families was
enormous, but we banded together.

Although actions speak louder than words, words have been
the main source of my income, and have always provided me
with inspiration and comfort when drawn together by amazing
minds. Around this time I found solace in Portia's speech from
The Merchant of Venice. The plot of the play is convoluted and
has more than a tinge of anti-Semitism, but her defence in court
of Antonio is sublime. Antonio is in debt to an angry Shylock,
who is threatening to take a pound of flesh from Antonio, as
the contract appears to allow, even though this would surely kill
him. I knew a thing or two by now about unreasonable conditions being placed on your person. Georgie's body, her health,
wellbeing and her very future had been exposed to the blunt
instrument of the law. It was she who would carry the cost of that
over the years to come.

And so, in my head, almost like a prayer or affirmation, I'd say these words:

> The quality of mercy is not strained;
> It droppeth as the gentle rain from heaven
> Upon the place beneath. It is twice blessed;
> It blesseth him that gives and him that takes:
> 'Tis mightiest in the mightiest: it becomes
> The thronèd monarch better than his crown:
> His sceptre shows the force of temporal power,
> The attribute to awe and majesty,
> Wherein doth sit the dread and fear of kings;
> But mercy is above this sceptred sway;
> It is enthroned in the hearts of kings,
> It is an attribute to God himself;
> And earthly power doth then show likest God's
> When mercy seasons justice.[1]

I was to repeat this speech many times in the eighteen months it took for a decision in our appeal to be handed down. So much for a speedy resolution. Every day I prayed that the judges would season justice with mercy.

11

Transcend is born

A month or so after the appeal was heard, I caught sight of myself in the mirror and registered that there'd been a downward slide in my health and wellbeing. The worst of my bad health decisions had been starting to smoke again, which I'd known the ill effects of all along but had done it anyway, quite compulsively. It was time to examine everything that wasn't working in my life, including infrequent exercise, and make some changes. There was no longer the need to devote hour after hour to the court journey, and given my lack of control over the outcome of the appeal I was itching to exert some personal power. My health was the top priority. I wanted to have some fun, I wanted the ache in my heart to dissolve and I also wanted to help others where I could.

I gave up smoking again, pretty much overnight. Almost immediately I began to feel better and not like a terrible fool for having started again. I started exercising gently. Not like crazy, but more than I had been. I tried really hard to stop obsessing about things I had no control over.

For a long time, Jane and I had wanted to start a support group for the parents of trans kids. We were sick and tired of receiving unwanted advice from people who weren't in our shoes. Parents like us needed a neutral space where we could just let go, not have to be strong for others in our families, not have to get everything right, not be castigated while we learned and stumbled over a new language for things we'd never experienced or thought about before, not told who our child is by a stranger. Jane and I envisaged creating a soft place to fall when it all got too much. A place to vent when overwhelmed by frustration. A place where we weren't assessed and scrutinised, judged or patronised. We needed accurate info, effective peer support and the space to celebrate our kids in a world that told us we should be ashamed of them or that we'd harmed them.

Although Jane was busy studying, we worked out a plan and did what we could together. We were total novices. Over several months we researched lots of different websites and thought about what we needed to include on ours. We had to register a domain name and come up with a name for ourselves. What about Transcend? We agreed that the word was short and memorable, and loved the sense of grace it conveyed: a promise that we could rise above the challenges.

Setting up Transcend turned out to be a fantastic project for me. It helped me to manage my anger and anxiety when I could redirect it into something positive; certainly, I released a good deal of pent-up energy. This was one of the best things for my health.

Slowly, and with some help, the website grew. Our vision was for the site to be a one-stop information hub run by parents for parents, a classic grassroots network. Already we knew that having supportive parents and access to good-quality information was a young trans person's best hope, and that remains true.

In my experience, these were the things that parents urgently needed to know when they were trying to get their heads around their child's identity:

Is it appropriate that I support my child?

If it is appropriate, where do I find the best professional advice?

Are there any families like mine? Can we meet?

Since those early days, the landscape has changed tremendously and it's rare that I'm asked the first question. Still, the realisation and expression of gender dysphoria is an overwhelming time for young people and their families. I'm yet to meet a parent who doesn't give full consideration to every aspect of their child's wellbeing.

The day-to-day running of Transcend consisted predominantly of speaking to new families and adding them to the parent forum so they could meet others. We also organised the occasional get-together, dinners for parents and family days for the kids. I began connecting with the community more broadly, meeting with the Health Department and other community groups. It was another big learning curve.

On the home front, I was prioritising positivity and trying hard not to think about when a decision would be made in our appeal.

Georgie and Harry were enjoying their final year of primary school and our routine revolved around their activities. On weekdays, I always looked forward to afternoon tea with them. It was the perfect opportunity to catch up on the day's events and get a feel for how the kids were travelling.

One day, Georgie came home proudly carrying a citizenship award. It was fantastic that she'd been recognised, but Harry, who hadn't even achieved the position of library monitor, was overwhelmed by emotion. He jumped to his feet, his voice shaky. 'I feel like everyone just sees right through me!' he gasped. 'Everything's about Georgie! She's in the newspaper; everyone's always asking about her; when people look at me, they see straight through me!'

There was no mistaking the rawness and honesty of his reaction. And it was true that much of our recent family life had been about ensuring Georgie's safety. It wasn't that we'd forgotten Harry: we'd checked in with both kids regularly. Perhaps we'd been too quick in telling ourselves he appeared to be doing all right. But of course all the stuff about Georgie was going to affect him, and I didn't pretend otherwise.

'You're right, Harry,' I admitted. 'We've looked right through you, and I'm so sorry.' I didn't want to serve him up a dish of platitudes. That wouldn't have been fair. I felt so guilty he was feeling this way and so sad for him. Many siblings do feel sidelined when their parents' resources are pouring into a child who needs extra care or protection. Then and there, I resolved never to make that mistake again.

Harry and I snuggled on the couch. 'What can I do to help change that? What would you like people to know about you? You're good at so many things.'

We talked a long time and by the end of our conversation, we'd decided on a course of action. Harry was going to run a comedy festival at school, and he was going to host it. When we pitched the idea to his teachers, they loved it. A date was set and posters put up around the school to advertise for participants. There were plenty of takers. Harry set about writing material as a segue for each act, and I purchased some joke books as prizes.

The event was a triumph. Harry was utterly hilarious, his jokes were solid and his introductions quirky and warm-hearted. I was incredibly proud of him, but more than that I was amazed. Harry was a genuinely good performer. He was an absolute natural.

Not long after that, Harry was named as a finalist for the Glen Eira City Council's My Brother Jack Awards. We were to attend a ceremony where the winner would be announced. A piece he'd written at school had been entered into the Hardie Grant Egmont Primary School Short Story Award. His story was called 'Barry Trubshaw and the Giant Blender', and was a rollicking tale of two friends, a murderous brussels sprout and the lengths the friends went to in order to defeat it. All in 500 words.

He won! When the judges delivered their summation – explaining why his piece had been chosen – they cited the fantastic structure of the piece, the well-drawn characters and the cracking plot. And then, at the ceremony, it was read by one of the judges to the audience. What an effect this had on Harry, to hear his story read out loud and the audience laughing and enjoying every unexpected twist in the tale. This more than anything else bolstered his self-confidence. The award confirmed

his talent for writing and, no longer invisible, Harry Stone had
arrived on the scene, fully formed and ready to go.

Mum used to say, 'You're only as happy as your least happy child.'
No sooner had Harry come good than Georgie started falling
apart; she'd begun to feel ostracised by her friendship group. Group
dynamics can be pretty febrile at this age for girls, but what seemed
to be fuelling this disruption was a rumour spread by a new kid
that Georgie was 'really a boy'. The gossip spread like wildfire. At
first, Georgie hadn't wanted to tell me, but Harry urged her to.

I was heartbroken for Georgie. Straightaway, I notified the
school about what was happening. By this stage we had a
new school principal and he wasn't on the same page as his prede-
cessor. We were asked to go in and discuss the matter; he suggested
we get the school counsellor in for the meeting; and he wanted to
talk separately with Georgie's psychiatrist. I wasn't keen on this
idea and discussed the proposed meeting with Georgie. She didn't
want a fuss made. All she wanted was to say – as she had, consistently – that she was really a girl and then to move on with life.

Georgie's time at school without her gender identity being an
issue had been so precious. Devastatingly, it looked as though it
might be coming to an end. Even though we'd known this might
happen, it was a shock. Certainly, none of us could face another
assessment by another 'specialist'. We were overwhelmed at the
thought of it.

I didn't rate this principal, but I told him that if he organised the appointment and let us know when it was, we'd attend.
It never eventuated. Much later, I heard that someone told him

our family had been through enough and to leave us alone. I was grateful for that.

The rumour died down without any intervention, but something had changed for Georgie. The safety she'd felt at school was gone and with it her confidence. Now she sat mutely with her friends, not feeling included or even liked. She began to spend lunchtimes crying in the bathroom. Her teachers noticed she was struggling. Girls can be brutally cruel to one another.

We'll never know exactly how much the gossip about Georgie changed everyone's perceptions of her, but it seemed to be reinforced when she wasn't allowed to stay in the girls' dorm on ski camp. We were told that there wasn't enough room, but Georgie and Harry could share a room if they still wanted to go.

Decisions must be carefully made about how you react to these moments. What the school was saying sounded like rubbish, but I didn't share my view with the kids. I simply asked them how they felt about the proposed accommodation arrangement and whether they still wanted to go.

The school's proposal touched a vulnerable place in Georgie's soul. Yet it didn't occur to her that it might have been because she was transgender, and I didn't want to put that idea in her head. Georgie already felt like enough of an outsider and she didn't want to be excluded even more. Though disappointed and slightly bemused, she was up for it; Harry, too. They still wanted to go skiing.

I put aside my anger and didn't draw up a battle plan. You have to choose your battles, and I truly didn't have anything left in the tank.

*

The evening I launched Transcend at my home, I invited members from the trans community and those working across a wide range of advocacy and support services. I also invited some of the staff from the RCH. It was on this night that I met Associate Professor Michelle Telfer, a paediatrician and clinical lead of adolescent medicine at the RCH. She was going to be working with many of the trans and gender-diverse young people accessing treatment at the RCH and I could just tell she was going to be amazing. It was the beginning of a long and effective advocacy relationship, one that continues to this day. To my delight, Michelle became Georgie's new doctor soon afterwards. She would go on to create the RCH Gender Service as we see it today, a multidisciplinary service that leads the world in transgender and gender-diverse medical care for children and adolescents.

Michelle Telfer is an excellent advocate for the service and the children and families it cares for. From the beginning of her tenure as the Director of the Gender Service, she knew that funding was key. I rallied Transcend parents, who wrote to their state local members asking for the service to be funded. We emphasised the important role it was playing in the health and wellbeing of our children, and our fear that the quality of service would decline rapidly without dedicated and adequate funding. Michelle was a dynamo. Calm, considered and persuasive, she was able to convince both the hospital and the state government to back her plan for a multidisciplinary service, with more staff, reduced waiting times and better outcomes. I know how hard Michelle worked to achieve that. And I know how pressing the need for a fully funded service was. Without it, the system as it stood wouldn't have been able to carry the cost. Few really understand how close it came to shutting down completely.

Well before Georgie and Harry finished primary school, Greg and I put considerable thought into which secondary school would work best for them. We'd made the decision not to send them to a school nearby. Georgie was still not confident she'd be treated kindly if people knew she was a trans kid. We did a lot of research and even looked at schools way out of our area, but in the end I sought the advice of the Department of Education. They had some suggestions for me. Elwood College was one, and it was un-zoned, so enrolling them would be no problem. That was good, but I had questions about interschools sports days: I needed to be sure Elwood wouldn't interact with feeder schools from our area, to minimise the likelihood that Georgie would be faced with kids who knew her story. As far as I could discover, there was nobody at the school from our two primary schools, so while we couldn't guarantee complete privacy, we were fairly confident we could achieve it.

The teachers and management at Elwood College were magnificent, and from the start I knew both my kids were going to thrive at the school. It was strong in the creative arts and had a growing academic reputation; we'd absolutely hit the jackpot.

Georgie and Harry settled in well, and before long they were involved in everything from house activities to the school production. Harry landed one of the biggest roles in *Guys and Dolls*, that of Big Jule. It was a pretty big deal for a Year 7 student.

Finally – and really, really truly – things were looking up.

*

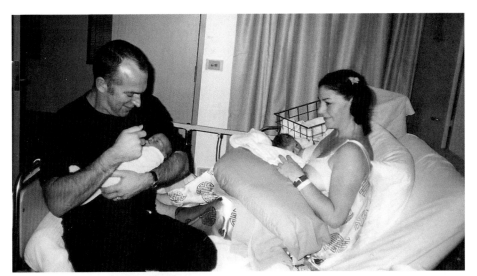

Babes in arms: Greg and me at the hospital with Harry and Georgie (above); with my mum, Jean (left); and me doing a tandem feed on the go (below).

All smiles: the kids have always been good in front of the camera.

Harry and Georgie with our beloved family pets: Roxy (left) and Lottie (right).

Georgie playing dress-ups through the years (with Harry, right). As you can see, Georgie embraced all her playthings, though no doubt she would have preferred a Supergirl action figure to the ones she has above.

Georgie after a 'makeover' by the kids of our very dear circle of friends. To them, Georgie's expression of herself just made sense.

In 2005, the kids were in kindergarten and life was all go.

Spot the tourists. On our trip to Bali in 2009; I think every single thing we have on, including sunnies, are from the local market.

First day of kindy and last day of school – what a journey was had between these two photos. Harry and Georgie thrived at their high school, Elwood College. It was a perfect fit – so much so that Georgie was co-captain of the school and Harry was able to develop his creative skills as a writer.

St Kilda Football Club

From fan to Pride Game Ambassador, Georgie has inherited a love for AFL – especially the St Kilda Football Club – from her family. Go you mighty Sainters!

We've had some fun on
our travels: (clockwise
from above) Stonehenge,
Butterbeer at Universal
Studios in Los Angeles
and meeting Mickey
Mouse at Disneyland.

All the world's a stage: our family grew out of the performing arts.

Greg and I fell in love while working on *Lady Windermere's Fan* at the Melbourne Theatre Company in 1995.

As Mae in *Cat on a Hot Tin Roof* for MTC in 2008.

The cast of *Taletellers*, a play written by Harry Stone.

Georgie busking at a local market.

Associate Professor Michelle Telfer has been a massive source of support throughout the years. She, Georgie and I became a persuasive team, advocating for changes to the medical and legal systems.

Georgie's final appointment with Dr Telfer.

I started Transcend in 2012 to better connect families and their trans or gender-diverse kids to professional supports, to help them feel less isolated. Peer support is a vital ingredient to better health and wellbeing outcomes for everyone in the family.

The work of Transcend continues:

At the Royal Children's Hospital, running a Transcend Auxiliary market stall.

At the RCH Foundation Celebration of Giving, full of gratitude. The following day was Georgie's final appointment with Doc Paul and the RCH Gender Service.

We've met some movers and shakers through the years for our advocacy work. In Canberra (above); with Victorian Premier Daniel Andrews (left); and Georgie with the very engaged and supportive Duke and Duchess of Sussex, speaking about her pride as a young trans woman, while Prime Minister Scott Morrison looks on (below).

2017 Voltaire Award Night

Award Winner: Gillian Triggs

Red-carpet glam: in the past couple of years, Georgie's been recognised for her advocacy with a slew of awards and has had the chance to meet the likes of Gillian Triggs (above), former president of the Australian Human Rights Commission.

Our proud family: Harry, me, Georgie and Greg at the Australian of the Year Awards. I think we scrub up nicely!

A quiet moment as Georgie and I wait for her gender affirmation surgery.

Mission accomplished! Celebrating Georgie and Harry's VCE results. Now for uni and everything else that awaits them.

Georgie, ready to take on the world.

On 31 July 2013, our solicitor rang me to say the finding in our appeal would be delivered the following day. Our agonising eighteen-month wait until that point had been punctuated by calls from families about to submit their court documents. 'Do you know when a decision will be made?' they all asked. 'No clue,' I'd reply. At long last, we'd know the outcome. The best possible result would be that no court involvement would be required to access Stage 1 or 2 treatment unless there was a disagreement between parties.

Our solicitor phoned me straight after the findings were released. The judges had said yes to Stage 1 but no to Stage 2. In other words, they'd found that the administration of gender-affirming hormones was still classified as a special medical procedure requiring an application to the Family Court – unless the young person was deemed to be Gillick competent. Proof of Gillick competence would have to be presented to the Family Court by the young person's doctors. If the young person was found to be Gillick competent, they could legally consent to their Stage 2 treatment. But if the court found the young person wasn't Gillick competent, then the court would make a decision about what was in their best interests.

Straightaway, we could see this would create another imbalance of justice for these adolescents. Some doctors took an evidence-based approach: if such a professional found that a young trans person wasn't Gillick competent, I would trust that assessment. But those with conservative views were never going to say a young trans person was Gillick competent, even if they were. The second issue was that the subsequent court process would then become a part of the 'risks and benefits' counselling that was required in order to receive treatment. For a young person who was already vulnerable and had precious little agency as it was, this was an enormous ordeal to have to undergo. It seemed punitive and pathologising, and I was infuriated that the Full Court had lacked the courage to change this discriminatory law for good.

It was hard to know how to feel. It was fantastic that the time-sensitive and fully reversible Stage 1 treatment was no longer deemed a special medical procedure. That reform was going to transform the lives of hundreds of young people who'd otherwise never have been able to access that treatment. But the Stage 2 outcome was a massive disappointment. The Full Court had decided that families like mine, who'd already been to court, would have to go through the whole long-winded and gruelling process all over again. Only to be told what we already knew: our kids needed this treatment.

For my family, the appeal decision had brought about no change in our personal circumstances. Georgie was already receiving the benefits of puberty blockers, and prior to the appeal we'd known that we would have to head back to court when the time came for her to access Stage 2 treatment. The thought of that had been horrendous in 2011 and it was horrendous now. It was like having an anvil hanging over our heads and waiting for it to fall. While the change in law gave others comfort, it gave us none.

I shared the news among the trans families in our community, few of whom knew that the decision concerned my child's case. All I told them was that a case had gone through that had been partially successful. There was a lot of relief and celebration, but for Jane and me it was bittersweet. Vanessa's application for blockers had already been heard and the financial burden of that had very nearly broken them. Neither of us knew how we would face going through court yet again.

But from those who did know *Re: Jamie* was our case, I began receiving heartfelt messages of thanks. The day after the decision came down, I heard from one family very close to me that their kid had just been given their first shot of puberty-blocking treatment that morning with no court involvement at all. Another family called to say they'd had a court date set for that week; it had been cancelled and an appointment made immediately for their child to have their first treatment. This news was totally uplifting and Georgie, too, was proud that something so positive had come out of what for her had been such a difficult time. She didn't want anyone to go through the fear and upheaval about treatment that she'd experienced.

Georgie and I were still determined to see the law about Stage 2 treatment changed, but timing is everything. There was a team discussion about whether to appeal the decision in the High Court and I was somewhat relieved to be advised against it. Relieved because, firstly, we'd put ourselves through a lot already; and, secondly, had we proceeded and lost, we may have been liable for the cost of the entire proceedings. That would have financially destroyed us. There was no benefit to exposing ourselves to further trauma and risk for a doubtful outcome.

For me, however, it was unfinished business. This mission was personal. Having come so far, and knowing the impact a bad law was having on good people, I simply couldn't give it up. I made an oath to myself that I wouldn't stop advocacy until law reform was achieved, and I began to gather the troops.

Slowly but surely after the appeal decision, the stalemate of our lives lifted and I could breathe more easily and think more clearly.

Throughout the past few years, Greg and I had continued to struggle to find a way through our relationship problems. It would be way too easy and completely wrong to blame our troubles on the challenges of having twins or raising a transgender child. Our children were an absolute source of pride and joy for both of us, and a reason to persevere. We were no different from most other couples faced with marital breakdown.

I can only speak for myself here, but for years the thought of ending our marriage paralysed me with fear. Knowing how much both our kids needed us was motivation enough to not be the cause of another moment of hurt or sadness for either of them. But I couldn't do it anymore. Greg and I decided to separate, but we agreed to remain living under the same roof. And we continued to live this way until 2016.

For some time, I'd been toying with the idea of taking Georgie and Harry to England to visit my sister Jessie, her husband Kevin and their daughter Priya. A Christmas catch-up in Blighty sounded like just the thing to bring about a reset. We arrived on Boxing Day and proceeded to have the most brilliant time, walking around the woods near their home, road-tripping to Stratford-upon-Avon (I was in heaven), Stonehenge and to various castles and dungeons. At the Harry Potter tour in Warner Bros. Studio, Georgie blew her entire holiday budget in one day, and then some! We had an absolute ball. We took the train to Cardiff to see the Doctor Who Experience and took in shows on the West End. We even saw a panto at Milton Keynes, *Snow White* starring Warwick Davis. It was a hoot.

Unexpectedly, Harry felt a powerful connection to England; it was as though he'd found his place. One day, his Uncle Kevin took him up in a small aircraft over Cambridgeshire, even allowing Harry to take the controls for a spell. We'd woken to a heavy frost, and it was a crisp, clear morning. They found themselves flying over a sparkling patchwork of fields and towns. Harry was enchanted.

All of us had a beautiful time and it felt as though some real joy was beginning to flow again. To my delight, I felt a sense of playfulness returning, of fun and optimism. How do we make that holiday feeling last?

It was a shock when I noticed within a month of term one starting that Harry didn't seem right. He didn't have much energy and was flat; his expression was monotone. Given that we'd just had such a great holiday in England, this seemed terribly out of place. When I asked him if anything was going on, he said, 'No, not really. Nothing's wrong.' To me it was obvious that something was amiss. However, I didn't want to press in case that pushed him away.

After a few days, he came back to me and said, 'I think I'm depressed.'

I didn't delude myself that we had the skills to help him out of the hole. Harry needed a professional, and I hastened to set up an appointment to give him the time and space he needed to explore what it was about. While he couldn't exactly put his finger on a reason for his depressed state, it seemed to have something to do with growing older, putting behind him the innocence of early childhood, and dealing with the grind of school, the cliques of student friendships, the feeling of being an outsider. And it was about masculinity. Harry was already well advanced through puberty and had inherited the Robertsons' genes for height – or lack thereof. The First World War enlistment records of my Grampie and his brothers put the tallest of them at a modest 5 foot 7 inches, or 1.70 metres. Grampie had been turned away the first time he'd tried to enlist for being too short. He was 5 foot 3 inches, or 1.60 metres tall. Eventually, they'd needed him more than they needed height. We Robertsons were Scottish Highlanders, sure-footed, stout, wiry and long-lived. Harry feared he wasn't going to grow any taller.

There were so many things at play, but it was telling that it bothered him when other people were quick to interpret his experiences through Georgie's. It was lazy to reason that Harry should be feeling depressed because having a transgender sister must take its toll. He found this hard to stomach: he couldn't even have his own depression, his own dark night of the soul, without somebody making it about Georgie. It was unfair to him and equally unfair to Georgie, who never wanted to be the source of a single moment's pain for her brother – and hadn't been. It was as though some people could only see our lives a certain way, and because of this Harry was denied his own identity as a loving, supportive brother and as someone with his own questions about life, identity and meaning. He was a young man working out who he was and what it meant to be him. His depression had absolutely nothing to do with Georgie or his parents' break-up.

I let the school know Harry wasn't doing too well and that he was receiving counselling. What happened after that shows why I hold Elwood College in high regard. Some of the male teachers took him under their wing a bit. One disclosed that he'd experienced a similar depression at the same age. Another drew Harry aside and in concrete terms told him how valuable he was: a kind and good young man, and such a clever writer. These inputs – along with counselling and time – helped Harry through this dark period. By the time the school production approached, he began to feel much more optimistic and hopeful. I'm grateful, truly grateful, that he had such good people around him, people who saw him and him alone.

Harry was given the role of Martin the pessimist in *Candide*, a role to which he could bring the lessons of this dark time. Later, like Voltaire himself, he was able to view his difficult period through a philosophical lens. 'I'm very glad,' he told me, 'that I went through it. I've never felt such deep emotion in all my life. I know now what it's like to really struggle and I know I can ask for help and I know I can work through it. It wasn't fun. But I'm grateful for it.'

The year before, 2013, Dad had been admitted into the aged-care facility where Mum was living. His decline into dementia was rapid. In late June 2014, the home informed Fe that they believed Dad was in the last stages of life. I flew to Tassie, met Fe at the home, and together we sat with him. Every now and then, Mum would pop in and nap in the armchair next to his bed. We don't know what recognition there was anymore, but she was drawn to the room. By then Dad was lying peacefully – he didn't wake at all. Mum patted him on the tummy. 'You're all right,' she said soothingly.

As we kept vigil, Fe and I chatted about the past, apologised for any pain we might have caused Dad and forgave him for the same. I read to him from the *Tibetan Book of the Dead*. Then I took my leave – I had to be back in Melbourne for work – but I wish I'd stayed. In the early hours of 24 June, Dad took his last breath. I put together a photo memorial for the service. As the keeper of the family history, I had access to loads of photos, and my sisters and I organised the service. Mum came with us and Jessie flew in from England.

Dad had been a vibrant, smart, infuriating, intractable, uncompromising, cheeky and complicated man – he'd want you to know he was also handsome. There was no piece of music that could do him greater justice as he took leave of this world than Tchaikovsky's '1812 Overture'.

For a few years, I'd been considering buying a property in regional Victoria and had researched two or three different areas. Thanks to my now-thriving voice-acting career, I'd saved a deposit and was ready to take a closer look at a few places. I'd never owned my own home before; I still rent in Melbourne. This place, once I found the right one, was to be my escape, my therapy and somewhere to just be.

The kids and I checked out a few properties and decided on one. It didn't need much work and was a short walk to one of the most amazing beaches our coastline has to offer. I made an offer and stuck to it. Years of negotiating wages for jobs had made me brave. They asked for more, I held my ground, and in the end they agreed to my price.

Now I had a place that was just mine – and the resident wombat's. The wrens that darted about in the long grass and trees, along with the cockatoos, kookaburras and kangaroos, delighted me. Roasting marshmallows in the fire pit and having the expanse of constellations twinkling above is my idea of pure luxury. Proximity to death reminds us of what's important in life; Dad's death made me understand my priorities better.

The media had discovered Transcend, and I was fielding requests – for quotes, comments, interviews and stories across all platforms. To my surprise, there were quite a few enquiries from artists wanting to explore gender in their next work. I was pretty unimpressed with some of their pitches. Requests to speak to 'someone who had transgendered' received short shrift, but I always responded with an email to explain why their request was denied. Who knows whether they understood fully the disrespect they'd shown: it was as though they were shopping for creative credibility and edgy notoriety: 'I really want to give transgender people a voice,' they'd say. I'd point out that transgender people already had their own voices. 'Drama Vampires,' I'd tell myself and roll my eyes.

Some media professionals were as bad. Requests from popular commercial publications to *tell Jamie's story, really sensitively* were roundly rejected, remuneration and all. If we ever told our story publicly, it would have to be with the very best and most reputable people. Then *Four Corners* got in touch.

Janine Cohen is a reporter and producer of many years' experience from the ABC. She contacted Transcend wanting to discuss a story she was researching for *Four Corners* about how the court process was affecting transgender teenagers. She'd read about the case *Re: Jamie* and wondered if Transcend was able to put her in touch with any families, including Jamie's. I said I'd see what I could do, obviously not letting on that 'Jamie' was my daughter. I contacted Naomi McNamara, who'd been a member of Transcend for some time, and asked if she might like to have a chat with Janine to sound out becoming involved. Naomi's daughter, Isabelle, was also seeing specialists at the RCH, and it seemed to me they were the perfect family to be at the centre of the story, if they chose to.

There was a lot of thinking to do. At this point in time, Georgie and I had to remain anonymous. The court required it, and if we were to violate those orders, we'd have been in contempt of court. But above all else, I was protective of Georgie's privacy, as per her express wishes.

The two of us discussed Janine Cohen's proposal and thought about it from every possible angle. It wasn't that Georgie didn't want to tell her story: she wasn't ashamed of herself in any way. But appearing on screen with a pixelated or shadowy face is for someone in witness protection or with something to hide; that wasn't at all the case with her. She wanted people to know what our family had gone through, our efforts to contribute to putting a stop to the distressing court process, so that others would understand. Georgie and I agreed to find out in more detail what the *Four Corners* team had in mind. But this meant we'd have to disclose to Janine that Georgie was 'Jamie' – in other words, to place our trust in her. Were we frightened? Incredibly. The backlash after our case had burned. Talking to a TV producer was next-level exposure.

With enormous empathy, Janine listened to our concerns. Her team had a small budget to hire a make-up artist, she said, and floated the idea of creating some prosthetic features for us. They could only afford for Georgie and me to have this done, which meant Greg and Harry wouldn't be interviewed. It was better than being pixelated. We also agreed that as I was a voice artist, and my voice may be recognisable, they'd slightly deepen my tone.

Well, we could live with that. This was too important an opportunity to pass up, and we took it. Naomi and her family were on board; Paige Phoenix, a trans man, was on board; and Georgie and I were on board. Filming started almost immediately.

'Being Me' went to air on Monday 17 November 2014. At the sound of the opening soundtrack to the *Four Corners* program, Georgie and I found ourselves supercharged with anxiety, mostly because the issue of court applications was about to be ventilated nationwide. This respected program, with its healthy viewer numbers, was picking up on a problem that was at the margins of society and putting it front and centre. When veteran anchor Kerry O'Brien invited the audience into this story, he suggested it had the potential to profoundly change the way Australians perceived transgender children and their families. Hearing this from such a familiar television figure, it felt like progress had already been made.

For us, it was riveting viewing. Isabelle and her family were incredible: considered, relatable, loving parents and ordinary people, they were able to convey with honesty and heart their family story, and their fears and hopes for Isabelle's future.

The perfect subject, Isabelle was natural, unaffected and articulate. She was excellent at conveying the experiences of so many kids. Michelle Telfer appeared, describing the treatment and standards of care that the RCH Gender Service provided and delivering an unequivocal message that the court process was harming children. Doc Paul made an appearance too. Paige related his story – one of family rejection, and of music as a source of resilience – and we told ours. It was an incredible show and one of *Four Corners'* highest-rating programs that year. Millions tuned in, and the feedback was overwhelmingly positive.

The screening of 'Being Me' took the plight of transgender children and their families into the homes of politicians, policy-makers and everyday Australians. Encouragingly, the New South Wales Police Force started using the program as a training resource for their new recruits. This was a positive example of progress in places of power.

The legal fraternity was also alive to the issue. *Re: Jamie* had had quite an impact in the world of law. The case was taught in university legal faculties around the country, and over the years Transcend has received a number of requests for help with PhDs on the subject. We were told that it was widely regarded in legal circles as the wrong decision, and that many thought the inter-pretation of *Re: Marion* had been wrongly applied. Once 'Being Me' was screened, offers of pro bono legal representation for families started being offered to Transcend and the RCH from law firms and community legal centres. Immediately, a number of individuals seeking Stage 2 treatment had a legal option where previously they might have had none. This was the most exciting outcome of the *Four Corners* program.

Another by-product of the program emerged from within the RCH itself. One doctor, after watching 'Being Me', could see the benefit to transgender females of a procedure he'd been offering to male cancer patients. An unfortunate consequence of some cancer treatment was sterility, and he and his colleagues were employing an experimental treatment for preserving the option of parenthood for the future. It involved removing a small section of testicular tissue and storing it in a cryopreservation bank. From the stem cells contained in the testicular sample, scientists had produced some viable sperm that had resulted in a baby. But this was from older patients; producing sperm from immature testicular tissue had yet to be achieved. While there was no guarantee it would work, it was definitely an option worth considering.

When Georgie was informed about this possibility and asked if she'd like to have the procedure, her reaction was subdued. It surprised me that she didn't seem enthusiastic, but I didn't make a big deal about it. It's always been better to leave Georgie be at times like this as it means she's processing and will talk to me when she's ready. She seemed very sad. Walking our beautiful but constantly ravenous white labrador Roxy one day provided us with the space to talk about it further. Whatever she was holding on to, it was something big emotionally.

'Lovie, what's going through your mind right now? It feels as if you don't like the idea and I'm wondering why.'

'It's not that I don't like the idea, Mum. It's just brought up a lot of old feelings that I thought I was over. I know this sounds stupid, but in some ways I'd almost forgotten I couldn't have my own children.'

Georgie lowered herself onto a park bench and began to weep. 'I feel silly, because of course I'm not going to have kids from my own body, but it feels like I'm grieving that loss all over again – or more consciously than I had before.'

We stayed at the park until she'd cried and talked it all out, and by the end of our walk she'd resolved to undergo the procedure. She understood it was experimental and that it might not result in her own offspring. It was, however, an option previously unavailable to her, and she intended to embrace the potential it held.

I also shared news of the procedure with Jane because it struck me as something Vanessa might consider. 'Give the hospital a call, Janie,' I suggested.

Subsequently, Vanessa and Georgie were the first transgender adolescents in Australia to have this procedure and the RCH was the first hospital to offer it. They were both admitted as day patients on the same day, and while they were in theatre Jane and I caught up in a café downstairs. It was always uplifting to spend time with her. When later we caught up with our kids there they were, side by side in the recovery ward, chatting away as if they'd spent the night on the tiles.

'I really like your scrunchie, Vanessa,' Georgie slurred.

'Thanks,' Vanessa slurred back, applying a hand gracefully to her ponytail. 'It's Mum's.' While the two patients fully recovered over the next few days, Jane and Vanessa stayed with us, and the girls played every single concert DVD they owned between them. They swapped information about their favourite singers and talked about songwriting, music and the future. Only rarely was being trans a topic of conversation for them. It wasn't the biggest thing these two friends had in common.

Our issues with the Family Court had entered the mainstream, and the screening of 'Being Me' generated opportunities and conversations. Transcend had a platform, and I made up my mind to use it.

Changing a law is hard, regardless of whether you attempt to do it through the court system or through legislation. Reform looks easy when an issue's time has come, but that's only because all the groundwork has been done beforehand. What I set out to do, along with Michelle Telfer from the RCH Gender Service, was to take every opportunity that came our way to educate and invite others to join us.

12

Roller-coaster

During the school year in 2014, the Safe Schools Coalition had visited Elwood College for the first time to help a young trans person who was joining Georgie's year level. Georgie, who was still not out at school, was interested to observe the reaction of her cohort. She was pleased to see her friends and classmates listen respectfully to the information being shared, eager to support this new student. They'd tumbled out of the session armed with practical information on how to be a good ally, and had been provided with stickers with which they proceeded to festoon their locker doors. It amazed Georgie how universally welcomed this student was, and she began to think that perhaps it was safe for her to be open about her experiences.

But before she had a chance to fully process those thoughts, the issue was brought to a head: a student had started at Elwood College who knew Georgie from primary school, and one of her classmates thought they recognised her from 'Being Me' and had taken her aside to confirm it. Now she felt pressured to make a quick decision and come out to her friends. She was angry and upset about the loss of her own safe space and the freedom to simply be Georgie; about being exposed again to the fickle business of the approval – or disapproval – of others. With that came the deep-seated fear of rejection, the unuttered words, 'This is me; don't hate me.' She sobbed and sobbed at the loss of this privacy, and we told her she didn't have to tell anybody if she didn't want to.

'No,' she said through gritted teeth. 'I'm sick of being at the mercy of others. I'm telling my friends.'

She picked the day she was going to tell them, and the night before she was in tears again, but they were softer now. It was scary to be making herself vulnerable to past hurts and rejections by sharing this intimate experience of herself; it was an act of faith in her friends, and she hoped it would go well.

'Just see if a good moment presents itself, Georgie. Don't force it. If it doesn't happen tomorrow, it will happen when you're ready and the time is right. You don't have to do anything if you don't feel right about it.' Those words were all I could offer her, and again I suffered the pangs of powerlessness. It was yet another of those days you send your kids off to school and hope they come back in one piece.

Georgie was looking drawn. Harry knew what might be happening that day and he was going to keep an eye out for his sister. All day long I could think of nothing else. *Please, please, please let it be okay.* I couldn't imagine her friends not being fully supportive. They were switched-on kids, smart, open and kind. I was very hopeful; but still . . .

After school, she bounced through the front door triumphant and excited. 'I told them!' she exclaimed. 'It was amazing. I found exactly the right time and place; it just happened. And the right people were there, the ones I wanted to tell, and they were great, Mum. They were really lovely, and I feel so relieved! They said they'd keep it private. And I said, "Tell who you want to; it's not a secret." And so I guess everyone will know soon.'

The impact on Georgie coming out to her friends was as subtle as it was deeply felt. Within our family there flowed a profound gratitude to these lovely kids and their excellent parents, and the school, who were aware that Georgie was now out to the school community. She received nothing but support, and in her time at Elwood College she was never bullied, either before or after coming out. Georgie being transgender at school was unremarkable; it didn't change the way people related to her.

Georgie's confidence blossomed. Her faith and trust in the people around her was a significant factor in that. She was enjoying the things that gave her pleasure and the things she was good at. Academically she was hitting her straps, and creatively she was writing more songs than ever. She sang everywhere she went, at whatever task she was undertaking, like a Disney princess. I could imagine all the woodland creatures following her as she walked through life. It was all a little bit magical.

Georgie had been on puberty blockers since she was ten years old; she was soon to be fifteen. Georgie's doctors were concerned that she'd been on blockers longer than anyone so far. They contacted the gender clinic in the Netherlands where the

'Dutch Protocol' – considered the most progressive and humane in the world – had been developed. The Netherlands was the first country to administer puberty blockers to transgender patients. The question our doctors wanted answered was this: did they have a child who'd been on blockers for as long as Georgie, and, if so, what was the impact on their bone density – as puberty closes the growth plates and strengthens the bones – and general wellbeing?

Although Georgie was getting on with life, she was noticeably behind her female peers in physical development. Blocking puberty doesn't stop growth generally, but it does slow it down considerably. Being behind her peers in this way set her apart from them at a time when she really wanted to be able to develop alongside them as much as possible.

Sex education was problematic for Georgie as she felt left out of the discussion. She couldn't join in when her friends talked about their periods or buying bras or any of the things that were up for discussion, and while she knew it wasn't their fault it was still difficult to handle.

When the Dutch clinic responded, they said they didn't have anyone who'd started blockers as young as Georgie, and nobody on their database had been on blockers for as long. The RCH team decided it was appropriate for Georgie to begin oestrogen, which would help her in a number of ways. First, her bone density would improve. Second, it would help with the ongoing struggle to keep her testosterone levels at bay. And, third, she'd begin to develop female characteristics like breasts, allowing her to feel more comfortable in her own body and be more in line with the girls her age.

What the doctors were recommending was Stage 2 treatment and, as you'll by now appreciate, getting it meant going
back to court, a prospect none of us was looking forward to.
Yet again, Georgie's young age could be a hurdle to justice. She
was still fourteen, and the age that so far had been stated as the
time to begin gender-affirming hormones was sixteen. Georgie
was pushing boundaries again, not through choice but through
circumstance. We phoned our lawyers.

January 2015 hit like a freight train. I was organised and
ready to go. We had an initial meeting with our lawyers early
in the new year because I knew we were in for a trying time in
more ways than one. My beautiful mum had been struggling
for the previous month with a persistent chest infection. She'd
been taking antibiotics but they were only holding it at bay, not
resolving it.

In mid-January, Mum had a fall. She was never going to
recover. My sisters Fe and Lou rushed to her bedside and between
them watched over her for the next few days. I caught the *Spirit
of Tasmania* and spent an uneasy night hoping I'd get to see her
one more time and thank her for everything she'd given me in my
life. I sat in my cabin, looking out at the magnificent wild seas of
Bass Strait, wondering if this was to be Mum's last night on earth.
I knew nobody loved me as completely as she did.

I arrived safely not long after 9 am, and was relieved to be
able to kiss her forehead and stroke her beautiful hands that had
worked so hard and loved so tenderly.

It is a privilege to witness the birth of a child and now I know
it is a privilege to witness the passing of a life. My 'butterfly'
had flown.

I didn't feel a shattering grief. It was Mum's time to go, and she'd loved fully and was loved fully in return. But now I was on this planet for the first time in my life without my mum, without my dad. They'd died within seven months of each other. It was a gentle grief, like a soft rain falling. Darling Georgie wrote me a song, which she called 'Tears Are Diamonds'. It was so beautiful that she saw I needed a little support. You can look the song up on YouTube. This is the chorus:

> It's okay to cry
> Your tears are diamonds, bring them to the light.
> Can't be strong all the time
> Just curl up in my arms and it's all right.
> Your heart is shining brighter than the moon and stars tonight
> It's okay to cry
> Your tears are diamonds, bring them to the light.

After I returned to Melbourne I drifted somewhat. I couldn't quite focus or concentrate on what came next. *Where was I up to? Where are we with the court process? What's next?*

I started working furiously on the support group, joining up an ever-increasing number of new members, trialling a Facebook group and making sure our court case was on track. I thought I was okay.

Georgie had an appointment at the RCH coming up for her regular shot of puberty blockers. The last time she'd had blockers was the day of her testicular biopsy several months earlier. She was on a double dose of blocking medication: two injections were predicted to last much longer than any of the previous combinations. I felt comfortable that we had all our ducks lined up as best we could.

From the look on Michelle Telfer's face as she read the blood results from Georgie's pathology test the previous week, I knew all was not well. Her testosterone levels were exceptionally high, double the levels that had terrified us so much when she was ten years old. The double dose of medication hadn't held for the time predicted, and Georgie was in full-blown male puberty.

None of us could compute what we were seeing. It was extreme and we were all shocked. The realisation began to dawn on us that something terrible was on the verge of happening to Georgie. We could see it in one another's eyes and feel one another's fear in the air. For now, all we could do was give Georgie her two shots of blockers, and we left clutching another pathology order for bloods to be taken in a few days' time. We needed to keep close tabs on her testosterone levels. We had to protect her in every way available to us.

Yet again, Georgie was at the centre of a drama not of her making and one she was unable to control. She was at the mercy of systems and other people, and the safety and security she'd only recently found was dashed. Here was yet another perfect example of why the court process harmed the children it was meant to protect. And why forcing our child to go back to court again for the same treatment plan was so monumentally unjust. Treatment would be delayed when it was clinically required, and urgently.

This system was leading not just to poor outcomes, but also to outcomes that made their mark permanently on the bodies and in many cases the minds of the young people. They deserved so much better from the justice system. The trauma was real. I know. My daughter lived it.

Too many families like mine, ordinary people, were suffering in a similar way to us. How could I convey to the Family Court the agony of waiting, in limbo, for a court date to be able to access the medical treatment that was recommended worldwide? It wasn't a special request. It was *the* treatment plan, agreed upon by medical professionals everywhere, based on medical evidence and peer-reviewed science. Why was Australia the planet's only jurisdiction that forced this onerous and discriminatory process on its transgender children? Who was benefitting from this? Nobody.

What if members of the Family Court could walk in our shoes, perhaps by staying awake all night, as some parents did, to ensure a kid didn't harm themself. Or tried to track down an absent and recalcitrant father, persuade them to sign court documents or support or acknowledge their child. It was tough to hold a child, yearning to promise them that everything would be okay, that the adults had it all in hand, but knowing that we didn't. It was a mess.

At night I would hold Georgie while we waited for her testosterone to drop down, rocking her and letting her weep. She was unsafe, exposed. 'Am I going to be all right, Mum?'

'I don't know, darling. We're trying hard.' I wasn't going to spin her a lie.

The day after we received Georgie's blood results, I was on the phone to our lawyers first thing. It takes a lot to make me cry, but I was pacing the floor at home and through my gulps of emotion asking that they urgently submit an order. By midday they had a draft; by the close of business they'd submitted it, requesting an urgent hearing.

It felt like we'd made no material progress over the previous four years. History was repeating itself, but this time our situation was worse. Georgie was acutely aware of what could happen to her with this level of exposure to testosterone, and she fell into the darkest place she's ever been. The last time, we'd been able to protect her from knowledge that would frighten her. This time around that was impossible.

Georgie became hyper-vigilant about possible alterations in her body. Was that an Adam's apple in her throat? Had her shoulder width expanded? Was the structure of her face changing? She was terrified her voice was breaking. She was no longer able to hit the high notes in the songs she'd written. About a month earlier she'd had a cold, but what if the catch in her throat wasn't because of the cold at all, but something more permanent and frightening? To test her voice, she kept singing and singing and singing, making her throat more inflamed, raw and tired. I took her aside and suggested she allow it to rest, let it heal. It was awful to listen to her go through that every day because you could hear her fear and desperation. Then the house fell silent. She stopped singing completely. No more woodland creatures.

A blood test early the following week revealed that her testosterone levels had not reduced rapidly or far enough. Immediately, she was prescribed cyproterone acetate to halt the effects of testosterone on her body. This was the same medication used as the safety net when she was ten, and would work almost straightaway. Fully cognisant of the court process ahead, Georgie was fearful and angry. She had blood tests every week to reassure her that what was happening inside her body was back under control and to help manage the spiralling anxiety she was feeling.

I informed the school about what was happening and they promised to keep an eye on her, but some days she was so distressed she had to stay home. For a high achiever like Georgie to take time off class, unable to focus on anything but her current predicament, was completely out of character. The court set a directions hearing for 5 June 2015.

In late May, Georgie and Harry's fifteenth birthday came and went. We had cake. There was nothing Georgie wanted for her birthday other than bodily autonomy and to be released from this hormonal holding pattern. Literally, her body had become a cage she was trapped in.

Somehow, earlier in the year, I'd fooled myself that this time the court process wasn't going to get to me. But after Georgie's recent experiences, I couldn't fool myself any longer.

Our QC had suggested that Georgie write a personal letter to Her Honour Justice Thornton to illustrate that Georgie was Gillick competent – and therefore able to consent to treatment – and fully engaged with the court process. All the evidence supported that, but if the judge decided to rule Georgie wasn't Gillick competent then she would make the decision to consent to Georgie's treatment.

The letter was written with our court date just days away.

To Her Honour,
I am a normal, cheerful, confident girl and I know who I am.
It's just that my exterior doesn't mirror my interior. I want

my body to develop alongside my peers', and I want my body
to match who I really am; a girl. It is simple, however it frustrates me deeply that I have to go to court to be who I am. It
frustrates me that anyone has to endure this. It shouldn't be
the court's decision. It is my body, and only I have the right
to decide what goes into it. It is acceptable for my family
or the experienced doctors to advise me, but in the end it
should all be up to me. However, this right has been taken
completely out of my hands. Not only have I experienced
much anxiety about going into male puberty four years after
I started puberty blockers, but I have absolutely no control
over my body. It is you that has control, so I implore you
to let me start Stage 2 treatment. Then, I can be who I am,
without this worry hanging over me.

Thank you.

There was also the question of whether the judge would allow
Georgie into the courtroom for the trial. We all agreed that this
would be of benefit to Georgie; we wanted her to be present to
see these decisions being made about her. However, it's very rare
that children appear in Family Court proceedings and a request
needs to be granted by the judge. We decided to wing it on
the day.

Enraged by everything about her predicament, Georgie asked
our legal team when she'd be able to identify herself publicly and
tell her story, identifying herself as 'Jamie'. This was a burning
question for her. Just as at school, her anonymity was no longer
experienced as a freedom but as a burden she had to shed, and
'Jamie' the pseudonym was no longer serving her best interests.

Like the laws preventing her from making her own medical decisions, the lack of agency in how and who she could tell her story
to was stifling her. She was on the march. Her request to identify
herself was added to the court documents for consideration.

It came to my attention that Pious Pete, one of the detractors from our appeal, was sniffing around the periphery asking
questions. He'd obviously seen the case listed. It appeared that
he was deciding if it was worth trying to intervene again, in case
we had a second crack at changing the law. When he circled
a few times, asked a few more questions but then faded away,
I was relieved. I honestly don't think I could have sat through
another detractor.

Jane became my lifeline once again. As usual, I swore quite
a lot, but as well as allowing me to decompress, she offered
me much-needed soothing. I always got off the phone from
her feeling less anxious. My sister Fe and I cried on the phone
together as I described Georgie's state of mind and body. Apart
from that, I isolated myself from most people during this time,
and that included everyone at Transcend. It was all I could do to
deal with this, my work and caring for my kids' daily needs.

Harry and Greg, all of us, were geared to one outcome alone.
United, we all arrived at the Family Court together. Our family
and friends were behind us, waiting hopefully for good news.

We met Greg's cousin Andrea at the court. We'd asked her to
come on the off chance Georgie and Harry were barred from the
courtroom. A comedian and writer, Andrea is a good egg, and
her sensitivity to situations has always been much appreciated.

She's been a much-loved constant in our children's lives and was the ideal person to have with us that day.

We waited in a conference room for what seemed like a considerable amount of time – the case being heard before ours was running late. Would today be a procedural hearing, I wondered, or could our legal team convince Her Honour to hear the case today? Would Georgie and Harry be given leave to sit in court for the proceedings? Would Georgie be given leave to identify herself? Would Georgie be permitted to consent to her own treatment? My expectation was that Georgie would leave the court able to begin oestrogen that day; no such application for medical treatment for transgender adolescents had ever been refused. Then again, she was younger than anyone who'd so far sought orders, and we knew there were no guarantees.

Eventually, the five of us piled into the court and sat in the middle of the first row of seats. Greg and I each held one of Georgie's hands. Greg looked nervous and emotional. Having the kids in the courtroom with us heightened our senses. It was as though he and I were seeing this process through their eyes. The courtroom was big and we felt so little.

'All rise,' said the clerk.

Justice Thornton entered the court and her warmth was instantly evident. She cast her eye over our family, then asked our counsel to begin. In the four years since our first encounter, the court process had become slightly less adversarial. There were no intervenors at this point, no Independent Children's Lawyer, and no longer were doctors required to be in court and cross-examined. But it was still the court process. Evidence was required; there were affidavits to be signed and sworn, court fees to pay and delays to be endured. When our counsel asked Her Honour if she'd consider the matter today as there was no controversy and no intervenors, she agreed to do so. Hurray! We'd have an answer today, and hopefully a good one.

The case moved so swiftly it was almost dizzying. Yes, Georgie, Harry and Andrea were allowed to be present in court. They were able to hear the evidence of doctors, who were unified in their view that gender-affirming hormones were urgently required and absolutely appropriate for Georgie. The doctors were also aligned in their assessment that Georgie was Gillick competent. The judge said that Georgie's compelling letter and her attendance in the courtroom that day both reinforced the case for her competence. In summary, the judge said, the assessment of the doctors as to Georgie's full and mature understanding of the treatment was in line with her own. In keeping with the findings in the *Re: Jamie* appeal, as Georgie was found to be competent, the court was not required to make an order.

We had it! Today Georgie could access those hormones that were going to make life so much better in every possible way for her. Additionally, the judge granted Georgie leave to identify herself as the subject of the application and as the child subject of the decision in the Full Court in *Re: Jamie*, in whatever manner she may choose.

Lastly, Justice Thornton addressed Georgie directly and acknowledged the difficulty of Georgie's experience and the love of her family. The judge offered her best wishes for the future of this young person full of potential. It was as positive an experience as we could ever have hoped for in a courtroom. For that, Justice Thornton gets a vote of thanks from me. We'd had a really rough trot and we appreciated the compassion she demonstrated that day.

We left the court elated and thanked our lawyers profusely. Again, they'd represented us pro bono. What legends. Georgie was so relieved. All of a sudden, the way was open to her again, a new chapter was about to begin, and the huge and terrible cloud of the Family Court was no longer hanging over us.

Now that Georgie could legally consent to her treatment, she did so that afternoon with Michelle Telfer, and next thing a script for Progynova 1mg – oestrogen tablets – was faxed through to our local chemist. Georgie and I headed to the shopping strip near home, asked for our script and waited while it was filled. Smiling broadly, we thanked the pharmacist, a gentle and kind fellow, as he handed over the packet.

Georgie and I were in the queue, about to pay, when we noticed the price sticker. All that pain, all that fuss, all that expense to taxpayers and ourselves, all that time wasted, all the agony Georgie had been subjected to over these many years had culminated in this packet of bog-standard hormones that were priced at $8.90. We both laughed, ruefully.

13

Advocacy

While it was the best thing that Georgie started Stage 2 treatment, the path to obtaining it had been a traumatising one. The impact stayed with Georgie for a long while. Her usual vitality and joyfulness were gone, and she still hadn't begun to sing again.

A few weeks after our trial, Georgie and I met with our legal team to discuss mounting a further challenge to the law. It was possible, they said, but on balance and given the enormous strain on Georgie and the family, they advised against it. It was sound advice and we took it, but that didn't mean we weren't disappointed. After our meeting, Georgie and I sat in the car and had a little cry. It was a mixture of relief and sadness that we weren't able to finish the job. Perhaps there was enough public awareness now to bring about legislative reform. Perhaps another courageous family would challenge. The latter did seem unlikely though. The fact was that as no orders for Stage 2 treatment had been refused by the court, there was nothing to appeal. Taking into account, too, that families were more routinely receiving pro bono assistance for their cases, it was unlikely there were the additional resources to mount an appeal.

More than anything, what Georgie and I needed was peace and quiet to recover from our latest ordeal. We took trips to our house by the sea and soaked up long windy walks, blowing away the cobwebs and heartache. We played Cluedo, which always made Georgie hysterical with laughter for some reason. Harry and I could never fully fathom that, but nonetheless her response made us laugh too. We cuddled our dear Roxy, who in her own beautiful way had made home a safer, funnier place to be. Her big brown eyes and exceptionally smelly breath let us know she was there for us. 'There's always hope,' she seemed to say whenever she laid a paw on our knee.

During this post-court period, I flew to Sydney to speak on behalf of Transcend at the Safe Schools Symposium at the University of New South Wales. The Safe Schools program was now federally funded and was rolling out across the country. From my perspective, that was a marvellous thing. The program was a vital ingredient in creating learning environments and school cultures that were healthy and inclusive for all. Those families in Transcend who'd accessed Safe Schools were extremely happy with the support they'd received. How I wished we'd had access to a program like Safe Schools when Georgie was at her first primary school. It would have made a world of difference.

In my speech, I emphasised that transgender students were challenged at every turn and faced exclusion and bullying. They needed supportive families, access to appropriate medical and psychosocial support and an end to court interference. The least they should expect was to be supported at school and to be free from discrimination in their educational settings. I was and remain a supporter of the Safe Schools program. After my speech, a person attached to the then Education Minister Christopher Pyne came up to me, offering assurances that the minister supported the program and would continue to do so. Hello, I thought. There's trouble brewing.

The Elwood College school production was underway, and while this year Georgie had decided not to participate in it, Harry had thrown himself in and was having an absolute ball. It was *The Wizard of Oz* and Harry had been cast as the Wizard. As always, he relished his role and gave it his own special brand of kooky charm. He was on fire creatively as he had written another award-winning story for the My Brother Jack Awards, a tale about a little blue alien called Alpaca, who needed a tinkle. The story was titled 'Destination Lavatory', and it won the Hardie Grant Egmont Junior Secondary Short Story Award. Harry really is a wonder.

Georgie gradually regained her spark. Time and distance were healing her, as were the visible signs of her body beginning to change with gender-affirming hormones. Now that her treatment plan was working, there were fun things to look forward to. Among them was a school trip to France. I so wish we had trips like this when I was at school. During the two-week tour, they were billeted in Bordeaux, visited Cannes, Nice and Avignon, and toured the battlefield around Villers-Bretonneux, near where my Grampie had fought. Georgie found the sights and sounds of Paris intoxicating, and loved exploring it in small groups of friends, buying lunch from a local patisserie and visiting art galleries. It was just the cure for a weary heart, and she came home with great stories to tell and memories made. She was back in more ways than one.

The year had been a difficult one for me in terms of managing Transcend alone. Jane's studies and family commitments kept her busy, and although I'd asked for help from other parents, many were too time-poor or struggling through difficult situations themselves. It was completely understandable. When I picked up the work of the support group again – after stepping away from it in order to deal with the court process and support Georgie – I wanted to rethink aspects of it. At the same time, Georgie and Harry were my priority, and the loss of my parents and the ending of my marriage contributed to the throbbing of my heart. In order to make sure my energies weren't too diminished, I needed to set up some good boundaries.

Every day I'd spend time speaking on the phone to new parents or current members who were struggling. I'm not a coun- sellor, and Transcend didn't offer counselling services, but I was a fellow traveller and wanted others working through unfamil- iar territory to make it. Often I was the first person a parent had spoken to about their child being trans, and I found – and still find – this a particularly privileged position to be in.

I'm regularly moved beyond words by the love I hear parents express for their children, even if they're struggling to accept or understand fully what their child's telling them about themself. I admire the determination with which those parents overcome feelings of grief, shock and fear for their child's future. I've seen mothers leave their jobs to support anxious, depressed and suicidal children, and I've watched those kids come out the other side. Some have not. Too often, I'm afraid, I've seen parents who've disagreed about what to do for their child, then suffered deep fissures in their family that are sometimes irreparable. I've seen parents – mothers, mostly – blamed by partners or family members for 'encouraging' their child to be transgender. I've seen supportive parents and their child excluded from their extended family. Invitations to important family events withheld. I've listened while parents wept on the phone because their child was being bullied at school and it was impossible to move to another. Christian parents have confessed their worries that they'll be rejected by their church if they support their child. I've borne witness to the care and unconditional love shown by parents of children who wouldn't leave their room, so frightened were they of being judged and harmed when beyond the safety of those walls. I've seen parents take in other people's rejected children and treat them like their own. Despite myriad barriers, parents and the children they love have persisted and changed the course of their lives through education and support.

At times, these conversations have left me feeling a little vicarious trauma and worry for a parent or child having a particularly difficult time. Some calls have stayed with me for days. Some stay with me still.

The court process was an enormous cause of distress, but I felt useful whenever I was able to connect families with legal representation or help them understand better what the process entailed. Over time, the legal and cultural context altered, and

I found the parents I was talking to knew they wanted to support their child, knew there was help available and were ready to access it. Everything was constantly and rapidly evolving; the language, the expectations and the quality of information were improving all the time.

Buoyed by the fact that I felt both Georgie and Harry were on track again, I was keen to be a part of the law reform process. With Georgie able to identify herself, we were in a unique position. We'd been through the court process completely, we'd launched a partially successful appeal resulting in a change of law, and Georgie, who was the subject of that appeal, was able to identify herself fully. We finally had a young person who'd been through this ordeal and could speak of the harms it caused.

First, I enlisted the help of the families of Transcend in a letter-writing campaign, appealing to federal politicians for support, sharing their stories and asking these politicians to help back legislative reform. Families wrote about their concerns that their child's mental health would decline while waiting for a court date; others cited concerns over the cost, or the difficulty for regional families to access the court system. The letters poured in.

It was Senator Janet Rice, representing the Australian Greens, who responded to our letters first. She is a member of the Parliamentary Friendship Group for LGBTIQ Australians and was keen to invite our families into her electoral office in Coburg. A number of us attended and we discussed the issues we faced.

Then followed more consultations with community groups, in which the RCH's Michelle Telfer was heavily involved. It was clear that a lot of education needed to take place around the court process and the medical requirements. We weren't going to convince those with the power and authority to help us unless we helped them to understand. Through Janet Rice's office and the Parliamentary Friendship Group for LGBTIQ Australians, we were given an opportunity to do just that. An event was planned for February 2016, to be attended by a large contingent of parents and children along with politicians of all stripes. Michelle Telfer and Professor Fiona Kelly, a lecturer in law at La Trobe University, would speak. Fiona had a forensic understanding of the legal precedents and what was required to legislate effective reform. Included among the many speakers were Georgie and me, along with Naomi McNamara and Isabelle, who'd appeared in *Four Corners*' 'Being Me' episode. We also had meetings arranged with individual politicians to put our case before them, and I was hopeful we'd have a positive impact.

Now fifteen, Georgie had emerged on the other side of her experiences stronger and more determined than ever before to be an advocate for young transgender people. Her first public speaking engagement was for the 2015 Youth Health Conference in Melbourne. As she spoke, I watched the faces in the audience; people were riveted by her account and her insights, many of them moved to tears. The Georgie juggernaut was just beginning. Countless speaking invitations followed, and she went from strength to strength with her presentation skills.

Georgie's development as an advocate was outstanding, but she seemed to be getting very thin. During the September school holidays, I noticed that she was skipping meals. She was exercising regularly, too. When I asked her about why she was skipping meals she insisted that she wasn't hungry, but I was concerned enough to flag it with Michelle Telfer at her next session. Michelle, who is also highly experienced with children experiencing eating disorders, was fantastic. Georgie was certainly underweight, but the advice we received was to maintain a no-fuss awareness of the issue without putting pressure on her. Georgie and I talked about why she might have arrived at this point. She said the weight loss was completely unconscious, that she hadn't planned on it or thought she was fat. She recognised that it had to do with the lack of control she'd had over her body. The trauma of the court case had manifested in this way and I could see the logic in that – of my daughter's desire for bodily autonomy and control.

Yet again the dreadful court system had extracted its pound of flesh from my daughter. She was quite literally fading away. Happily, with the very best of support from the RCH Gender Service, and with gentle, loving care, over time Georgie returned to a healthier weight. A Telethon Kids Trans Pathways Research paper released in 2016 showed that 22.7 per cent of young trans people had been diagnosed with an eating disorder. I was so grateful we'd had such effective guidance from the RCH, which helped resolve what could have become an entrenched issue for her.

I'd registered Transcend for our first ever Pride March, to be held at the end of January 2016. Pride March is Melbourne's answer to Mardi Gras and a celebration of survival, community and resilience. Transcend was to be the first parent support group for children to march in an LGBTQI+ parade in Australia. Many families were not comfortable being visibly out, so only a handful of us put our hands up for it. That was fine. I was so excited that we'd finally be a presence after four years of hard work to build Transcend. We were at a point where we were stepping out of the shadows to join the rest of the community.

But it was not to be. A small number of parents, for reasons best known to themselves, decided they were going to march under their own banner, splitting an already tiny group in two. Effectively the families of Transcend were being forced to make a choice between one group and the other, and some of our members were really hurt and confused. I was absolutely gutted and heartbroken. I didn't want anyone to feel conflicted in what should have been a really positive moment for our families, so I withdrew Transcend from the march.

Transcend was now no longer the only peer-support group for parents in our small and very fragile community. At the end of the worst year of my life, I had no more fight in me and decided that for my wellbeing and that of my children, I would step aside from peer-support work. I'd worked so hard to establish Transcend, and had contributed a considerable amount of personal funds into its running – I hadn't received a cent of government funding – not to mention the thousands of hours I'd put in. But I was done. I had experienced what I now realise was total burnout. I was sad, angry, ashamed I couldn't continue. But I wasn't confused. I could see exactly what had contributed to this. And I knew I would still go to Canberra to advocate for law reform in 2016.

Greg, Harry, Georgie and I retreated to the beach house for the summer holidays and, as always, the healing power of the ocean worked its magic on me. The hours we spent diving through the pounding surf cleansed my soul, but I was defeated.

It was Georgie who noticed I'd had the stuffing kicked out of me and needed some love. 'Mum, you don't have to run a support group anymore, but don't stop advocacy. You've done so much and you've still got so much to offer, especially around law reform. Stick with the people you trust and me, and we can keep going. Just in our own way.'

I cupped her face gently in my hands. She was right.

14

Renewal

It was a blessing to be able to experience daily life now that many of the stressors that had been affecting us were gone. Georgie and Harry were heading into Year 10, taking on one VCE subject each and gearing up for their final years at school. Our lives were already so busy. Georgie and I had resolved to do whatever advocacy we could around law reform and creating a more positive narrative about the lives of young transgender people. What was obvious to me and those working professionally with trans kids was that, with support, their health and wellbeing outcomes were the same as children in the general population. In other words, remove entrenched institutional and social discrimination, surround them with love and affirm who they know themselves to be, and our kids are just fine.

Georgie and I had a positive story to tell. We'd overcome every obstacle, forged a path through unknown territory and left maps for others. We'd maintained our sense of humour and fun despite experiencing many dark times during which we'd gritted our teeth. With Georgie free to tell her story, it felt as though the windows were being thrown open after a long winter. It was so freeing to be able to talk about the things we'd undergone. Although some memories were still quite fresh, we knew that by sharing them, we could start to change hearts and minds.

Greg and I now set up separate homes. We'd lived together as separated co-parents for the previous two years and this was an important step to establish our own lives.

Once the school year began, the routines of life fell into their natural rhythms. Pick-up and drop-off, work and extracurricular activities, and weekends for Harry and Georgie at their dad's new house. Before we knew it, 22 February was approaching and it was time to head to Parliament House, Canberra, to lobby for law reform.

It was an interesting day from start to finish. Malcolm Turnbull was prime minister, in the first year of what would become another short-lived incumbency for which Australia has become famous. At our event, the room was packed with politicians from all parties and the crossbench, plus advisors, lobbyists, families, health and legal professionals and media.

Welcomes were made, and first to present was Michelle Telfer to talk about the medical perspective, giving an overview of the treatment and why the court process was compromising good outcomes for young trans people. Professor Fiona Kelly then spoke about the legal precedents, outlining how we had found ourselves in this position and how we could find our way out of it, via legislation or another challenge along the lines of *Re: Jamie*.

Then we heard from parents, children and youth groups about the impact this law had had on all our lives.

For me, this event validated the years of hard graft; it was gratifying that our key message was being communicated in the halls of power. This was a significant opportunity to make our case. In my speech, I tried to convey how inappropriate a place the Family Court was for making this sort of medical decision, taking the power away from doctors, parents and most significantly the young people themselves. 'Biology is fast, the court process is slow', my pithy one-liner, was picked up by the media.

I'm positive, though, that the most powerful part of the day for those assembled was hearing testimony from the young people themselves. I doubt that many gathered in the room had met in person or even seen in the media a transgender adolescent or child. I believe that being introduced to our kids that day had a huge impact, perhaps more than any of the persuasive presentations. You cannot deny someone's existence if they're standing right in front of you.

We'd arranged our meetings with individual members of parliament to take place either before or after the Parliamentary Friendship Group for LGBTIQ Australians presentation. We had a good meeting with Mark Dreyfus, the Shadow Attorney-General, who listened intently. He was both across the issue and supportive of reform, and impressed as a particularly well-groomed politician. Also on board with reform was Liberal MP Warren Entsch, a Parliamentary Friend of LGBTIQ Australians, storyteller and warm fellow, and Catherine King, the Shadow Minister for Health.

At the last meeting for the day, we found the advisors to Attorney-General George Brandis well apprised of the issues as they currently stood. They'd attended the presentation and had an advanced level of understanding, though were not wildly confident of reform happening quickly. Brandis was notoriously difficult to get a meeting with and his reputation was as a fairly combative conservative figure, as evidenced by the public and longstanding feud between himself and the then president of the Australian Human Rights Commission, Gillian Triggs.

Before our group disbanded, we met up at the Queen's Terrace Café at Parliament House. Many families had travelled to Canberra for the day. It was fantastic to catch up with friends I'd known for years and to meet people whose names I recognised from online interactions. It was a significant day: here we all were in Canberra, around fifty of us, openly and proudly advocating for our children. What we'd all achieved through this momentous day mattered. It really was a turning point and we felt the impact was going to be significant, if not in terms of speedy law reform.

Some of our families had been tempted to believe those who said that law reform should be relatively easy through legislation. But I found that assertion somewhat irresponsible as it raised people's hopes. Generally speaking, support for law reform within Parliament seemed to me to be soft at best, despite the declarations of individual members across party lines we'd witnessed that day. The deep chasm between the highly conservative fringes in the Liberal–National Coalition and the more moderate voices within the parties meant that it would be next to impossible for the Coalition to agree to legislative reform. The Coalition was already deeply divided on same-sex marriage; ever-growing vocal opposition to any reform of the Marriage Act had paralysed its progress through Parliament.

I concluded that for our agenda, this visit to Parliament House was the beginning of a much steeper climb.

At the very time we were presenting our case for reform in Parliament House, Cory Bernardi, the ultra-conservative senator from South Australia, was meeting the prime minister. He delivered a petition signed by 1421 people demanding that the Safe Schools Coalition be defunded, citing concerns over their 'political agenda'. The petition was tabled the following day in the Senate and debate blew up across the country. Social media was set alight. The Coalition Government had funded the national roll-out of the program and politicians scrambled to work out what their position was. Some supported the program; others called for a review; others still thought it should be scrapped.

There's no doubt in my mind that the Safe Schools program was highly effective in fostering inclusivity and respect for LGBTQI+ students in schools. But the politics of one of its founders, Roz Ward, became the relentless focus and – according to detractors – evidence of a radical Marxist 'gender theory' with which vulnerable children were being brainwashed. Backed by certain sections of the media, the neo-conservatives of the Coalition successfully linked in the issue of same-sex marriage and wrested back control of the party from moderates.

It was a particularly nasty episode. Benjamin Law's excellent *Quarterly Essay*, 'Moral Panic 101', does the subject better justice than I can do here. Suffice to say that our trip to Canberra was completely eclipsed by this new and present danger to our children: to their safety, acceptance and inclusion at school.

In response to this confected moral panic playing out in newspapers and on television, the very real panic generated among the trans kids and their families was intense. Here were our nation's leaders doubling down on negative stereotyping of the lives of LGBTQI+ children. Their message was that parents' rights were being restricted; that freedom of speech was being denied. Trans and gender-diverse children were being characterised as mentally ill predators in bathrooms, whose mere presence at school could confuse children into becoming transgender themselves.

Apparently, there were grown adults around who believed fervently that gender identity in children is so febrile that the mere mention of gender diversity would flick some internal switch and suddenly the *whole* school would be trans. Innocent children could, in this ludicrous scenario, catch 'the transgender' easier than the common cold.

Things to get rid of at school: head lice, bullying, plastic.

Things to support at school: diversity, friendship, versatile uniforms, freedom to learn.

Two days after our trip to Canberra, the premier of Victoria, Daniel Andrews, and minister for equality, Martin Foley, came to Elwood College to reaffirm their commitment to the Safe Schools program. Georgie, who was involved in the Student Representative Council, and Harry were part of a small selection of students who met the pair. Georgie was able to say that she'd never been bullied at Elwood College and she attributed that in part to the school having been involved with Safe Schools.

Nevertheless, the sudden appearance of politicians indicated that real damage was being inflicted politically. The ones likely to suffer most were the students the program was designed to protect. That was the travesty of it all. The kids, yet again, were collateral damage in the wars of adults.

The Project on Network Ten contacted Georgie and me through the Office of the Premier in Victoria and we appeared on the show later in the week. Safe Schools wasn't the issue we'd expected to be talking about days after our trip to Canberra. What a week.

In this volatile atmosphere, I wasn't sure how we could tackle law reform. It seemed impossible to imagine a rational conversation taking place in our federal parliament. The pollies had all lost perspective. The cruelty being inflicted on children through the policies of successive governments and politically motivated 'charities' was inexcusable. I'll never understand how this hacking-away at the dignity and rights of children was allowed to occur over this period of time, as the nation came to realise that our leaders were a pack of power-hungry plonkers. While they whipped up division to shore up their base, kids on Manus and Nauru suffered, First Nations children suffered, LGBTQI+ kids suffered, kids with disabilities suffered. And all while the planet burned and they chuckled about Pacific Island nations sinking into the sea.

After the *Four Corners* episode 'Being Me' went to air in 2014, Georgie and I had received a beautiful letter from Assistant Commissioner Tony Crandell of the New South Wales Police Force, a champion of diversity within the force. In it, he thanked Georgie and me for our contribution to law reform and reassured us that through our work we were saving lives. I wrote back, thanking him for his generosity, and said I hoped one day we might meet.

On Saturday 5 March, Georgie and I were to attend the Sydney Gay and Lesbian Mardi Gras. Aside from the event's significant history, I'd had a soft spot for it since stumbling upon the parade in 2001, when Greg had a job in Sydney which meant that we were living in Surry Hills for five months. On my regular walks, I'd wheel the double pram all over the area. One balmy summer evening, while Greg was working, I took a stroll up to Oxford Street, having totally forgotten it was the night of the parade. The babies were about six months old at this point and were sitting up quite alert and taking it all in: the glitter, chaps, leather, feathers; a throng of people in all their gloriousness. The atmosphere was intoxicating, wonderful. In the face of all the hate directed towards the LGBTQI+ community, they showered love and a bit of magic all around them. Those little kids were soon covered in stickers from every possible community group and organisation, the pram decorated with glitter and balloons. The glow I felt as I wandered home lasted for days.

I thought I'd reach out to Tony Crandell to see if we could be involved in some way. In short order, we were invited to speak to the officers marching at Mardi Gras that year. Interestingly, Tony had just delivered an apology on behalf of the NSW Police Force for the way the original protest in 1978 had been mishandled by the police.[1]

While there, we were also given a fascinating tour of the command centre. Every angle, every street, every nook and cranny of the Mardi Gras route was being monitored. It's a massive, impressive operation. After sharing a meal with the gay and lesbian liaison officers (GLLOs), a cohort that includes personnel from all around the state, Georgie and I were escorted down to the assembly area, where we had the honour of marching with the Inner City Legal Centre, a non-profit community legal service located in Kings Cross. Increasingly, they were representing the families of trans kids in court on a pro bono basis, and would become a significant player in legal reforms.

I met many families who were a part of the wider parent community; in particular I remember meeting the indomitable and magnificent Lisa Cuda, a woman who had created parent support from the ground up in New South Wales, just as I had done in Victoria.

Back in Melbourne, the school play was being cast and rehearsals were about to begin. This year's theatrical feast was *The Mouse That Roared*, based on the novel by American writer Leonard Wibberley and adapted for stage by Christopher Sergel. Despite the fact that our schedule was packed with school events, we were maintaining a fairly balanced existence.

It was impossible not to notice the negativity that had attached itself to the Safe Schools program. Georgie and I attended protests and wrote letters in its defence, as did so many others. It particularly disturbed me how, in this anti–Safe Schools environment, our kids' very existence was being rejected – denied completely. The argument sounded to me epically contradictory: 'You're transgender, you don't exist.'

Junk science was being bandied about. Detractors were writing opinion pieces quoting from publications that weren't evidence-based or peer-reviewed. Liars and their lies were tweeted and retweeted. Should anyone call out the assertions of far-right extremists who didn't have a fact to save themselves, those extremists would claim that they were being bullied and maligned. How fragile they seemed to be, all the while whipping up hatred.

And it was the hatred that was unforgivable. Imagine being an LGBTQI+ child during this debate and discovering that your existence was seen as disturbing, unnatural, infectious, a political agenda, a Marxist plot, a mental illness, or that you actually didn't exist at all, that you were a fad and fashion.

More sinister still was the claim that parents were abusing their children and making them trans. Can you believe that this was in 2016? By which time Australia had already declared in poll after poll that it supported same-sex marriage. But no. These demigods were going to let Rome burn and they were going to do it at a time when the Royal Commission into Institutional Responses to Child Sexual Abuse was in full swing. Think about that. The testimonies coming out of that Royal Commission were heartbreaking, devastating. Many of the same institutions that were under a microscope for turning a blind eye to the cruel treatment, abuse and gaslighting of their victims were quite prepared to denigrate a new generation of children, by shaming them for their sexual orientation or gender identity, shaming the family they belonged to, or by telling them that their same-sex parents didn't deserve the same rights and responsibilities that others enjoyed.

Around the Easter school holidays I received a phone call from Janine Cohen, the reporter who'd worked on 'Being Me'. Janine was always mindful to follow up from time to time with the people she'd interviewed for *Four Corners*. Just to check in. It was a rare journo who did that, and I always really appreciated it. More often than not, it was a grab-the-story-and-go approach.

Janine asked how the kids were doing and what was going on in life and in the world of advocacy. I told her that law reform had all but stalled after the Safe Schools attacks had begun. Nothing had been accomplished and we were no further along than before. The narrative around our kids' existence was toxic and I didn't see how it was going to improve. I talked too about Georgie's Stage 2 application the year before and how, after that court case, Georgie could now identify herself publicly and tell her story in any way she liked.

Janine had recently moved from *Four Corners* to *Australian Story* and wondered aloud if perhaps this was a story she could cover. She asked me to leave it with her, but added that if the story was picked up, production likely wouldn't be taking place until later in the year. Within a few hours, however, she called back and said they wanted the story as soon as possible. How quickly were we able to start filming? Fortunately, we had a week of school holidays left and we could work around anything else her team needed to do beyond that.

It was like a whirlwind. A great deal of planning goes into creating a story like this for television. It's an incredibly detailed process with an overarching plan of how the story will be told and broken down into scenes, which shots and locations will be used and who will be a part of the story. It was the first time I had heard the term 'guilty buildings', a phrase used by television documentary-makers about the shots taken of the buildings where events in the story unfold. There were a great many 'guilty building' shots taken of the Family Court. Those interviewed would be Georgie's doctors Doc Paul and Michelle Telfer, family friend Victoria Eager, Georgie's friends Leah and Alex, her high school principal Rhonda Holt and the Chief Justice of the Family Court, Diana Bryant. And, of course, Georgie, Harry, Greg and I would be interviewed.

It was a tremendous opportunity to put law reform back on the agenda, but it came with a risk, as all these things do. We wanted to tell our story as honestly and as responsibly as possible, so that there would be a positive response. What I've realised, though, is that there's always a negative response from some-where. The prospect of personal criticism was less concerning than ensuring we accurately represented the issue and the impact the court was having in the lives of families across Australia. Of equal importance was establishing Georgie as the main voice of the program. Having been rendered silent throughout the court process, she was the one person we should listen to the most.

Prior to shooting the *Australian Story* program, Georgie and I had done quite a bit of media, but this was unlike anything else. For the four of us in our family, the process was fascinating and challenging. For example, we had to restate the question as part of our answer. An example of this might be, 'When did Georgie first tell you she was a girl?' I'd reply, 'Georgie first told me she was a girl at the age of two and a half.' It was a useful technique for editing and storytelling purposes, but it often felt unnatural and stilted.

Neither Greg nor I sat in on the interviews with Georgie and Harry. We wanted the kids to be free to talk about whatever they wanted to. Being able to share our story in this way was at once a real privilege and extremely daunting. There were very personal components to the story, such as the early discord between Greg and me and the impact that had on us and Georgie, and the court case and the impact it had on Georgie and the well-being of her twin brother, Harry. Some of these parts of our lives we hadn't yet fully processed or we still felt terribly guilty about, so being interviewed was confronting for us all. But we were willing to expose that rawness so that we might break through judgement and open some hearts. We were just an ordinary family, trying to do our best under enormous pressure not of our own making. We were trying to help others understand and connect with the issues. We wanted viewers to be on Georgie's side.

There was some media in the lead-up to the story going to air. The *Australian Story* episode was to be called 'About a Girl', and when the promos started running on the ABC and across social media platforms the week before, we all started to get nervous in earnest. This felt incredibly exposing and we hoped it would work out for everybody. The program was to go to air on 15 August 2016.

Meanwhile, on 13 August, the Australian Football League was to hold its first ever Pride Game at Etihad Stadium (now Marvel Stadium). The St Kilda Football Club, the Saints, were playing the Sydney Swans. There had been significant backlash against this move, but footy fans like Georgie and me couldn't have been prouder or more excited. The Pride Game was inspired by the advocacy of Jason Ball, an openly gay footballer who was challenging the AFL to tackle homophobia in the sport. Jason would go on to found the Pride Cup and be named as the 2017 Victorian Young Australian of the Year.

Georgie and I were rapt that it was our club, the Saints, who instigated the Pride Game. We'd watched our team rise to the top of the ladder only to be defeated in the AFL Grand Final in 2009 by the Geelong Cats and again in 2010 by the Collingwood Magpies. Don't even go there; it still hurts. The Pride Game was such a meaningful and bold initiative that in my home it eclipsed the disappointment of premierships lost.

This was corporate citizenry and leadership done well and I was incredibly emotional leading up to the game. So much so that I was moved to write to Matt Finnis, the CEO of the Saints, to tell him why the Pride Game meant so much to Georgie and me. For such a big organisation to be visibly supporting the LGBTQI+ community in the vitriolic atmosphere wafting like a toxic miasma from Canberra across the country was truly uplifting. In my letter I wrote of how the initiative made me think of our team song, 'When the Saints Go Marching in', and how loaded with meaning the lyrics are:

> The Saints' team song is, as you know, an old gospel song, sung originally by African Americans, the survivors of terrible dehumanisation, oppression and lack of opportunity, longing for the day they would be free and accepted as human beings, equal in both Heaven and on Earth. It's a song of yearning and longing for inclusion. I was pondering yesterday the hatred towards LGBTQI+ people from certain individuals and organisations. It gave

me a lovely sense of hope that on 13 August, we can sing our song with its remarkable history, festooned in the colours of the rainbow, and truly say that LGBTQI+ people ARE among that number when the Saints go marching in.

I was thrilled to receive a reply to my letter, and was glad that I had taken the time to thank Matt and the club. Saying thank you is really important when people are sticking their necks out.

The Saints weren't to win that night, but we had a ball anyway. It was thrilling, a beautiful feeling, to be there in that crowd.

Monday 15th came around all too fast. Georgie and I spent the day doing media for 'About a Girl'. Already, the odd salty comment was cropping up on social media pages, expressing revulsion and disgust at either Georgie's existence or our parenting. *Please, let this not blow up.*

We hadn't seen the program prior to it going to air, but we had read through the transcript of what our family had said. When we sat down to watch the program on TV that night at eight o'clock, all of us were as nervous as we were excited. The first face we saw was that of Victorian Premier Daniel Andrews, who did the introduction. Then the story rolled.

It's surreal to see your family story on screen. Some of your own story resonates and some of it doesn't, like mismatched socks after a wash. After it was over, we sat quite breathless. We felt we'd survived something. The piece was well constructed and well told. It made the point for law reform effectively. Georgie's voice had been amplified.

Instantly, texts started coming in from friends and family saying how much they had loved the program. Overwhelmingly, the response of social media was positive that night. It seemed to have reached a wide audience. Yet the following day, when I watched it again on my own, something about it made me feel quite fragile. I couldn't work out why. Even though I knew it was impossible to convey all the nuance and detail of such an experience in twenty-six minutes, the absence of those subtleties made our story feel slightly alien.

By the time I watched it for a third time on Wednesday morning, I was feeling unsettled. I took a shower and stood still as the water hit my body, hoping it would wash away these feelings. I knew we'd chosen to expose ourselves and our wounds beyond the confines of our immediate circle, to relive the pain of our lives so that other ordinary Australians might understand. I hadn't anticipated the avalanche of emotions after submitting our story to public scrutiny. Watching a version of our story reflected back to us on screen had ripped open freshly healing wounds. It was absolutely re-traumatising. I found myself on all fours in the shower, sobbing tears of rage. It was as though the past five years were screaming out of me from depths I didn't know I possessed. In those places I must have hidden even from myself the pain of supporting our kids, fighting battle after battle at school, disappointments in our relationships with others, the current political climate and the toll exerted on us by the court process. Soon the water had run cold and my body was exhausted from heaving out these black, malignant, primal cries. Now that all that grief had coursed its way through me, I felt hollowed out.

I never watched the program again. Not that I didn't think it was good or useful, but because I didn't need to put myself through it anymore. Greg, Harry, Georgie and I all felt similarly – so glad we'd told our story, but the sense that the telling of it came with a sting. It hadn't been for our benefit, but for others', and in that sense it was a resounding success.

Thanks to *Australian Story*, the issue of reforming the law and removing the jurisdiction of the Family Court in the medical decisions of trans adolescents was put firmly back into the minds of those who might effect that change. The program gave us further access to organisations and people to shore up support. And it introduced Georgie to a much wider demographic and enabled her to start a Change.org petition seeking a commitment for legislative reform. She planned to take it to Canberra and deliver it to the major parties.

We were profoundly grateful to have had the opportunity we'd been given. It's a rare thing to be able to educate people on that scale about the lives of transgender children, and we weren't going to squander it.

Throughout the year, Roxy had been persistently unwell. I'd taken her for oodles of tests – for unexplained vomiting, fevers and urinary tract infections, among other things – to no avail. Now she was getting me up four or five times a night to let her out for a wee and she wasn't improving at all. Having tried every-thing I could, sparing no expense, to help our beloved pooch back to health, now I was at the end of the road. The months of disturbed nights were bringing me undone, and after a particularly bad night I called our vet in tears.

'I think it might be time to say goodbye to our girl,' I said. 'I feel so bad; I love her so much, but I can't take it anymore.'

'I know, you've done your very best for Roxy,' he said. 'And I want you to know that I watched your *Australian Story*. You're good people. She's been a lucky dog.'

I arranged a day to bring her in to be euthanised. The kids were spending the weekend at their dad's and I made sure they'd have some time with her before we said our final goodbyes. I spent the weekend cuddling and chatting with her. We didn't bother going for walks as it hurt her old bones. I whispered into her ear, 'Roxy, my love, you have to help me. It's so hard to say goodbye to you. It's breaking my heart. Help me know that I'm doing the right thing.' That night she stopped eating and drinking.

As a family, we took her to the beach one last time and she seemed to be doing it for our sake. She was happy to be with us all, but wasn't keen to walk on the sand. She made it to the water's edge as if to say, 'Okay, I came to the beach. Now let's go,' and wandered back up the path to the car.

Our pets offer us unconditional joy and solace. Beautiful Roxy had comforted our family since Greg and I gave her to Georgie and Harry as their fifth birthday present. What a gift she was to all of us. She was always there with a kind nuzzling nose and a reassuring paw. She delighted us with her extraordinary yoga poses, legs akimbo, and was the most stubborn creature. When she didn't want to be walked home on her lead, she'd fall to the ground and not budge, especially when she found a morsel of food she liked: her penchant for possum poo and wombat poo might have contributed to her demise. As we waited in the surgery, all four of us said thank you to Roxy for every ounce of love she'd given us. I ran my fingers over her beautiful buttercup-coloured ears, the smooth dome of her head, and gazed into those liquid brown eyes. All of us watched on as the vet talked us through as he went, gently and kindly inserting the needle and bringing her sweet life to a close. She relaxed, lay her head down quietly and was gone.

We cried for days.

In October, the Federal Government announced it wouldn't renew funding for the Safe Schools Coalition Australia, even though the Louden review of the program, released on 18 March that year, had found that the program's resources were consistent with its aims. The intense attacks on both the program's contents and the SSCA staff had a devastating impact. Victoria vowed to maintain it. But even the LGBTQI+ community became conflicted on how best to manage the situation – and, therein, one of the aims of the detractors was achieved. Division. It was a shameful chapter in the bitter marriage equality debate, of which SSCA had become the first victim. But, again, those who suffered most in the fallout were children. I will never forgive the mendacity that brought that harm about.

In the months prior, it had been suggested to me that I nominate Georgie for a Gay and Lesbian Organisation of Business and Enterprise (GLOBE) Community Award. When I looked into it, I discovered that GLOBE is a not-for-profit community group that aims to support and empower LGBTQI+ Victorians in their professional interests and in developing their businesses. It also annually holds community awards celebrating the achievements of individuals and organisations in the Victorian LGBTQI+ community.

The only category in which Georgie more or less met the criteria was the GLOBE Person of the Year. Even that seemed a bit much for a sixteen-year-old, but I filled out the nomination form and submitted it. I also nominated the RCH Gender Service for the Health Providers category, and Georgie nominated me in the Straight Ally category. All of us were shortlisted.

The GLOBE Awards ceremony of 2016 was Georgie's first introduction to the wider LGBTQI+ community. Before that we'd mostly mixed with other Transcend families, so it was amazing to meet so many incredible people on one night. Matt Finnis was there from the St Kilda Football Club, a finalist in the same category as me, along with Premier Daniel Andrews and absolute hero Angie Greene, the founder of Stand Up Events, an organisation dedicated to fighting sexual and gender discrimination in sport. To be in such illustrious company was an honour.

The Person of the Year was the last award to be announced, and as the anticipation built Georgie started to look nervous. Up until then, she'd been mingling happily and enjoying the food. Now she looked slightly blanched. Martin Foley, the Victorian minister for equality, stepped onto the stage and read out the names of the finalists. When he announced, 'The winner of the 2016 GLOBE LGBTI Person of the Year is . . . Georgie Stone!' it seemed that everyone in the room leapt to their feet as one. Until that moment, we'd been unaware of how much Georgie's *Australian Story* episode had entered people's hearts. The outpouring of support for our beautiful girl was overwhelming.

Having seen herself as an outside chance, Georgie had only prepared a few dot points rather than a speech, but what she said was impressive. Breathless with surprise and adrenaline, she dedicated the award to 'all transgender people who don't feel safe, loved or treated fairly'. It was an incredible night. The first of many.

This award was about more than Georgie, though. A breakthrough was happening in the telling of transgender stories, and momentum was building rapidly. Social and cultural progress and its backlash were happening in parallel. Right now, we needed to avoid becoming bogged down in negativity or diverted from the work of law reform. Georgie was building an impressive advocacy skill set for one so young and was gathering allies and access everywhere she went.

By now, the years of advocacy for law reform by Associate Professor Michelle Telfer, Professor Fiona Kelly, Georgie and myself – along with others at different junctures – were starting to add up. Our modus operandi was to meet with and speak to influencers – people who had a seat at the table of power – and at events we sought opportunities to connect with anyone who might play a positive role in reform.

I arranged for Georgie, Michelle Telfer and I to meet with the Australian Human Rights Commission. The organisation had argued against Stage 2 law reform in the *Re: Jamie* appeal and I was fascinated to see what would be said. But every connection was an opportunity and by this time I was convinced the Human

Rights Commission had evolved in its understanding of the issues. It felt to me they understood now the full impact, consequences and harm that the decision in *Re: Jamie* caused. Should the opportunity present itself through the courts to review the law, it was my feeling they may argue differently.

There was unequivocal evidence that the judiciary was awake to the harmful nature of the law. In the December 2016 ruling of a Family Court case named *Re: Lucas*, Justice Tree, in finding the young person competent to consent to his own treatment, made these observations:

> As if the general turmoil and challenges which being a teenager in our modern world generates are not enough, the additional burden of requiring an already vulnerable and highly marginalised group to individually litigate to vindicate their identity seems inhumane. No other group of adolescents is required to do so. Having already traversed a far more difficult path than many of their peers, it can only serve to further increase their burden.[2]

Tree added that the process appeared to be 'of no benefit to the child' and 'anything but in their best interests'.[3] Justice Tree continued:

> The difficulty is that it is unlikely that *Re: Jamie* will be revisited in the near future, simply because as I have indicated, the court invariably accedes to the applications. Therefore, in my view, there is an urgent need for statutory intervention in order to undo the consequences of *Re: Jamie*. The sooner

that children such as Lucas and their families do not have to endure the ordeal of litigation in order to get on with their lives, the better.

Therefore, in my view, there is an urgent need for statutory intervention in order to undo the consequences of *Re: Jamie*.[4]

I'd really like Justice Tree to know how much this statement made my heart sing with hope. I was also desperate to undo the consequences of *Re: Jamie* as soon as possible.

Requests continued to come in almost every day for Georgie to speak or appear in media. Magazines were lining up to feature her, high-profile podcasters wanted to interview her, and she was invited to speak at all kinds of events. We couldn't accept even half of them. Soon I was having to get up at 6 am to check my emails just to keep up with the requests.

Georgie has always been a studious person and it mattered to her that she didn't miss out on school if at all possible. We stuck to this rule pretty strictly. Besides, it was never Georgie's or my intention that advocacy should take over her life in any significant way. People are often surprised to discover that being trans is not the biggest part of her life. In her daily life, it barely rates a mention. She gets on with the things that are about creating the future she imagines for herself, like any ambitious young woman her age. At this point of the year we were excitedly planning a big reward for surviving the last few years with our sense of fun still intact: a trip to the USA.

But boy, had things changed. Hillary Clinton's shock loss of the US Presidential election had left the world stunned. Donald Trump, the most unsuitable man ever for any public office, let alone leader of the free world, was now the forty-fifth President of the United States of America. The world had officially gone mad.

We flew into a country that was holding its breath, braced for an uncertain future, but one many rightly predicted as chaotic and divisive.

Oh, America! What have you done?

15

New York, New York!

On Boxing Day 2016, the extraordinary Carrie Fisher, aka Princess Leia – actor, author, comedian, mental health advocate – collapsed. Harry, Georgie and I were driving around Beverly Hills, kilometres away from the hospital where cardiac specialists were trying to save her. Sadly, they couldn't. Not that we realised that as we cruised along Rodeo Drive. I felt strangely dislocated. A few hours ago, we had stepped off the plane, and now we were in a parallel universe. Everything was familiar but ever so slightly out of whack. The next day we caught the train to Universal Studios and passed a small shrine that was forming to honour the late star on Hollywood Boulevard.

At the Harry Potter section, we downed a butterbeer then hit the rides. By day's end, we'd familiarised ourselves with Jurassic Park and Springfield, but we skipped the *Walking Dead* walk-through experience; zombies are a bit much when you're jet-lagged. As we headed back to our hotel, we noticed that the makeshift shrine to Carrie Fisher now overflowed with flowers and keepsakes. A crowd was keeping vigil, holding candles. Her mother, Debbie Reynolds, would join her beloved daughter in death the day after.

That's the day we spent at Venice Beach, where we enjoyed the less frenetic pace but were shocked by the number of homeless folk we saw. Everywhere we went in LA, we saw the walking wounded, which made me ponder the entrenched inequities that cause and perpetuate the visible lack of health care. I thought about how difficult it would be to support a transgender kid without universal health care.

Donald Trump was still yet to be inaugurated as president, and his declaration that he was the biggest, most stupendous supporter of LGBTQI+ people was yet to be tested. (SPOILER: he isn't.)

This was not the time to dwell on anything negative, however. One of my strong philosophies is that no matter what's happening – good, bad or middling – life is to be lived. We'd come to the States to play.

It was exciting to fly into New York, where my sister Jessie and my lovely niece Priya joined us for our week of fun. Our nephew Ben lives there with his partner Jeni, so it was a lovely catch-up with family in the city that never sleeps. New York was still decorated in all its Christmas trimmings and everything had an air of whimsy about it. We took in all the usual sights. Times Square was cold and bright and full of energy. What a dazzling cacophony of sounds, sights and smells. Central Park! What an absolutely stunning place. We wandered into the Central Park Zoo, where it started gently snowing as a snow leopard loped through its enclosure. We visited the Statue of Liberty, the Empire State Building, 30 Rockefeller Plaza and, only by way of proximity, a heavily guarded Trump Tower. It was beautiful to spend time with family, with my funny and very dear sis. This was food for the soul.

By New Year's Eve, we were so tired from our adventures we didn't make it out the door of the hotel. I was starting to feel like I was coming down with the flu, so we took it easy and played games in the downstairs bar until midnight struck. What was in store for us all in the new year? We fell into a deep and much-needed slumber to the sounds of New York City 2017.

The following morning, New Year's Day, we woke up full of anticipation about seeing our first Broadway production, *Kinky Boots* by Cyndi Lauper. It didn't disappoint. For those of you who don't know the story, it goes like this: Charlie Price returns to his father's shoe factory after his father's death and struggles to find a way to keep the business going. Fate intervenes when he meets Lola, a drag queen who needs shoes that will suit her needs. An unlikely friendship and business partnership is formed, but there are hurdles and hatred to overcome. It all culminates in a fabulous glittery explosion of love. It was truly a beautiful show and my heart was mush after the curtain call. The final song, 'Raise You Up/Just Be', has lyrics that just killed me. Look them up.

The audience went wild; we stood and applauded, wrapped in a warm blanket of acceptance and love. The curtain fell and I flopped down in my seat. I can't remember who asked me if I liked the show, but I burst into tears and had to bury my face in my hands so I didn't let out big sobs. It was such a relief to be in a space where difference was celebrated. Where surviving the brutality of life was elevated to the heroic. Where having a heart was the only badge of honour worth wearing, along with an awesome pair of Kinky Boots. They were tears of relief and of happiness.

Jessie and Priya headed back to England; our time in New York City had passed too quickly. We left it knowing that the citizens were heading into a dark time. One thing's for sure: NYC will outlast Trump. You can't keep the Big Apple down.

Disneyland beckoned. The long-promised visit to the 'Happiest Place on Earth' was a reward for all the hard work and persistence of 2015–16.

As we walked through the gates of Disneyland I remembered myself as a child, watching Disney on Saturday nights and seeing those twirling teacups and happy children with Mickey ears on, so tempting and completely unattainable. The USA was the magical kingdom far, far away, and everything I saw on TV showed me the kind of dream life that was impossible in 1970s Tasmania. Some of my friends went to the Gold Coast for holidays in winter and came back with suntans. This was the height of privilege and cool. To have a natural tan in Hobart in winter meant you had money. Sometimes, I would hear that a kid from my school had gone to Disneyland and that was like being told they had gone to Mars.

Number-one priority was to buy ourselves some Mickey ears. If you go to Disneyland and you don't buy Mickey ears, did it really happen?

Our first ride was the classic It's a Small World. Thrill level: zero. Cheese level: no measurement currently exists for the extreme cheese this delivers. It was magnificent! A phantasmagoria of animatronic theatre, of racial and gender stereotyping, of Christmas cheer and full-frontal earworm. Fifteen minutes of lazy riverboating through scenes depicting celebrations from almost every culture on the planet. We loved every second. Actually, Harry wasn't so fond. His imagination was filled with horrible scenes of animatronic dollies becoming murderous. Horror movies have a lot to answer for.

Georgie and Harry were greater thrillseekers than me, and they took themselves off for the rides they wanted to experience: Matterhorn Bobsleds, Space Mountain, Splash Mountain, Indiana Jones and Pirates of the Caribbean. I amused myself with more gentle pursuits, not being a big roller-coaster fan, and my back was giving me grief so I wanted to take it easy. Instead, I stayed in Fantasyland and went on all the rides I'd wanted to go on as a kid. The Mad Tea Party, the Dumbo ride and the King Arthur Carrousel. I know; I'm a wild child!

When the kids came back saying they thought I'd like Pirates of the Caribbean and Indiana Jones, I was sceptical but curious enough to take a look. Oh heck, I thought, you only live once. I loved them. We kept going back for more, and afterwards I took them on the kids' rides I'd loved in Fantasyland. We had so much fun. We had a photo taken with Mickey Mouse, ate chilli dogs and ice cream. It was three days of silly fun, junk food, zero good coffee and LA sunshine.

Exhausted on our third day, we fell asleep on a park bench in Disney California Adventure. That's no small feat, given the number of people around. Dear Harry was coming down with the cold I'd caught in NYC and all of us were beat from two weeks of wall-to-wall activity. So we flew home to Melbourne, feeling so fortunate and full of new memories to carry with us always.

We stepped straight back into meetings, appearances and projects. The Georgie juggernaut continued unabated, and I was receiving far more requests than we could possibly accept. But there were projects that we'd already agreed to, and happily so. We put our support behind a Justice Connect program to help trans teens access free legal support for the Stage 2 court process. And we continued to push for legislative reform through Parliament.

The weekend before the kids went back to school was the Pride March in Melbourne, which we'd missed out on the year before. We'd been looking forward to this event immensely. We were so excited as we marched proudly with the RCH's Gender Service – our second family, and the people who had saved so many lives. Marching at Pride is amazing, a giant hug from a crowd of community members and allies. The friends marching with us helped make the day even more special. It's wonderful to see the kids wearing their colours proudly or T-shirts with affirming messages written on them. We were one of many groups representing a breathtaking array of community and corporate groups.

The cheers the RCH received as we walked by further warmed my heart. As did the smiling faces; the crowd gave out so much love. All of us had dreamed of equality and were working to make it reality.

*

Around the time Georgie and Harry began their penultimate year of school, invitations for Georgie kept arriving thick and fast. The things I turned down ranged from speaking at an awards event to making a comment on the legacy of Germaine Greer. That was easy to decline; Ms Greer is no friend to the trans community. It was also a 'no, sorry' to magazine features: we simply couldn't fit them in with school and extracurricular activities. There had to be time for Georgie to just be a kid.

Georgie and Harry were beginning to get itchy feet, I'd noticed, and life beyond their school years was starting to excite them. They had a yearning to focus on what they loved doing and were good at, and to find the people who would become part of their adult lives. They were in their second year at the 16th Street Actors Studio Youth Program, a professional training program for young actors between the ages of twelve and seventeen years. Harry had also applied for and been selected as a Melbourne Theatre Company Youth Ambassador, which gave him access to current-season productions and creatives. It was an excellent opportunity.

For both Georgie and Harry, there was no doubt in their minds that their future would involve storytelling in some form. Greg and I were obviously very supportive of that. In this world, you must do what your heart calls you to. Talent is important; hard work and application, though, will make you 'lucky'. The harder you work, the luckier you get.

I was feeling the approach of the finish line, too. Though the relentless routine of school was starting to drag, we were feeling a sense of forward momentum in every aspect of our lives. Our family, despite Greg and me being separated, was still a functioning unit; my work life was stable and generating a decent income – the voice work remained consistently good. The advocacy that we'd been a part of was bearing fruit, despite the continuing challenges. I'd been making steady progress with shoring up meetings in Canberra to present Georgie's petition.

One Friday afternoon not long into term, I received an email from the principal, Rhonda Holt. She'd received an email from a person outside the school community warning that a YouTube clip was circulating that contained very disturbing and inappropriate content. Georgie was the subject of the clip. Rhonda said she'd send me the link.

Leah, Georgie's best friend, had come around after school – she was staying for the night – and we were heading to the pool for a swim. Harry was coming, too. The girls had been looking forward to this for days. Leah has been Georgie's friend since their first primary school days, and she'd appeared in 'About a Girl'.

There's so much about Leah that is endearing, but what springs to mind immediately is that she actually forgot Georgie is transgender. So irrelevant was that bit of information to her, so little did it play a part in their friendship, that it completely slipped her mind. One time, Georgie shared some of her feelings about her early childhood experiences. 'You're trans!' exclaimed Leah. 'Oh, yeah. That's right!' She's a darling girl.

While we were at the pool, I received the link but I didn't want to view it with others around, and I hadn't told Georgie about it yet. Instead, I sat in the spa that overlooks the main pool watching these three gorgeous young people chatting and having fun. I observed in myself an extraordinary sense of detachment. I felt calm. I knew that I could report this to the Office of the

Children's eSafety Commissioner. I don't know if the years of direct and indirect abuse had made me tough, but I knew we were going to handle it.

We got home, I made pizzas, and while they were in the oven I watched the clip. It was awful. Absolutely disgusting, threatening, demeaning and vicious. The guy behind the video was making an attempt to belittle and dehumanise Georgie in particular and transgender children generally. There was a grotesque mockery of Georgie's voice and quotes of hers that had appeared in the media. I was going to get this guy. I was not for one second going to tolerate Georgie being used in this way, but first she needed to see the clip and we needed to seek assistance.

My Scottish heritage plays some part in my personal mythology, and there's something of the plain-speaking, hardy Highlander in me. I thought of the war cry of Clan Robertson (*Donnachaidh*), one of the oldest clans, from which my ancestry is drawn: 'Fierce when roused'. At that moment I felt like a giant that had been shaken awake. She was rock-solid and could smell bullshit from a mile away. Her senses were alive to the elements. She could tell the way the wind was blowing; she knew the terrain; and she'd parlayed with former foes to bring about peace. If someone was hurting her family, she'd handle it. This giant woman was an embodiment of all I'd learned and absorbed – certainly through my own experiences, but even more so from the experiences of the families who became a part of the Transcend community. Every parent is written into the story of this giant; every line on her craggy face has been carved by the same pressure my family faced. If at this point you think my family's experiences are exceptional or out of the ordinary, please know that our challenges are similar to those of many families supporting a transgender child. All of us were once alone, isolated and scared. But we found one another, took solace in one another, found strength with one another and fought side by side to save our kids and keep them safe. When discrimination and fear are preventing your child from realising the full scope of their humanity, you grow bigger. Transcend came about because parents needed a place to retreat to when the world became too harsh. Now we'd gained back our strength and we were on the march. These families are my clan. Fierce when roused.

I showed Georgie the offending clip, and her first response was laughter. 'Oh, he's a sad little keyboard warrior, isn't he?' she said. 'What a badly constructed piece. It's not even informative.'

But we both agreed: it needed to be taken down. Georgie was still a minor, and protecting children from being bullied and demeaned, especially by adults, is vital. With no further ado, I contacted the Office of the Children's eSafety Commissioner and made a complaint to YouTube, providing a URL to assist them with investigating it further. It took several weeks and a couple of failed attempts, but the material was deleted.

So much work needs to be done on ensuring respect and safety in virtual spaces, and improving the tone of public discourse. Many large media organisations have allowed abuse and threats directed at specific people to continue unhindered with no moderation or care for the object of that abuse – even if the object is a minor. I'm glad I have taken screenshots of the abuse directed towards my daughter and our family over the years, cataloguing the individuals who posted them and the organisations that allowed that abuse to occur.

It's like the wild west of old out there. After the terrorist attacks in Christchurch on 15 March 2019, questions were raised about the contribution of social media and other virtual platforms to providing safe harbour for extremists and the white supremacist movement globally. So many of the issues we currently face – climate change, gender equality, racism, inequity and LGBTQI+ rights – intersect with the rise of hate speech and these extremist ideologies.

The time was right to take Georgie's petition to Canberra. I'd been liaising with the offices of the main political parties to set up meetings, and ensuring that Michelle Telfer and Fiona Kelly could be present and that the timing worked with Georgie's school commitments. Everything had been organised as quietly as possible. We didn't want any publicity, just to slide in and out of Canberra without fuss.

There was a good reason for doing this: fear that our visit would be sabotaged by lobbyists. Just over a year had passed since our last visit to Canberra, when noisy debate around Safe Schools had drowned out our calls for law reform. This time, Michelle, Fiona, Georgie and I were determined that the advancement of the rights of transgender children would not be halted or overshadowed by the big debates raging around us. The need for law reform was urgent and we'd reached a point where our advocacy had travelled every possible avenue of influence for reform. We had one more to tick off our list:

the highest lawmaker in Australia, federal Attorney-General George Brandis.

He was late. We sat in his library with its famously large collection of legal tomes and made small talk with his advisors. Just when it started to look really doubtful the meeting would happen, the senator bustled into the room, apologising for his tardy arrival. George Brandis struck me as one of those parliamentarians who was a complete political animal. Bluntly and without looking at her, he asked Georgie to explain why she wanted to see him.

Far from being daunted, my daughter was on fire. She placed before him in a white folder the names of the almost 16,000 people who were calling for legislative reform, along with papers written by medical and legal specialists and a letter outlining Georgie's own account of her personal story. She explained to him with perfect clarity why the law was bad and how changing it would improve the lives of transgender adolescents and free up precious time in the Family Court. She said that everyone involved in these cases was now in agreement that there needed to be law reform, and the sooner the better.

All the while Georgie was speaking, the Attorney-General didn't look at her once. He rolled his pen around in his hand. I hoped he was listening, but part of me wanted to say, 'Hey, George. *Look* at her.'

Georgie concluded and the A-G put his pen aside, turned to her and said, 'I absolutely agree with you. This is a legal anomaly that needs to be corrected.'

We were stunned. He then proceeded to talk about the ways reform might be achieved. It was obvious to us that his party wasn't functioning in a unified manner, and that legislation wouldn't be easily passed through the party room and tabled in Parliament. But there was more than one to way to achieve our goal. The fact that the Attorney-General was in favour of reform was significant.

With the key players now primed, all we needed were the perfect circumstances to bring this baby home. We got it when Justice Watts asked for clarification on the law in a case he had presided over, *Re: Kelvin*.[1] The case was a typical application for Stage 2 treatment, with the applicant's father supporting his son, who was given the pseudonym 'Kelvin'. Justice Watts had accepted that Kelvin was Gillick competent and able to consent to hormonal treatment, but referred the case to the Full Court, asking for confirmation of the court's decision in *Re: Jamie*. A hearing was eventually set for 21 September 2017. It was our best hope in a long time.

International Day Against Homophobia, Transphobia and Biphobia in 2017 fell on Wednesday 17 May, and the Victorian LGBTQI+ community was full of excitement. The Governor of Victoria, the Honourable Linda Dessau AC, had contacted individuals and organisations across the state, inviting them to celebrate our community, a much-appreciated vice-regal welcome to a marginalised community that was under intense pressure.

It was the first time Georgie, Harry and I had been to Government House, so we were full of anticipation.

The place was packed. Every single person who'd received an invitation seemed to have accepted.

Something personal was compelling me to attend this event. The governor, our host, had been the judge in our first court case. She'd never met Georgie, and I wanted her to; it was important to me. Many parts of our life were now coming full circle, quite organically. It felt as though the events that had thrown us around were finally reaching their natural conclusion, and I wanted desperately to be at peace with our past.

After all the official speeches, we were able to wander through the state apartments freely. There were plenty of friends to see and chat to but we gradually found our way to the State Drawing Room, where the governor was meeting people. We waited to be introduced; I was feeling shaky. It was the first time I'd set eyes on this person since our day in court in 2011. What did I actually want to say?

The governor's aide-de-camp drew her towards us and introduced me. It was up to me to introduce her to Harry and Georgie and explain a little about Transcend. 'Your Excellency, Georgie is a transgender advocate and is also Jamie,' I said.

The governor understood immediately who Jamie was. Our eyes met, then we spoke quite personally. I don't feel right to say more than that in this book. Before we moved away, I asked if it was appropriate to give her a hug. She nodded and we embraced, one mother to another. We were all glad to have had the chance to meet, and I was proud to introduce my children to her in a context unrelated to our previous encounter.

Everything about that evening was uplifting. I felt I was putting the past firmly behind us – not with bitterness but with love. Georgie, too, felt hope that everything was changing, and for the better.

More love entered our lives with the arrival of Lottie the Love Puppy, a truly adorable little black labrador. She had eyes that could melt solid steel, and was such a quick learner at puppy school, but had a bladder like a colander. It cheered us all up to have a dog around again. We missed Roxy terribly, and we missed the way she brought us together. Our family seemed to function better with a dog. Our cat Joy, too, had lost the plot without Roxy to protect her territory, and we were getting visits from the neighbourhood bullies. Joy, who can be more than a little contrary, was begrudgingly accepting of this gentle ball of energy. We were besotted.

2017 will go down in Australian history as particularly brutal and divisive. We'd had many of those years in a row. Every once in a while, I'd disengage from Twitter and the relentless news cycle so I didn't drown in negativity. Thankfully, Georgie and Harry were focusing on their schoolwork; being otherwise engaged kept them away from the nasty stuff in the media about trans people. Georgie was an advocate, but she was also a school student and a kid, and we always prioritised those needs ahead of any other.

As soon as she turned seventeen, Georgie was able to book an appointment with a surgeon to discuss gender affirmation surgery. She had all kinds of questions to ask, but there was so much information and she didn't quite know how to process it. She didn't want to feel negative about the risks of surgery and the long recovery, but recognised that it was a big step. Her attitude was admirable, yet it was evident she was struggling to come to grips with how she felt.

Afterwards, I encouraged her to articulate her feelings. Was she overwhelmed by the unknown? About how hard surgery was really going to be? Would she be all right? The surgeon had been confident Georgie could expect a great outcome. It was another of those occasions when Georgie needed to be left alone to process her thoughts in her own time.

Meanwhile, I'd been working towards Transcend becoming a Royal Children's Hospital Foundation Auxiliary. This would allow Transcend to come under the umbrella of the RCH Foundation and to fundraise specifically for the RCH Gender Service. It was a fantastic opportunity to give back to the hospital that had given us so much.

Another year, another school production. This year, it was announced, there was to be no musical; it was decided it would be a kind of showcase. All the kids were disappointed by that prospect, but one of the teachers went ahead and selected some songs. Then it was suggested that they be woven into a loose narrative, and Harry was asked if he'd be able to write something. What he ended up developing was an exquisite narrative about a post-apocalyptic world populated by benevolent witches, show-folk, lost children, a lonely boy and an unhinged count. His story brought the songs together beautifully and the result was a triumph. Both Georgie and Harry performed in it, too. The performers loved the production because it was written by one of their own, and Harry had given them all great roles and a wonderfully strange world to inhabit.

After the closing-night party, I was driving them home and Harry said he was the happiest he'd ever been in his life. I was flooded with joy.

*

In 2016, not-for-profit research organisation the Telethon Kids Institute surveyed the mental health of trans kids. The report, called 'Trans Pathways', offered insight into the experiences of trans and gender-diverse Australians aged between fourteen and twenty-five years. The results were truly confronting:

79.7% had self-harmed

74.6% had been diagnosed with depression

72.2% had been diagnosed with anxiety

22.7% had been diagnosed with an eating disorder

78.9% had experienced issues with school, university or TAFE

25.1% had been diagnosed with post-traumatic stress disorder

89% had experienced peer rejection

74% had experienced bullying

68.9% had experienced discrimination

22% had experienced accommodation issues or homelessness

65.8% had experienced a lack of family support

48.1% had attempted suicide[2]

This is the reality of trans and gender-diverse young people in this country today. We must ask ourselves why we've left them to suffer for so long, because in no possible scenario are these numbers acceptable. The impacts of those very harmful outcomes can continue in a myriad of ways for people's entire lives. Studies like Trans Pathways are incredibly useful as they tell us the extent of the problem. We then have to go about finding a solution.

There is very good data on what happens to people when they are not given the supports they need, when they are rejected and discriminated against. What is missing is good data on the

outcomes for young people who are supported, who have access
to affirmative health care, learning environments and loving,
accepting families and social groups. Anecdotally, we can say that
affirmative support for trans kids manifests in social inclusion,
academic achievement and mental health being at the same level
as children in the general population. It's for this reason that,
in mid-July 2017, after many requests from parents who had
previously been members of Transcend, I re-established the peer-
support group. It was like we had come home to one another.

The RCH Gender Service is undertaking one of the biggest
studies of its kind in the world, Trans20. Researchers will track
the health and wellbeing of participants from their service over
a twenty-year period. The results will allow us to see a better
picture of the health and wellbeing outcomes longitudinally of
this cohort, and what can be learned about how to improve the
care of trans and gender-diverse young people in a medical setting
as well as in their day-to-day lives. This very important research is
why I'm committed to supporting Trans20 through fundraising
for years to come.[3]

During the winter, I nominated Georgie for the Victorian Young
Australian of the Year award. I didn't know how she'd go; all
I knew was I wanted people to know how hard she'd worked on
law reform and that she'd done so while still achieving well at
school and in her other passions. I submitted it hoping she'd get a
thrill from the nomination at least.

It was a pleasant surprise to discover Georgie was selected as
a finalist and we were to return to Government House for the

ceremony. That day, Greg, Harry and I were beaming as we walked up the driveway with our darling Georgie. She'd endured so much, worked so hard to overcome discrimination and injustice for others while simultaneously fighting for her own rights and justice. She'd dedicated her whole adolescence to the cause and still managed to be bright, kind and caring. What a proud family we were.

After a short reception in the drawing room we were led into the ballroom to take our seats. ABC Radio host Jon Faine was the master of ceremonies, and the first award announced was the Victorian Young Australian. The nominees were all incredible people. We heard a citation for every finalist and each one walked to the governor and the premier to receive a certificate and have a photograph taken. Then the recipient was announced: 'The 2018 Victorian Young Australian of the Year is . . . Georgie Stone.'

She received rapturous applause. It was another full-circle moment as Governor Dessau presented her with the award for her commitment in advocating for legal reforms. We could never have predicted the strange and wondrous serendipity of life.

From there, life became a whirlwind. It was truly staggering how we hurtled through the next few months.

21 September *Re: Kelvin* was heard before the Full Court of the Family Court. Intervenors of note were the Australian Human Rights Commission, the Attorney-General of the

Commonwealth and, perhaps most significantly, the RCH.
The Inner City Legal Centre was counsel for the applicant. Also
participating were detractors, there to argue against overturning
Re: Jamie. We all held our breath and hoped that the court would
be persuaded by those who really understood the impact of this
law: the RCH Gender Service, whose doctors saw the impact on
young people every single day.

7 November The results of the Australian Marriage Law Postal
Survey were announced: Australia had unequivocally voted for
same-sex marriage. Advocates had worked for years. Many of
them had been campaigning solidly since the 1980s. Celebrations
broke out across the country. It was beautiful to see. I don't think
anyone will forget the image of Senator Penny Wong waiting for
the results. Every fibre of her being was held in that moment, and
when she realises the yes vote has won she remains stoic for a few
seconds before her head falls into her hands and she sobs. This
image will always stay with me. Her parliamentary colleagues
place their arms about her and drape a rainbow flag over her
shoulders.

30 November The findings from *Re: Kelvin* were to be delivered.[4] Michelle Telfer from the RCH asked if Georgie and
I would like to wait at the RCH with her to hear the news.
There was nowhere on this earth we'd rather have been at that
time. As good fortune would have it, Isabelle Langley – who,
along with her family, was the main subject of 'Being Me' – was
going to be at the RCH that day for her regular appointments.
It was so right we should be there together on that day after all

the advocacy Isabelle, Naomi, Andrew and Hattie had contributed to the cause.

We gathered in the RCH Foundation office, and staff from the Gender Service began to pour in, as well as the RCH legal team who had been a part of the case. It was a nervous wait, but I think we all felt quietly confident. The tide was turning gradually towards justice. The room became subdued when Michelle took herself out of the room to receive the phone call. It seemed like a long time she was gone, but it might only have been five minutes. When she came back in, my heart was racing. Georgie and I were sitting together and I felt her energy beside me, tense and quivering.

'We got it,' Michelle announced. 'We won.'

The air burst from my lungs. It was done. Finished. The quiet gave way to sounds of relief and exhalation. I hugged my darling Georgie, who'd contributed so much of herself to the fight. Big hugs with Isabelle and the family. Then the tears that had sprung up were followed by laughter and sheer unadulterated joy.

My thoughts turned to Kelvin and his dad, the people at the centre of this landmark case. I remembered only too well how it felt to be in the middle of the maelstrom when people were extremely invested in the outcome of your case. I hope they know how grateful we all are and how we wish them well always.

From early on in our advocacy journey, I'd vowed that I wouldn't give up until law reform was achieved. Now it was, I could feel the years of tension begin to slip away, like a deep unwinding of sinew.

7 December Same-sex marriage was written into law in Australia. The scenes at Parliament House were jubilant. But many in the community were feeling battered and bruised. During the previous few years, a lot of harm had been done to LGBTQI+ people. For Parliament to have subjected its own citizens to this process was disgraceful. Many will never forgive them for that. The politics surrounding the survey had caused particular damage to transgender people – and children especially – who were thrown under a bus for political gain.

Also, while same-sex marriage was achieved, marriage equality wasn't. Many transgender people, depending on the laws of their state or territory, were still required to undergo gender affirmation surgery to legitimise their marriage in the eyes of the state, or were forced to divorce their life partner. There was still much work to be done and many fences to mend.

8 December Georgie and I flew to Sydney for the Australian Human Rights Awards. She was a finalist for the 2017 Young People's Human Rights Medal for her contribution to law reform and fighting for the rights of transgender and gender-diverse young people in Australia. And she won!

Her work was being widely recognised. In the past year, Georgie had also won an Australian Defence Force Long Tan Youth Leadership Award; the Making a Difference Award, presented by the Anti-Defamation Commission; the inaugural Young Voltaire Award, presented by Liberty Australia; a place in the Kwong Lee Dow Young Scholars Program, presented by the University of Melbourne; she'd been made the RCH Gender Service Ambassador; and was named the 2018 school co-captain of Elwood College.

It was as though the exhausting and unforgiving uphill climb was over. The view from the top was divine.

*

2018, the final year of school, rolled around. It was going to be a big year. There was no avoiding it. At least we could try to make it as pleasant as possible. We cut back drastically on Georgie's advocacy commitments, leaving only a couple of important dates in the diary. Harry and Georgie also made the decision that they wanted to live with me full-time in this exam year. I know that Greg understood why, and supported them, but it was difficult for him nonetheless.

As a family, we headed down to my beach house and had a very lazy Christmas day. No commitments, no dressing up for lunch, pyjamas all day. Time away from work and the regular routine was just the ticket.

The Australian of the Year Awards were to be held in Canberra on 25 January, but the official proceedings began two days prior to the award ceremony. It was such an exciting event to experience with Georgie, and we were both looking forward to meeting all the truly inspiring finalists in every category. We researched them all to make sure we fully appreciated their contribution.

Upsettingly, some online attacks were made against Georgie and there was criticism of her inclusion as a finalist. There was denial of her identity and blame was laid against her allegedly child-abusing parents. The attacks were sustained over a period of several days, a wildfire that fed off its own energy. This experience reinforced my understanding that the hatred unleashed towards transgender people during the same-sex marriage campaign had left people like Georgie utterly exposed and undefended. That so-called debate had allowed people to say whatever they liked about trans people without sanction. It had been a mean free-for-all, allowing people to vent long-held enmity that they wouldn't have felt free to express before. Reports from some parents in Transcend reflected this shift, with previously supportive family or friends beginning to say uncharitable things about their children. It was a consequence of permission being granted by our government to open the floodgates of prejudice.

The online trolling aside, heading to Canberra for the awards was exciting. For Georgie, it was remarkable to reflect that only three years beforehand, she wasn't even out to her friends, let alone publicly advocating as a visible and proud young transgender woman. Now she was a finalist for the Young Australian of the Year.

Georgie and I arrived in Canberra on a hot Tuesday. I'd brought with me my microphone and computer in case work needed me – and it turned out they did. It was lucky they got in early; over the next few days it would be hard for me to find the time to record anything. The schedule was packed. So I set up my portable studio on my hotel room bed and spent the afternoon recording retail scripts.

It was good to know that Harry and Greg were driving to Canberra, having a lovely adventure along the way, and would arrive soon. Georgie was meeting her fellow finalists. It was a relaxed and convivial atmosphere; she was having lots of fun and looking forward to going to Government House in Yarralumla for an evening hosted by the Governor-General, Sir Peter Cosgrove, and Lady Cosgrove. The weather was beautiful. Lake Burley Griffin stretched out beyond the green lawns, still and silent. A jazz band played and people mingled and chatted in the glow of the late afternoon. Georgie was introduced to the governor-general and it was wonderful to see her hold her own in new and such illustrious company.

The following day's program consisted of a morning tea reception at The Lodge with the prime minister and Mrs Turnbull, a luncheon hosted by the Commonwealth Bank and the awards ceremony in the evening. It was a whirlwind.

Georgie made her way to the foyer of Parliament House to join the other finalists, looking stunning in Carla Zampatti black trousers and a royal-blue asymmetrical cropped top with extravagant full-length train flowing behind. There was no sense of who might be the recipient of each category. But the honest truth is, I don't believe anybody thinks it's going to be them. It's not unusual for everyone in the running to experience impostor syndrome – the sense that somehow you've found yourself in the midst of all these amazing people and you don't quite belong. This pattern seems to repeat itself every year. Georgie was simply soaking it all in and enjoying the moment. It wasn't important to her whether she won or not; it was only important that she savoured the moment and represented her community with dignity.

The 2018 recipients were revealed: Samantha Kerr was named as Young Australian of the Year for her achievements representing Australia in the Matildas, the Australian women's soccer team. Senior Australian of the Year was Dr Graham

Farquhar AO, a biophysicist and one of Australia's leading scientists. Eddie Woo, the dynamic and engaging maths teacher, was Australia's Local Hero, and Professor Michelle Simmons, who'd pioneered quantum physics research that may lead to a quantum leap in computing, was the 2018 Australian of the Year. All were worthy recipients from among many outstanding and inspiring finalists.

Those few days made an indelible impression on us all. We left with happy memories and Georgie with new friends. Our feet hurt badly, but our hearts were full.

16

Bring it on

Transcend was to march in our first ever Pride March as a group on 28 January 2018, and the families and allies who'd made it such a supportive and generous group were all there. It was an absolute thrill to be in the colours of trans pride: pink, white and blue. Factorie, the clothing outlet, had sponsored us by printing a hundred T-shirts with a design created especially for us: a fingerprint in the trans pride colours, symbolising that just as every person's fingerprint is unique, so too is their gender identity.

One of the best things about community celebrations like Pride March and Mardi Gras is witnessing the diversity expressed across so many organisations. These parades were born of protests against discrimination, and even though there's a contagious sense of celebration, for the LGBTQI+ community there is still protest, still defiance, still the acknowledgement that there is more work to be done to achieve equality. To participate as an ally is an enormous privilege. To participate as a parent is intensely meaningful. When words fail to fully express how we feel about our children, the depth of respect we have for their honesty and courage, the way they've transformed us so completely, so profoundly, then we march. We march to show we are rock-solid allies for our kids, so they can see they're worth fighting for and so we can say without equivocation, 'I'm a proud parent and I'll always have my kid's back.'

And . . . the final school year began! It was the same as every other year except it was overlaid with future focus, ushering in a gateway to a uni, a course, a potential career. Heads were down, in the books. But there was other big stuff: Georgie's surgery was booked for the end of the year, post-exams, and we'd all but set aside any advocacy for the year apart from a couple of things with which we had a special affinity.

Building on the runaway success of his script for the previous year's musical, Harry had been asked to write a full play for the school production. He'd spent the summer holidays drafting and redrafting scene after scene. He put in a tremendous lot of work and it looked extremely promising.

As every key date came and went on the calendar, a big word was attached to it: 'last'. We had the last welcome back to school, the last swimming carnival. Between so much 'last' and 'next' existed our daily lives. That's where Greg and I came in.

My role for the year was to keep Harry and Georgie well fed, washed, relaxed but effective, to help them plan and take breaks when they could. Greg was the taxidriver, purveyor of quality viewing and Saturday night family dinners. We both provided plenty of love and understanding.

Georgie's commitment to her studies was admirable, and she had no qualms about politely turning down offers to participate in events. It really tested her resolve, however, when she was asked to audition for the role of Dreamer, a transgender super-hero in the CW's *Supergirl* TV series. Ordinarily, she'd have revelled in the chance to audition for it. Nicole Maines was cast, which we thought was a fantastic choice.

When Matt Finnis invited Georgie to be the official 2018 Pride Game Ambassador, this was one opportunity she didn't want to pass up. In our family, football was central to wintertime and family life. When I was growing up in Hobart, every week my Grampie and his friend Mr Hobday would walk down the road to the North Hobart Football ground and watch a match. When they returned after the game, Mum would put on after-noon tea for them, and we'd sit by a raging open fire with a freshly baked cake or Anzac biscuits and watch the telecast of the VFL matches out of Melbourne.

Mum was an avid follower of sport of any kind. She'd sit up late and watch motor-racing and kept the wireless on all summer for the cricket. But football, somehow, was the best. Her team was Carlton, Grampie's team was St Kilda, Dad's team was Geelong. Footy represented family and belonging, rituals of kinship and stories of hope. Games were theatre, high drama, the clashing of titans. A mind game. Footy is a great social equaliser, and because of that it has the chance to tell a story of the values that unite us.

Something that worries me in our current political climate is the 'othering' of the vulnerable, the attempt to negatively classify groups of people outside our own personal narrative. It happens with First Nations people, Muslims, refugees, queer people, trans folk. We see it directed at women all the time; the trolling of

AFLW players is a recent example. Anti-Semitism is on the rise. Hate and division are on the rise.

Australian Rules football is an awesome game. It will be better still when the AFL can come to terms with the fact that trans women are women. There is a great deal more work to be done in this area; football needs to be inclusive and it needs to evolve. But the spirit of the game, for me, will always be about family and belonging. The motto for the 2018 Pride Game was 'I'll Stand by You'.

Being the Pride Game Ambassador was a wonderful experience for Georgie and, by association, me. We filmed a package which covered a little of our story, our love of footy and our reasons for supporting the Pride Game. Georgie delivered a beautiful keynote address before the game to a room full of dignitaries, and we were lucky enough to pop down to the players' room before the match. As Saints supporters we are really proud of our club, and as advocates we hope the message we shared was a powerful one.

This is Georgie's speech:

Good evening everyone,

I am deeply honoured to be the 2018 Pride Game Ambassador and feel privileged to have the opportunity to speak to you today.

Firstly, I would like to acknowledge the traditional custodians of this land upon which we are gathered here today, the Wurundjeri people of the Kulin nation, and pay respect to their elders past, present and emerging.

Minister Foley; Commissioner Ro Allen; Matt Finnis, CEO of St Kilda; Andrew Ireland, CEO of the Sydney

Swans; representatives of the AFL; sponsors, stakeholders, distinguished guests and fellow community members:

I would like to acknowledge my LGBTQI+ elders and thank them for their service, contribution and wisdom. Without their hard work and dedication, days like this would be impossible.

'Impossible' is such an inspiring word, though, don't you think? There is nothing more exciting than proving 'impossible' wrong. I turned eighteen two weeks ago and I've been reflecting on my childhood and the things I thought were impossible back when I was a little person struggling to be heard and understood. Bullied and excluded, but holding dear an impossible dream that one day I could be who I knew I was. Who I know I am. As a kid I loved dancing, but I stopped totally, vowing only to return when I could present as myself, a girl. I loved sport, but I had no opportunity to play a team sport because of my gender identity. I missed out on things that are viewed as vital to growing children because I wasn't understood and I wasn't safe.

My love for the St Kilda Football Club came from my mum and my great-grandfather. Mum has said that footy is the rhythm of winter for our family and that is so true. It's Saturdays listening to the Coodabeens on the radio, and every car trip over the weekend, short or long, we listen to Grandstand. Sometimes Mum will have the telly on as well as the radio coverage, keeping track of two games simultaneously. And while she is listening, she's preparing dinner or baking, so it's mixed with the comforting smells of home for me.

I began going to the footy when the Saints were on the rise in 2008. It was Robert Harvey's last game and Mum thought she should get me along to see a great. Every time the ball came near him the crowd would cheer. I caught the excitement of being at the ground and part of a tribe.

Except I wasn't quite. My childhood has been spent fighting for my rights and the rights of other trans and gender-diverse children. I have had periods where my health and wellbeing were compromised by laws that did not protect me and in fact harmed me. I have had to change schools because of bullying. I haven't always been able to enjoy the full scope of my education because I couldn't participate in sport fully and I was too worried about being me to learn. Swimming lessons and carnivals were hell for me. I have had people say that I should be thrown off a cliff and endured online abuse that was disgusting. To some people, my very existence is impossible.

If you listened to some of the current commentary about transgender people, we don't exist. And for trans women especially, our motives for being female are given nefarious and menacing meaning. This commentary is ill-informed and dangerous. Why? First, because it's wrong. Second, because children are watching and listening to everything. They learn how to deal with difference from behaviour modelled by adults. They learn acceptance and generosity by how it is modelled by adults. They learn inclusion by how it is modelled by adults. They learn to value themselves by what is said about them.

The narrative around trans lives can be so limiting. Yes, we experience outrageous levels of discrimination, and the effects of rejection and isolation are well documented. But that is not the whole story. I know I am a very lucky person and experience privileges that others don't have. I have the luxury of not having to think about being trans most of the time. It is one part of my story, but far from all of it. In my day-to-day life, I go to school, I work hard, hang with friends or my brother, Harry, binge too much on Netflix, dream of life after school, of relationships, of having my own family, a successful career. A life of meaning and endeavour. The positivity and optimism I have is a direct result of my family's love for me. This love has rippled out into my school life, my health care and extracurricular activities.

Despite all the challenges, I have always had my family by my side and consequently I have been able to overcome every single challenge I have faced. Not only that, I've had the privilege to advocate for others. In order for any of us to reach our full potential, we need family, friends and allies to stand by us. I am part of an emerging generation of trans and gender-diverse children who have had family support and therefore enjoy much better health and well-being outcomes than previously. We have a lot to learn from our elders, a lot to say ourselves and a lot to contribute to our community.

When the Pride Game first began in 2016, it made me so happy and so proud of my football club. I had just turned sixteen and my *Australian Story* episode 'About a Girl' was to air the following Monday. It felt to me that Australia was finally beginning to want to hear our stories and perhaps think that a kid like me was not impossible after all. Haven't the last three years proven that the impossible is the best challenge to take up? We now have marriage equality for same-sex couples and a growing number of states reforming their laws to include marriage equality for trans and gender-diverse people as well. From the point of view of a trans young person, in the last six months we have finally achieved the greatest advance in the human rights of trans young people in this country by removing the onerous and harmful laws around accessing medical treatment.

To be named the 2018 Victorian Young Australian of the Year meant a lot to me, partly because I understand that while it was my name that was called out, it was an acknowledgement of the challenges trans and gender-diverse young people have faced for a long time. After years of our identities not being recognised and accepted, it felt to me that I and the many hundreds of other children like me were finally being seen as fellow citizens making a positive contribution to our country. Personally, I hoped that young trans people would see themselves in this new possibility of visibility and service to community and aim for more than they ever dared before. Visibility has a subtle but potent impact. Imagine what we can harness when young people can reach their full potential, regardless of their backstory? What brilliance will be unleashed! We get to enjoy the benefit of their talents, skills and contributions.

Throughout the last few years, I have had experiences and met people I would never have had access to previously.

I have met the most incredibly humble people, who have informed me, shared their wisdom, offered encouragement and ignited in me a daring fire. To imagine my work as a visible young trans advocate with a much wider and more creative scope than ever before.

I have always embraced the opportunities that have come my way. But now I feel I can *create* opportunities and invite other young people in to amplify their voices, and nurture their creativity and leadership skills. We all need to use our skills, circumstances and imaginations as a starting point for improving the lives of others. Through enormous grit, determination and most often love, our lives are improved by those who take action. And it is love that is the strongest motivator, the wildest creative inspiration and the most sustainable legacy.

So many of the stories featured over the past few years of the Pride Game have been about love. I have learned in my life that if I proceed with love in my heart, then more things are possible than without it. It is totally transformative.

In the short term, my future is about surviving Year 12, which I am in the midst of right now! But the next few years involve university and, I'm sure, a few surprises. I plan to continue the work I have done so far in improving the lives of trans and gender-diverse children. As the Royal Children's Hospital Gender Service Ambassador, I will continue supporting their incredible life-saving work and raising funds for their excellent research program, Trans20. It is vital that trans kids are given every opportunity to flourish.

The little person I was, who imagined a life she knew was impossible for her, would be amazed at what has actually transpired. She would be so proud of the people who put aside their fears and opened their hearts.

Love will continue to inspire me and drive me forward to a better day.

Thanks to my family for saying I'll Stand by You, and my footy club St Kilda for saying I'll Stand by You. To the Swannies for saying I'll Stand by You.

I hope love continues to inspire us all to achieve the impossible.

Around this time, Georgie was already thinking of future possibilities and had pitched the idea of introducing a transgender character to *Neighbours*. The producers were interested, and had lined up a meeting and an audition for her. We would wait and see what might unfold.

July brought us a Pink concert at the Rod Laver Arena. One of our favourite artists ever, she never disappoints. Her music has been the soundtrack to the best and worst moments of our lives; a comfort and an inspiration. We sang with all our might.

Harry's play, *Taletellers*, hit the stage in early August. It was a beautifully constructed, wild ride through a narrative peopled with characters who fought against the constraints of the roles they were forced into. The play opens with a B-grade novelist trying to write his great work of fiction, but the characters rebel, mainly because the book is so generic and predictable, the characters so formulaic and the writing so laden with well-worn tropes. As the play unfolds, the characters learn more about their own motivations. One character is constantly being killed off, returning with a different name but the same character traits; others are misunderstood and mistreated; some end up on the cutting-room floor and stage a rebellion. The play resolves after a dark and dangerous journey to steal the writer's computer and to prevent Cliché (the antagonist) from condemning them to a tale of dull limitation. The characters free themselves from the stereotypes that limited them and they are all able to choose how they'll tell their own story.

'Are you Harry's mum?' the kids kept asking me as I helped serve lunch for their final dress rehearsal.

'Yes, I am,' I replied proudly.

They told me how clever they thought he is, how much fun they were having, and would quote their favourite lines to me. I could see in all of them a real joy and I was moved to know that my boy had a great deal to do with creating that feeling. Theatre is a team effort and it relies on everyone to pull their weight and be supportive of the story and each other. These kids were all that and more to each other, and the result was stunning.

Greg and I saw all three performances and burst with pride at every single one of them. The audience loved the play. Every night we had family and friends come along to see Harry's show performed and Georgie and Harry perform in it, along with the brilliant cast.

It's extraordinary to see your child grow into themselves. All of Harry's 'stuff', all his quirky individualism, all his teenage pain and questioning, his love of words, his search for meaning, his philosophical ponderings, his immersion in stories, had been part of the development of this mind and this talent.

Harry had put in his one and only preference for university: a Bachelor of Arts in Creative Writing at RMIT. We filled out the application together; he assembled his portfolio with an incredible variety of writing styles. Greg, Georgie and I all agreed that if they didn't accept him, they didn't deserve him.

Georgie put in her preferences, too, and top of her list was the University of Melbourne Bachelor of Arts. We'd attended the open days of both universities and were convinced that the kids had chosen wisely for themselves. All we could hope for now was that they consistently worked towards their goals. They could only do their best. The rest was out of their control.

Jane and Vanessa, our dear long-time friends, arrived in Melbourne for Vanessa's gender affirmation surgery. Their arrival brought into relief an array of feelings that had been humming under the surface all year. The day of Vanessa's surgery, Georgie and I couldn't think of anything else, and were relieved to hear from Jane that everything was fine and Vanessa was safe, well and recovering. I didn't want to impose on what is an intensely private time, but Jane invited us to visit about four days post-operation, for which we were very grateful. Georgie was to have her surgery in the same hospital, and we knew we'd be there both as supporters and as observers, filing impressions and information for future reference.

Georgie was, of course, keen to hear from Vanessa about how she was feeling, if she was experiencing much pain – anything that would give Georgie an insight into what might be in store for her. It was useful to be in the ward and get a sense of the place. Seeing the drains and lines Vanessa had attached, the leg compressors and the regular visits from staff, gave us a sense of the well-oiled machine Georgie would have at her disposal. We could also see how tired Jane and Vanessa were, so we kept our visit to thirty minutes.

I will always be eternally grateful to Jane and Vanessa for being our buddies on this seriously enormous road trip. We've been in convoy the whole time, with each of us taking turns in the lead, keeping each other safe, chatting on the two-way, warning of what's ahead, carving safe passage through the dark. Jane was and is my rock, and she never let me down. Threes and eights to you, good buddy.

On the way home in the car, Georgie and I talked about what it might be like when it came to her surgery date, how we might feel. After having felt overwhelmed earlier in the year, I was expecting her to perhaps be more subdued in her response, but she wasn't.

'I know it's going to be tough, but I just want to bring it on now. I'm ready.'

17

The Final Countdown

A viral video that circulated some years back made me laugh with recognition. It was an in-utero view of twins, one of whom was singing 'The Final Countdown', complete with air guitar and fist pumps, to the annoyance of their twin. It could so easily have been Georgie and Harry, not because there was any special similarity between them and the twins in the video – my kids certainly didn't bicker – but because the last holidays before the Victorian Certificate of Education (VCE) exams felt a lot like this pressure-cooker situation. Georgie and Harry were once again sharing a bubble as they prepared to go through a threshold, but this time they were preparing for adult life.

They were studying together and each dealing in their own way. At face value, Harry appeared quite relaxed, while Georgie, always the perfectionist, was piling the pressure on herself. Fortunately for them both, they were studying the same subjects – English, Theatre Studies, Literature and History Revolutions – so they could discuss content in detail. All their subjects required them to write essays, and they revised by writing practice essays, finding the gaps in their knowledge and revising again. They had the advantage, being twins, of being tuned in to each other's moods. They were highly supportive and wanted each other to do well. In terms of stress, it helped that they had both completed a subject the previous year, so already had some runs on the board.

One of the worst aspects of the VCE is the pressure to achieve a high Australian Tertiary Admission Rank (ATAR) score. Focusing on achieving a particular mark in order to get into the course you want has become a torturous whip for many, and places absurd pressure on students. Sure, this is one of those rites of passage that are meant to toughen kids up for the so-called real world, but given the huge impact it's had on the mental health of so many young people and its decreasing relevance to both employers and universities, it seems to be time to take another look.

Luckily for us, at Elwood College the emphasis was on effort and getting the best out of yourself, and while the pressure was on, the teachers' care of the kids was amazing. Most kids wanted to do well and were driving themselves hard. By this stage of the year, all the students were so highly calibrated in their under-standing of how to achieve the best marks that the slightest variation from that could create undue anxiety. To a VCE student, the difference between an A and an A+ in a practice exam can mean an agonising revision of their efforts so far and can cause fear that, under pressure in their exam, they'll crumble. In our home, the philosophy was to keep on top of the workload, to do your best, and everything else would take care of itself.

As these days of study unfolded, Georgie and Harry – or sometimes the three of us – would have long, tantalising conversations about the future. We'd take Lottie for a walk at our local park, throw her the ball and imagine that they'd both got into their first-preference course. The talk would be about how they'd meet in the city for coffee between lectures or catch up at the pub with friends they'd met in class.

Inevitably, these discussions would also bring us to Georgie's surgery. She'd waited for this all her life, and suddenly it was only months away. 'I'm just excited now,' she'd say. We had a sense of light at the end of a long, long road of school, of doctors' appointments, of injections and blood tests and psych appointments, and of meeting the criteria for everyone else to accept her as who she's always said she is and waiting for them to sign off on the truth.

How long does someone need in order to prove themself? If you're a trans person, it seems like you need a lifetime.

Dotted through the year's study schedule were Georgie's many specialist appointments leading up to the surgery. She required two psychiatric evaluations from two separate psychs. She required blood tests and bone density and CT scans. She required visits to the GP and to her surgeon. And on top of all this, she underwent the hair removal process that the surgeon required prior to surgery.

Every fortnight, Georgie presented herself for electrolysis and laser treatment on the most tender part of her anatomy. To anybody suggesting that being transgender is a trend, may I suggest they have a year's worth of hair removal by these means on their genitals and see how trendy they actually feel.

*

Our lives have always tended to be busy at the best of times, though I'd tried to cut down our obligations for the VCE year. Even so, during this period before the final term of school, the kids had holiday lectures to go to and Theatre Studies practical exams to prepare for: they needed to practise and fine-tune their monologues. And I wasn't sitting around much myself. I ran a Transcend Family Day – at my home – which many families came along to for the first time. The Transcend Auxiliary held our first stall at the RCH, selling our T-shirts and other merchandise, and lots of delicious fudges and jams. Georgie, Harry and I celebrated the AFL Grand Final at the home of our mates Vic and Saunders – a rare get-together in a crammed year.

Because we had a few quite glam events coming up, I made appointments to tidy our scruffy hair and brows. The GLOBE Community Awards took place the evening of the kids' last full day of school, 19 October. They'd spent the previous month in full-blown revision mode, but they graciously came along to support me as I was up again for the Straight Ally award.

That afternoon, Georgie and Harry had come home from school with two letters they'd written to themselves: one they had written when they first started high school and the other they had written at the beginning of Year 12. They read them out loud while we were getting ready for the evening. What a journey.

Harry's letter from the beginning of his VCE year was truly hilarious. We were crying with laughter as he read it to us:

> I'm putting myself through Yr 12 for your nuts. I'm going
> to be taking all sorts of bullcrap and loving it anyway so

you can get that friggin' course. You F— owe me. So don't
waste this bloody thing you dingus. Don't be a little wuss,
don't feel sorry for yourself and don't whinge about intellectual inadequacy. You've done all three of those things you
big schlong. You're still a teenager, you're not supposed to
have reached the pinnacle. Keep learning, keep working
to learn, please. Don't take yourself so seriously you plonker!
You're a little man on a little blue speck full of loads of other
people who think they're important. Sorry man, neither are
you. Just don't beat yourself up about it eh? Remember to
be kind, honestly. Kindness is a good thing. Not enough
people are kind. In the words of the great Tommy Wiseau,
'If a lot of people love each other the world will be a better
place to live.' He was a complete twat but you get the idea.
Keep up your talents, don't waste 'em. Talent is bullcrap if
you don't use it. Don't get cocky. You're still a teenager, you're
not F— bulletproof. Brace yourself for failure, and enjoy
the wins when they come. Embrace the people in your life
you actually care about, okay? Don't feel like the world owes
you anything. Newsflash, it doesn't owe you squat. Anyway,
enjoy your life, fill it with fun, and always show compassion.

Now excuse me while I go finish Year 12. Screw you.
Goodbye.

Lots of Love,

YOU xoxo :-)

PS: For god's sake help me!

Georgie's was full of her characteristic work ethic and self-
care:

Dear Georgie,

You made it! You did it! You're free . . . I hope you will, or have, gotten into the university of your choice. I hope you will get the score you want. You've worked really hard. I know it.

Wow, what a massive year. Vic Young Australian, a life-changing operation, other stuff I don't know about yet!? I really hope you're ok. I know it is going to be tough. But hey, you've been through worse. Suck it up princess.

My advice for you here on in is to – wait for it – follow your dreams. Do what you have always wanted to do. Honour 10-year-old Georgie by not being scared or slack. We owe it to her. Let's make adulthood as fun as childhood by being the best version of me we can be. Got that? Good. Now go have fun. Relax. Take a load off.

from Georgie

PS: I hope the P!nk concert was really good!

Each letter was so true to the writer's nature. Harry never ceases to amaze me with his wit, and it didn't surprise me – but it did delight me – that Georgie referred to her childhood as happy. She's always looking towards the light. She reminds me that, throughout all the challenges she faced, the dark times and the uncertain times, we made the best of it and tried to keep enjoying life, keep laughing, keep playing.

That night, it was a bonus to go to the GLOBE Awards as my heart was already overflowing. I rocked up with my ex-husband and our two well-rounded children and enjoyed an evening of celebration. Although I didn't win, it didn't matter a jot.

*

Even though we did our best to keep close to home base throughout 2018, there were some invitations no one would turn down. Georgie was presented with three opportunities to meet the Duke and Duchess of Sussex on their visit to open the Invictus Games in late October. One of these was as co-captain at Elwood College, and two were through her role as the 2018 Victorian Young Australian of the Year. She chose to go to Government House in Melbourne, which gave another Elwood student a chance to meet Meghan and Harry, and attended the Prime Minister's Luncheon in Sydney a couple of days later.

So it was that she and I flew to Sydney for the day, on the Sunday after the GLOBEs. As we made our way from the airport to the venue, Georgie was in a perky and chatty mood. I left her at the entrance to the venue with Professor Patrick McGorry, whose extraordinary work in the mental health sector was recognised in 2010 when he was named the Australian of the Year. Then I found myself a shady spot and watched the dignitaries arrive: politicians and their families, com cars, police and, finally, the Duke and Duchess of Sussex.

The buzz around the royal family is something to behold, the air crackling with anticipation. When they pulled up, it was quiet except for the sound of car doors closing, camera shutters clicking and the cheers coming from the Invictus Games playing out behind us in Hyde Park. I saw them go inside, cool as cucumbers, poised and relaxed, and thought of Georgie in there with our socially conservative prime minister, Scott Morrison. Mere weeks ago, he'd made some unsavoury comments about 'letting kids be kids' and used the term 'gender whisperers', which was a totally offensive, snide and scornful term for just about anyone who acknowledged the existence of or who deigned to support gender-diverse students. Nevertheless, Georgie was at the luncheon as one of Australia's young leaders, and she is always mindful that she represents herself and her community well, with dignity and respect, even if it isn't reciprocated.

The guests were arranged in groups, and the royal couple were chaperoned from one group to another. Georgie was in a group of Young Australians of the Year, and as Meghan and Harry approached, they turned to Georgie and she extended her hand. During their brief conversation that day, Georgie thanked Harry for founding the Invictus Games and told him that its message – of unity, connectivity and determination, even in the face of daunting challenges – was so uplifting. The message offered hope not just for those involved directly but for those watching at home who were dealing with their own struggles. She added that she found it personally inspiring as a proud young transgender woman, and as she said this she turned and looked the prime minister in the eyes. The photos captured of this exchange were interesting, and the conversations she had subsequently that day with several of the main players in our political world were enlightening.

Even after this extraordinary experience, there were still unmissable social events on our calendar, and the following day it was the school's valedictory dinner, a fabulous celebration of a magnificent cohort of kids. Some year levels just have a chemistry about them, and these kids had shown potential-plus from the start. Among Harry and Georgie's year were some talented, intelligent souls. It had been a privilege for us parents to watch one another's kids grow into adults. At the dinner I thought of how exciting it was that these kids were being launched into the world.

And may I say, again for the benefit of those hecklers in the back, that my daughter's presence and use of the female toilets hadn't made a single student confused or transgender. What it did do was generate understanding and friendship and love and respect.

When we began at Elwood College, it wasn't a Safe School. It didn't even have the great reputation it has now. But the school leaders and staff were open, and it was a fresh start for my kids. In the time that we were there, we witnessed an amazing transformation, not just in the amenities of the school with new buildings and new uniforms, but also in the school's culture. It's a credit to the principal, Rhonda Holt, and the school council, but also the willing and engaged school community.

Georgie was never once bullied at Elwood College – either before she came out as transgender or after, or before Elwood became a Safe School or after. At school, she didn't even think about being trans. Let that sink in: it wasn't a daily part of her life at all. Surely that's what we want for our kids, isn't it? To simply be able to go to school and learn, not learn to hate or be made to feel 'less than'.

Everything was ending and beginning at the same time. The following evening, Georgie and I went to the Victorian Australian of the Year presentation at Government House for the 2019 recipients. I found it uplifting that so many individuals like Georgie herself were turning their personal challenges into a powerful force for change.

A few days later, I delivered a speech at the RCH Foundation Spirit of Giving dinner. That night, I walked onto the stage feeling immense love and gratitude. I carried my truth as a mother, my vulnerability and my absolute pride in being invited to speak to this crowd after all those years of slog and heartache and triumph. Here is a snippet:

> This is Georgie's final year of school at Elwood College, where she is College co-captain, and her final year at the Gender Service. We have been coming to the RCH for over eleven years. It's a long time, and so much has changed. The staff are like family to us, the hospital a second home, so familiar and such an oasis from the sometimes cruel world outside.
>
> How can we leave such a place? How can I ever thank those who not only saved my daughter's life but helped give her a life she embraces? That is why we established Transcend as an auxiliary, so we could go on working with the RCH and the Gender Service for years to come, ensuring the generations who follow have the benefit of sound evidence-based and peer-reviewed medicine and research.
>
> I'm proud to be part of such a strong and powerful tradition of giving through the RCH Auxiliaries, and proud to support such a new and developing area of medicine. I'm grateful we have been so warmly embraced. And I am proud beyond words of my darling daughter, Georgie Stone.
>
> Thanks so much.

It was a truly wonderful night. Another ending, another beginning.

It was with the same mix of gratitude and readiness that we drove to the RCH the following day for Georgie's final appointment with Doc Paul. Here was the man who'd been our life raft from the start, his hair even more silver than when we'd first met him. The appointment was the final obligatory step in order for the surgeon to go ahead with the procedure. Doc Paul would need to send a report confirming Georgie was healthy emotionally, physically and mentally, and that there was no reason she couldn't proceed.

For this milestone day, we took with us gifts for those who'd worked closely with Georgie and given us so much of their time and their hearts. I dropped in to the RCH Foundation office and picked up the raffle tickets for the next Transcend Auxiliary raffle. Despite the hundreds of hours we'd spent in both the old musty hospital and this beautiful new one, I was glad it wasn't over for us really, that like so many families who've benefitted from the amazing work this hospital does, we too were dedicated to preserving and enhancing that work out of gratitude and love.

Once the formal part of their session was over, I was invited in to see Doc Paul, as had long been the routine. But this time, nothing was routine. We watched Doc Paul open his gift and I thanked him from the bottom of my heart. He was the lighthouse for us in the isolation of those early years, and thanks to him we'd been able to find our way to safety. He'd cared for Harry, too, as a little boy trying to work himself out. And look what happened: my kids have been loved and listened to. Valued and protected. Treasured and challenged. They can talk about their feelings; they can empathise with others; they're able to put themselves in other people's shoes; they listen; they're respectful.

It takes a village, they say, to raise a child. In our case, it has taken a small city. I'm humbly grateful to everyone who, with an open and sincere heart, helped us.

We drove away happy. No regrets. Nothing unfinished. Georgie's surgery was scheduled to take place in exactly one month's time.

Harry, Georgie and I were all so tired by that stage and we were ready to get off the treadmill of advocacy and study. Now we were at the start of the final push, so we had to dig deep. The following week, the kids would sit their English exam. Everything was building to a crescendo: Georgie was required to stop taking hormones four weeks prior to surgery, and the date happened to fall two days before her first exam.

Harry and Georgie went through the highs and lows of the exam period, which lasted two weeks. Through all this, Georgie continued with the painful hair removal, not skipping a single session, even in the midst of exams and exhaustion. She genuinely doesn't know how amazingly resilient she is. One day, I know she'll reflect and realise how extraordinary that was. After every one of these appointments, we'd walk out of the salon arm in arm back to the car, and every time, without fail, she'd thank me for bringing her to the appointment and for holding her hand.

The final exam, for Literature, was on Monday 12 November: two weeks exactly until surgery.

Although we were all spent in the post-exam period, the year hadn't finished with us yet. The following day, Georgie and I attended the launch of Lush's wonderful Transgender Awareness Week campaign. Transcend and a fantastic organisation named Minus18, established to connect young LGBTQI+ kids socially, had been selected as the recipients of money raised from the sale of a specially created product, the Inner Truth bath melt. It was completely delicious, and all profits from the sale of this product were to be shared equally between the two groups. Having a business like Lush support the trans community marks a profound shift in attitudes from only a few short years ago. A growing number of organisations and businesses are doing the work of supporting diversity and inclusion. Corporate citizenry and philanthropy are beginning to bridge the appalling gap in resourcing in the LGBTQI+ community and fulfil the need for visible allies. But we need so much more financial support. Governments need to catch up. Transcend's share of the Lush campaign was donated directly to the RCH Gender Service via the Transcend Auxiliary.

We decided to put the Christmas tree up early, on 14 November. We were anticipating that, by the last day of November, when we'd normally have done it, Georgie would be in recovery. Her doctor said the operation would take between four and five hours, that she would be in hospital for up to ten days, and it would be another six weeks before she was back on her feet. My overwhelming feeling was one of happiness for Georgie, who had been so patient all her life. I knew the surgery wasn't a defining moment for her, merely an essential step in a long journey, but it would be a physical ordeal that would affect us all.

Every year Transcend has its Christmas picnic in Melbourne's stunning Botanical Gardens. Every year the picnic gets a little bigger, and 2018 was no exception. It was a beautiful day, attended by many families who were new to the group and those of us who've known each other for years as well as the trailblazing trans elders we invited, who've carved a pathway for our families and our kids through their own blood, sweat and tears. What makes me particularly happy is how generous and delighted so many elders are at the possibilities available for many young trans people today.

Of course, we have a long way to go in pretty much every aspect of advocacy for trans and gender-diverse people, but there's no doubt progress is being made. Via workshops, consultations, panel discussions and sharing our stories – working with councils, governments, faith-based organisations; educational, sporting, medical and legal institutions; corporations and businesses – we're helping people to understand and shift old, harmful assumptions about transgender people. Slowly but surely, we're seeing the people we reach put in place programs and policies that allow for greater equity and inclusion in all aspects of life.

Nature unfolds and we adapt, I remind myself. Above all, as I looked at the faces of the beautiful kids at the picnic I knew that they'd already made a huge impact in their own communities by standing for their own truth. It's an act of enormous courage to keep showing up when the world says you shouldn't exist – and these kids do, day after day. It was and remains Georgie's courage that fortifies my own determination. Our children bring entire communities with them as they grow, and that's the kind of advocacy that changes society profoundly and forever.

It would benefit us all if more people in leadership roles were as brave as trans and gender-diverse kids are forced to be, if they were to eschew populist thought bubbles and opt for integrity. Abandon division. Choose patience and respect first. There are few people I admire more than the many transgender people I've had the privilege of meeting over the years. There are those who lost their families and children, their livelihoods and their homes; there are those who, without the supports available today, have endured almost unbearable childhoods. They have taught me so much through sharing their experiences and their wisdom. There is wide diversity within the trans community, and I've been challenged and am grateful for all that has been taught to me.

The day following the picnic was the Elwood College presentation night, which took place at the St Kilda Town Hall. Georgie, as co-captain, was one of the MCs. I'm sure all parents share the sense of achievement and fulfilment I felt that night when they've successfully supported all their children through the school years, especially the final boss – to use gaming parlance – of Year 12. I was so excited for Harry and Georgie about the opening of the next chapter of their lives, and so grateful to a school that had taught my children so much more than just the curriculum. They'd learned how to be a part of a community, how to make a contribution and, more than anything, that they were valued.

Both Georgie and Harry picked up awards that night. Georgie won the academic award for English and Harry received the Artistic Contribution Award for his work over the entire six years at school.

Again, I looked at these beautiful young people, the class of 2018 at Elwood College, thinking back to how they'd been in Year 7 and watching them grow over the years since into stellar people, and I felt such a pang of pride and love. The evening finished with a rendition of 'Here Comes the Sun', that exquisitely hopeful song written by George Harrison. Georgie performed the song with three friends. She'd performed with them on countless occasions over their school years, and that night they did it one more time – with feeling.

It was four days until this cohort would vote in their first state election and one week exactly until Georgie's surgery – not that her life was to be carefree and idle in that week.

20 November marked Transgender Day of Remembrance, a solemn day of commemoration for all those who've been murdered as a result of anti-trans bigotry and violence. Around the world, communities honour the memory of people whose lives have been cut short by hatred. The day reminds us of the vulnerability of the trans and gender-diverse community, the marginalisation of its people and the many layers of discrimination they encounter. On Transgender Day of Remembrance, we reaffirm our responsibility to make the world a safer place. I always think about my daughter, but this year in particular I thought of her leaving the protection of a supportive school environment to go out into the wider world. I also thought of the children of the families I've come to know and treasure. We want our kids to be safe – literally, physically and psychologically unharmed. We want them to be active participants and contributors in their country, not kept hidden – out of harm's way – or shunned and corralled into invisible corners. We want them to be free from discrimination, hatred, violence, misinformation, marginalisation, lack of equity or access to a place to call home, work and education. We want them to have the rights and responsibilities of full citizenry. Former US Vice President Joe Biden said back in 2012 that transgender discrimination is the

'civil rights issue of our time'.[1] He repeated this statement in the foreword of transgender equality campaigner Sarah McBride's excellent memoir, *Tomorrow Will Be Different*. I urge you to read it; you'll be doing yourself a favour.

On 21 November, Georgie flew to Sydney to deliver a keynote address for Woolworths employees. She came home that evening pleased with how the event had gone but absolutely pooped. The nonstop intensity of the year was beginning to catch up with her. Luckily, she only had a couple more things to do before she went into hospital the following Monday.

One of these was an interview with the Pinnacle Foundation, which had shortlisted her for a scholarship to help her with her university costs. The Pinnacle Foundation was established to help LGBTQI+ young people reach their full potential by supporting them in high school or tertiary education. The interview took place via Skype on Friday morning. Once it wrapped up, Georgie was waiting not only for her exam results but also a scholarship application and surgery. If she was scared, she didn't show it. I think she just felt lucky.

Later that day, the kids and I cast our votes in the Victorian state election. It wasn't a tough choice for us. When the results were announced, it became clear that the people of Victoria had unequivocally endorsed the government of Daniel Andrews.

A day out from surgery, a quiet calm descended on our house. There were instructions that we needed to follow to the letter in preparation for Monday. So often there's an obsession about the genitalia of trans people and inappropriate questions about whether they have had surgery or not. It's invasive, totally unnecessary and, may I say, pretty creepy. What I will describe now, with Georgie's permission, is how it felt and how Georgie fared in the eight days in hospital post-surgery.

A few days before, I'd created a text message group for close friends and family to update them on Georgie's progress. It was a practical way to make sure everybody got the same information at the same time. I knew our loved ones supported us and were willing everything to go smoothly. It felt like we had everyone gathered around us.

21 November Good morning folks. I've put together this text message group to keep you updated on Georgie's surgery, which is next Monday. Her operation will begin around 12.30 pm. Don't expect to hear anything before 5 pm. The surgery will take 4–5 hours. Greg and I may not be able to answer all texts coming in straightaway but will try our best to make sure you all know how she is doing. Georgie is ready, excited and the most patient person I know. We're all very positive and know she is in the best hands possible. Five more sleeps. Love you all, Beck

The day arrived. I'd slept soundly and woke up at 5 am, showered, got Georgie up, fed the animals, collected our belongings and set off. We didn't talk much in the twenty-minute drive to the hospital. It was early and the day was going to be long. Although it had been hard to conceive of how this day might feel, once we were there, in it, we just dealt with the practicalities: donning comfortable clothing; grabbing phone chargers and a reusable coffee cup; finding a good parking spot. In the background to all of this was a shimmering sense of the significance of the day.

Georgie had worked towards this day since, at age seven, she'd found out it was possible to have gender affirmation surgery. She was always unwavering, unequivocal and completely at peace with her decision to have the surgery. Over those many years, she received counselling in regards to fertility, the option of not having surgery, the irreversible nature of the procedure, and the usual warnings about the risks of surgery in general and this surgery specifically. She listened to and considered all the information presented to her. This was her story, her life, and, as an adult, the decision was hers alone to make. Her twin, her dad and her mum were, and are, rock-solid standing with her.

We arrived at the hospital at 6 am, too early. There wasn't anybody there to admit her yet. But before long we made our way to the ward and were shown the room that would be Georgie's home for the next nine to ten days. We set up camp, put her few items of clothing, almost exclusively nighties, in the cupboard, and placed her toiletries, books and technology in her bedside table. We waited. We cuddled. Harry and Greg were to come at 10 am. No point in all of us getting up so early.

7 am Day 1 Georgie and I are here at the hospital. Admitted. Waiting on a blood test, surgeon to do his rounds and the coffee shop to open! That's for me, not poor G, who obviously can't have anything at this point. Georgie is second on the list today. She's in good cheer and even got some

sleep last night. Will let you all know when she goes in.
Love Beck

My thoughts turned to the day Harry and Georgie were born. I'd avoided thinking of Georgie's surgery as a rebirth; that isn't what it meant to Georgie, nor is it how I felt. But there were parallel emotions. I visualised Harry gasping for breath surrounded by medicos, and Greg and I knowing in our hearts that no matter what happened we'd love him and look after him. No matter what, a parent has to have their child's back. If you're reading this and happen to be a parent who's unsure about supporting your child, I'd encourage you to think deeply about that sacred parental duty. You cannot fail or abandon them. They're pleading for your love, not your judgement. They want you to *see* them.

> **9.09 am Day 1** Georgie has had a beautiful warm air blanket on her. Because of the fasting, she was a bit dehydrated and cold so it was difficult to find a vein to take blood. Toasty warm now. They've just successfully taken blood and she's napping. All good.

Greg and Harry arrived with coffee and breakfast. Occasionally, a nurse came in, introduced themself and gave some instructions on what was to happen next. Mostly, they acknowledged that this would be a long wait. Georgie was lying on the bed and the rest of us tried to find perches for ourselves in the small room.

Finally, a nurse came in and asked Georgie to put on her gown and go to the toilet. It was nearly time. There was to be no pre-op sedation, no fuss; the process would be efficient, kind and respectful. Then, in an unobtrusive moment, it was time to go.

'Can I wait with her?' I asked hopefully.

'Yes, of course.'

Georgie hugged and kissed Greg, then Harry, and said goodbye. There was lots of love from the two main men in her life.

Georgie and I walked along the hallway, past reception, along another corridor, then were ushered into a more clinical setting. We sat propped up like a couple of Victorian ladies, straight-backed and politely nodding to all the people in the room who were busily preparing. More questions and checks of Georgie's identity band followed. She was shivering, and was given another warm blanket. We waited for about ten minutes. I tried to crack some corny jokes.

'Okay, Georgie. Shall we go in?'

We got to our feet, hugged, kissed. 'I love you,' we both said. I detected a tiny waver in her voice, but then she turned and walked resolutely into theatre and I retraced my footsteps to the ward. Somehow, I'd pictured myself struggling to master a flood of emotions at this point. But no. Everything felt matter-of-fact. I needed coffee.

Greg and Harry went for a walk and to search for something to eat. I told them I'd call when Georgie was out of theatre.

About 3 pm, I started to get restless again. The air shifted as the ward became busy. Afternoon tea was being served, day patients were being released and those staying overnight after their procedure had visitors popping by.

I received word that the wait wouldn't be too much longer. I let Greg know it was time to come back. He and Harry were back with me within half an hour.

3.59 pm Day 1 Georgie is out of theatre and in recovery. All very successful. Will know more later but for the moment all is well xxx

It's been so wonderful receiving all your emojis and positive thoughts today. Thanks everyone. We love you!

From along the hallway came the sound of wheels, and someone popped in and said Georgie was about to arrive. We all piled out of the room as they had to wheel in her bed, with her in it. There she was, pale as a sheet.

'Hello Georgie. Hello, darling.'

She opened her eyes. 'Hello,' she said groggily. All three of us felt reassured.

We tried to keep out of the nurses' way as they settled Georgie in to her room, primed equipment and checked lines. She had calf compressors on her legs to ensure correct blood flow and prevent clots forming. They made a noise that formed the soundtrack to the following days, beating out the time. Over the following days, we learned it by heart.

Greg and Harry headed home, exhausted, but I stayed until a problem with the cannula in her right hand was resolved. It became clear Georgie would be asleep for the remainder of the night and at about 9 pm I, too, made my way home. I was numb.

Every morning from here on, I made sure I was at the hospital by 6.30 so I didn't miss the doctor's rounds and could be on hand if Georgie needed the company. Greg usually arrived just before breakfast.

8.09 pm Day 2 Georgie's just had some extra pain meds. Her pain was up to about a 6 out of 10, but now she's comfortable again. She has been so well cared for. She wasn't too fussed about dinner tonight but she'd had a big lunch. She's starting to get sick of lying down. So tomorrow she might make it upright. Her legs and bottom are a bit sore from the pressure and she's been trying to move in the limited range she has. I've given her a few little massages. I'll sign off now. She's sleeping soundly xxx

8.30 pm Day 3 Georgie has been up and about for the second time today. Walked to the bathroom and cleaned her teeth. This is real progress and she's feeling pleased with herself. We had a lovely visit from her doctor at the RCH, Michelle Telfer.

4.40 pm Day 4 G had a good night's sleep last night. Her pain was zero. But she peaked early. After breakfast, wash and walk she started to feel nauseous. This has continued for most of the day. A couple of vomits have made her feel pretty down and uncomfortable, especially as she has to lie at no higher than 30 degrees, so vomiting is difficult and painful. Her very clean lifestyle means that her system isn't used to the cocktail of drugs being pumped into her, plus her body has been through such an ordeal, it's no wonder she's feeling so poorly. Even the anti-nausea medication makes her feel ill as it's being administered, and the smell of the antibiotics as they're injected into the line is pretty foul. But now that the medication has kicked in, she's better and resting comfortably.

Overall, Georgie still has no appetite. She's exhausted. She is very much locked into this experience on her own. We're all passengers. She's missing home very much, missing Lottie and Joy and various little things that sustain her. But she is gently pushing through what seems today like an overwhelming physical ordeal. Greg and Harry will be here soon. Dinner is in an hour and then I'll read her a couple of chapters of *Sense and Sensibility*, which has become a nightly routine.

9.32 pm Day 4 Before we left tonight Georgie was much improved and laughing at our dumb-arse jokes. Greg has discovered Nihilist Dad Jokes. They're pretty funny. She had a bit of dinner and hopefully will get a great night's sleep.

8.11 pm Day 5 Georgie was unfortunately still dealing with nausea this afternoon, but not as bad as yesterday. On the upside, she has walked again this evening, further than ever, and was unassisted – aside from the nurse who chaperones her to manage all the tubes and bags that come with her. Every day there's more progress. Thanks for all your encouragement and cheering Georgie on. I read out to her all the messages you send.

3.21 pm Day 6 It's a beautiful warm sunny day today and Georgie has been out and about twice to the courtyard. The second time we wandered through the café/reception area, which is closed today. She dreamed of ordering an iced coffee: currently, her food options are very limited so it's off the menu. I bought a few cups of microwave rice and she tucked into one today after she couldn't face a ham-and-cheese toastie. She can go for walks now as often as she likes. She's still struggling with nausea but being upright resolves it. Also, she's getting restless, so the walking helps with that, too.

Tomorrow is a big day. She has her dressing removed for the first time. After that she can sit up higher and start eating whatever she likes to get her body fully functioning again. All going well, she'll also have her catheter and IVs taken out.

It looks like Tuesday will be the day she gets to go home, but they have to be confident she's able to manage. She's very excited about being back with Harry, pets, Netflix. And to our house, which is festooned in Christmas decorations.

9.59 am Day 7 Good morning on this fine Sunday. I said yesterday that today would be a big day and G would make some big leaps. And it has been a really significant day. When I arrived at 7.30 am, Georgie's leg compressors had already been removed. She'd taken some sedation medication as the next stage of the process can be a little uncomfortable. At about 8.30 am, the surgeon and his specialist nurse removed all of Georgie's dressings. Also removed was the drain and all

IV drips, leaving only a catheter that G has full control of. Freedom! She is so happy and bubbly.

This was also the first time she was able to see the results of the operation. I cannot describe fully the depth of emotion she experienced. It's not about how long she's waited, which she certainly has, very patiently. Nor is it about how hard the road has been at times, which it certainly was. It's all about a beautiful young woman who can now fully be herself, be comfortable in how she chooses to express herself in the world and in her intimate relationship with herself, body and soul.

She's had a challenging week physically and mentally. She's met that challenge every day, and this morning she said through tears of pure joy, 'It was all worth it. I have a vagina and I love her.'

5.20 pm Day 8 This is likely to be nearly the last big text I send out. Our girl is improving by the minute. She's eating better since the heavy-duty drugs have ceased. This morning her catheter was removed and she's been given the okay to go home tomorrow. She is in a great frame of mind and her body is getting stronger. She is enjoying cups of tea again.

We want to thank you all for your love and support over this last week. It's been such a huge part of her recovery to hear you willing her on and we've felt your hearts with us every step of the way. In a few weeks' time, someone needs to take me out and buy me a few drinks then tuck me into bed. I'm done in! Thanks so much again for all your flowers and love. What a week we've all had together. B xxx

12.22 pm Day 9 Georgie is home! We left the hospital about 9.30 am with after-care instructions and medication. She's already done her morning care routine and has had a proper shower and washed her hair. The kids have now settled down to watch Christmas movies. First cab off the rank is *Elf*. Thanks everyone. Signing off now. xxx

It was wonderful for Georgie to be home. Hospital was an alien space despite the warmth of the nurses, and Harry and Georgie especially found it hard to communicate with each other in there. At one point Georgie had asked me if Harry was okay. She'd noticed he couldn't look her in the eyes and he wasn't very chatty. I reassured her that he'd been missing her so much that he had been knocked slightly off course. In fact, Harry and I had talked about how difficult it was in hospital to relax and banter, which is the way he and Georgie like to interact. Happily, now the two of them could set about starting their summer holidays with a Christmas-movie-palooza.

The after-care was daunting, and now that she was home Georgie allowed her emotions to flow freely. 'When is the good stuff going to happen, Mum? I feel like my life has been about jumping through hoop after hoop, and the hoops keep getting harder! I wish I wasn't trans. I wish I'd just been born a girl without all of these hurdles. When is the fun stuff going to start? I'm a young person and should just be having fun.'

Surgery isn't for the faint-hearted, as Georgie's experience demonstrates. The recovery is hard and long. It's important to recognise and understand that not every trans person wants to go ahead with surgery. Some folks simply don't see it as necessary for themselves in order to feel comfortable; others may not be able to have it for medical reasons; some may find the cost too much of a barrier. Indeed, without private health insurance, it would have been financially impossible for us.

At the time of writing, only four remaining states in Australia require a person to have had gender affirmation surgery before they're able to make a change on their birth certificate. Tasmania, South Australia, the Australian Capital Territory and the Northern Territory have amended their laws. New South Wales, Victoria, Western Australia and Queensland have yet to do so. Trans and gender-diverse people are often unable to conduct the business of life without documentation, of which birth certificates are usually the primary source, that reflects how they present to the world. Fortunately, gender-diverse people have been able to have their sex recorded in accordance with their gender identity in their passport for some years, and this had been Georgie's primary document for a long time. Now that Georgie was home, I applied for a new birth certificate. More hoops, more statutory declarations of support, visits to our local police station to have documents certified. But then it would be done. Female.

Meanwhile, I focused on feeding Georgie so she could get her strength back. Initially, she was frail, fragile and teary. Since she'd been home, not a day had gone by that didn't have her crying at some point. It came in waves. The rest of the time she was cheerful and grateful.

As each day passed, I saw her strength returning. By Day 4 of being home, she was no longer teary and was starting to look to the future, in small and big ways. Greg came over every day, bringing new movies to watch, and the lead-up to Christmas was as fuss-free as possible.

Georgie had been home from hospital for a week when we went back to the surgeon for him to check her progress. She was doing great, he pronounced, healing well and coping with her care at home. It was an incredible relief to have this reassurance. With such a major operation, even the slightest change could cause alarm and Georgie had some concerns, which were all allayed. She came away feeling much more confident and with peace of mind. How truly vulnerable this process had made her at times.

The next day Georgie and I rose early. It was the day the kids' Year 12 exam results and ATAR scores were to come out. Nervous, excited and a little scared, Georgie and I sat on her bed as she checked her emails. She had a raw ATAR of 86.7! We were so excited, but I think I detected a little flash of the perfectionist in her eyes that said, 'I wish I'd done better.'

I went into Harry's room to wake him. He hauled himself out of bed somewhat reluctantly, not just because of the early start. As we'd edged closer to this moment, he hadn't really rated himself. When I'd asked him a week or so before how he thought he'd go, he predicted an ATAR in the sixties for himself. That'd be fine, I thought, but I reckoned he was selling himself short.

'Oh wow,' he said in his characteristically understated way when he logged in. 'It says my ATAR is 82.6.'

Georgie and I hugged him really tight, then the kids texted their dad to tell him the good news. I texted Greg to say we'd given birth to geniuses. Harry and Georgie had worked so hard all year, and now they'd achieved marks that were clearly in the range for the courses they wanted to study at university next year. Phew! Then began the wait for the release of first-round offers on 16 January.

Christmas was spent in our pyjamas again. We'd made no arrangements to visit family, and for the first time since 2011, we'd be spending it at home. A pyjama-clad Greg came over to our place and we had no plans to dress for lunch. We had a delicious meal that lasted all day. In the afternoon, we played Pie Face Cannon, a messy, hilarious game that involves whipped cream, and Harry was an ace. Somehow, he'd mastered the art of surprise, and turn after turn, we others found ourselves copping a splodge of cream.

2018 had been exhausting, and the intensity of the previous few weeks had taken its toll. I slept for most of the afternoon, woke up for pudding, then slept some more.

Every day, Georgie became stronger and more capable of getting about on her own. New Year's Eve came around and I dropped her at a girlfriend's house for a party. The fun was just beginning.

One of the loveliest things I've discovered over the past few years is waking up to a new year without a hangover and with no regrets. New Year's Eve isn't my thing. Not only do I hate crowds, but I'm not a fan of new year's resolutions. Too much unnecessary pressure. Yet with the calendar clicking over to 2019, I took the chance to pause and reflect on all that had happened and could still happen.

What would lie ahead this year? My thoughts turned to my advocacy work. It can be tough going. The work can wear you down; the negativity, the abuse and the conflict all take their toll. Although my experiences with advocacy have changed my world-view, there are times when I am overwhelmed by the enormity of the challenges ahead. As a volunteer, I have no professional support for my wellbeing. The time I took off while Georgie was in hospital and throughout her recovery was instructive, giving me time for some quiet reflection about my future and the renewal of Transcend.

Georgie and Harry eagerly awaited the release of first-round offers. There would be no second prize; both of them had stated that if they didn't get their first preference, they'd take a gap year and reapply for the 2020 intake. Harry hadn't even stipulated any other preferences. The Bachelor of Arts in Creative Writing at RMIT was his one and only choice; writing has always been his only desired vocation.

The day before the offers were made, we cuddled up on my bed together and talked about how the wait was making us feel, and the uncertainty of how this year was going to pan out.

'I've realised,' Harry said, 'that for the first time in our conscious lives, we don't have our year mapped out for us by school. That has been a constant. If I don't get into university, what do I do?'

Georgie, too, was feeling the pressure. She'd received two scholarships for her university studies: one from the Pinnacle Foundation, and, to her surprise and gratitude, she'd also won a scholarship from the University of Melbourne; she'd been notified about it the day the ATARs and exam results were released. But the scholarship was no guarantee of a place. It's well known that the Bachelor of Arts at the University of Melbourne is the most in-demand university degree in Victoria; for the 2019 intake, according to an article in *The Age*, 2275 applicants had listed the course as their first preference.[2] Georgie was one of those hopefuls, and self-doubt had begun to creep in. There was a part of her that worried she might let down people who'd placed faith in her and her potential. But underneath that was a hungry, curious mind and a youthful spirit that had discerned the place in which it wanted to bloom.

After an anxious wait the morning of the 16th – results were due out at 2 pm – I suggested that all three of us go for a coffee or a walk to distract us.

'Sure. Good idea,' came the muted response, and Georgie and Harry went slowly upstairs to get ready. It was close to midday. Minutes later, a shocked-looking Harry loped back down to where I was waiting, clutching his phone, looking stunned but ecstatic. 'Holy frickin' shit balls!' He gasped and showed me the message: 'Congratulations. You have been accepted into the Bachelor of Arts in Creative Writing.' Georgie, Harry and I erupted into excited shouts and started dancing around the living room. Lottie caught the excitement and started dancing, too.

'Call your dad,' I suggested.

'Oh, Harry, good on you, man! I'm so proud of you,' Greg said. All of us were absolutely elated for Harry.

But still no email had come for Georgie, and while she was completely overjoyed for her brother, she was also desperate to know what her future would hold. An email would come, she knew, but would it offer her second choice and not her first?

Meanwhile, I'd invited Greg to come over sooner rather than later. I had champagne in the fridge ready to go. There was nothing else to do but wait. I suggested we watch some TV to keep our mind off things, but I fell asleep within moments of curling up on the couch. I woke to Georgie patting me gently on my arm.

'Mum, I got in! I got the email. I'm in. I got into Arts at Melbourne Uni!'

I sat bolt upright and squealed. Harry heard and came rushing in to join us. Arms were thrown around shoulders; there was hugging and kissing. Yes, I jumped up and down and clapped.

Georgie phoned Greg, who was on his way. When he arrived, we popped the champagne and toasted the effort our kids had put in and the brilliant potential that 2019 held. Dreams had come true; hard work was rewarded; adult lives had begun to take shape. I felt immense happiness and contentment. Done. Mission accomplished.

Epilogue

I feel weightless, as though I'm floating above my life, searching for another place to land. It's a beautiful sensation. The difficulties my family have encountered already feel like an echo growing fainter by the day. It is resoundingly true that Georgie being trans has never been the issue. The difficulty has always been the hostile world she has had to navigate. I've tried to help my children transcend every obstacle we faced, as well as overcome any bitterness that arose towards the struggle. I recognise my own privileges that have enabled me to do that. I've attempted to remove those obstacles for others in similar situations, and if I haven't been able to remove them, I've left a warning sign for those who follow. I want all our kids to flourish and reach their full potential. The world needs them.

I've learned many important lessons over the years. I have learned that there is no pain worse than the pain of resisting change. I've learned that this world can punish those who are vulnerable and brave enough to be themselves. I've learned we must be true to ourselves anyway.

I've learned to be curious and open. We must try to be alive to other people, other perspectives; curious before we judge, not after.

I've learned that help and support can come from the most unlikely of places, and that the most awful pain can be inflicted by those closest to us. I've learned that people can choose to be better, can reassess and heal wounds. I've learned that some people simply don't deserve your time.

I've learned that hatred left unchecked is corrosive, from governments through to us ordinary folks. And that silence is not the answer.

I've learned that hope alone cannot sustain people indefinitely. Keeping your eyes on the long game is vital. If you lose faith in your fellow human beings, look again.

Finally, above all else, I've learned that I will do whatever is in my power, at any time and anywhere, to protect my children from anyone who seeks to harm them or diminish their rights and dignity. I will always do this.

To my fellow parents: I wish you all well. I know you can make it through. Find a support group in which you feel comfortable, and proceed one day at a time. Try to be as brave as your child. Keep your ears, hearts, minds and arms open to them. You are their best hope.

To transgender, non-binary and gender-diverse young people: you are so loved. I'm a better person for having you in my life and I thank you with all my heart. It's been one of the great privileges of my life to have advocated for my daughter and for families and young people across Australia. Parents are vitally important allies in the quest for equality and inclusion. But more important still are your voices, and I encourage you to use yours if you can. It's essential, if Australians are to truly understand, that we listen, learn and take action. It's important you create your own platforms to speak, share your experiences and perspectives, and have your ideas heard and voices amplified. No more living in shadows. No more being silenced by louder, better-resourced voices. No more being told to wait your turn, or told you have no right to exist. You can never be erased.

The rest of us just have to quit the fear and learn how to be good allies. Transgender people are here, they've always been here and they're taking their rightful place beside us as equal citizens of the world.

Gender diversity is simply not a big issue for Georgie and Harry's generation. Gender equality, climate change and access to education, housing and meaningful work are the pressing issues for this generation. They are less concerned with how someone identifies or chooses to express themself, or what bathroom someone uses, than older generations. They want to know how we're going to save the planet.

A good deal has been said, in recent times, about this emerging generation and the potential they have to disrupt the current political and social culture right across the world. Young people are communicating more with each other than ever before, and it would be a disservice – and inaccurate – to say that their communication lacks substance or is banal. They are engaged politically across borders. They're listening to one another, building movements, creating solutions, collaborating with others whose experiences are different and finding where these intersect with their own.

We can play a part in this generation's success by supporting them and offering our resources, leadership skills and opportunities to grow. More than anything, however, we really need to listen. I want to be alive in the future our young people create, one that embraces diversity as its great strength.

For now, I'm drinking in the presence of my two gorgeous adult children and enjoying their happiness. Greg and I and our not-so-small village have guided Georgie and Harry through what seemed like impossible terrain at times, through surprising and uplifting times, through dark times and all the relentless ordinariness of life in between. Now we've raised them, I cannot wait to see what happens next.

I feel a deep sense of gratitude for the here and now. This is a moment of perfection.

Georgie and Harry have made it through childhood safely and their future has just arrived. Isn't that what we want for all our children?

Whoever they are.

Acknowledgements

I never thought I would write a book. And, once I started, I never thought that I could finish it. I've found the process of writing *About a Girl* at times excruciating, but I've shared it in the hope that you and I could meet somewhere suspended in the air, in the quiet spaces where hearts are open and understanding can be reached. I want to thank you, the reader, first and foremost, for taking the time to read this book and opening yourself to an experience you may be unfamiliar with or that you wanted to understand better. Thank you for joining me.

To everyone at Penguin Random House, thanks for giving me this amazing opportunity. Thanks to Sophie Ambrose for your guidance and your patience, Tom Langshaw for your sensitive and insightful editing, Anne Riley for your much-needed guidance and Louise Ryan; you really were the ignition point.

To Harry and Georgie, your unwavering belief in me is so appreciated. A big shout-out to my kids' proud dad, Greg Stone, and my beautiful sister Fiona Trzeciak for reading the first draft. To the Stone and Robertson clans and our brilliant inner sanctum of friends who have always been there for us, thanks a billion.

Humble thanks and much gratitude to our trans and gender-diverse elders, including our First Nations elders, for paving the way for the generations to come. I acknowledge the sacrifices you have made and the struggles you have endured. We stand on the shoulders of giants.

Thanks to Associate Professor Michelle Telfer for your generous preface for this book, and for reading the manuscript and giving advice when I asked. You have been a wonderful, attentive doctor and an advocate with so much determination and integrity.

To the Royal Children's Hospital Gender Service, how can I ever thank you enough?

Thanks to Professor Fiona Kelly for sharing the advocacy journey with us and providing such clear and cogent explanations of the law and how we might achieve reform. Thanks too for providing some reference points for this book.

To the Langley-McNamara family, you are such valuable friends. Naomi, thanks for reading the manuscript. Your feedback was really important to me.

To Jane, thanks for all the phone calls, laughs and friendship.

To the families, young people and allies who make up the Transcend community, thanks for your trust and your generosity.

Thanks to Maya Newell, who has documented so much of this story. I look forward to seeing what you and Georgie create.

To my girl gang: you know who you are, and you know how much I love you.

To Mum and Dad, thanks for all you gave me. I hope you're proud of me.

Ten per cent of the royalties from this book will be donated to the Royal Children's Hospital Gender Service.

Notes

Chapter 9: Court orders

1   Reasons for Judgment, *Re: Jamie (Special Medical Procedure)*, (FamCA 248, Justice Dessau, 28 March 2011), 17.

2   'Being Me', *Four Corners* episode aired on the ABC on 17 November 2014. Full transcript: abc.net.au/4corners/being-me/5899244

3   Kelly, F., 'The Court Process Is Slow but Biology Is Fast: Assessing the Impact of the Family Court Approval Process of Transgender Children and Their Families', *La Trobe Law School – Law & Justice Research Paper Series*, Paper No. 16-4.

4   Reasons for Judgment, *Re: Jamie (Special Medical Procedure)*, (FamCA 248, Justice Dessau, 28 March 2011), 14.

5   Reasons for Judgment, *Re: Jamie (Special Medical Procedure)*, (FamCA 248, Justice Dessau, 28 March 2011), 16–17.

Chapter 10: The appeal

1 *The Merchant of Venice*: Portia, Act 4, Scene 1

Chapter 14: Renewal

1 Jones, Jesse, 'That Should Never Happen Again', starobserver. com.au/news/national-news/new-south-wales-news/ nsw-police-apologise-lgbti-persecution/169836, 25 June 2018

2 Court reference: [2016] FamCA 1129

3 Ibid.

4 Ibid.

Chapter 15: New York, New York!

1 Court reference: [2017] FamCA 78

2 Strauss, Penelope *et al.*, 'Trans Pathways: The Mental Health Experiences and Care Pathways of Trans Young People', telethonkids.org.au/globalassets/media/documents/brain- behaviour/trans-pathwayreport-web.pdf, 2017

3 For more information on the Trans20 study, see: blogs. rch.org.au/news/2017/11/13/australian-first-study-into- transgender-youth-launches/

4 Court reference: [2017] FamCAFC 258

Chapter 17: The Final Countdown

1 Bendery, Jennifer, 'Joe Biden: Transgender Discrimination Is "The Civil Rights Issue of Our Time"', huffingtonpost. com/2012/10/30/joe-biden-transgender-rights_n_2047275. html, 31 October 2012

2 Cook, Henrietta and Butt, Craig, 'The Most In-Demand University Courses This Year', theage.com.au/national/victoria/the-most-in-demand-university-courses-this-year-20190115-p50rjc.html, 16 January 2019

Resources

Transcend has a comprehensive resources list for each state and territory in Australia. It includes international resources as well as suggestions for further reading. See more at: transcend support.com.au

If this book has raised difficult emotions and concerns for you, you can contact one of these excellent support services:

Lifeline: 13 11 44
Beyond Blue: 1300 22 4636
Switchboard: 1800 184 527
Headspace: headspace.org.au/
Kids Helpline: 1800 55 1800
QLife: 1800 184 527

Key terms

Terminology used to describe trans and gender-diverse people is rapidly evolving. Below are some current terms that are frequently used. However, many more terms exist, and it is important to ensure that people are given the opportunity to express their individual preferences for the use of terminology to enable respectful communication.

This list has been sourced from the Australian Standards of Care and Treatment Guidelines for Trans and Gender-Diverse Children and Adolescents, and is printed here with permission. See more at the RCH's website: rch.org.au/adolescent-medicine/gender-service/

Gender identity: A person's innermost concept of self as male, female, a blend of both or neither. One's gender identity can be the same or different from their sex assigned at birth.

Gender expression: The external presentation of one's gender, as expressed through one's name, clothing, behaviour, hairstyle or voice, and which may or may not conform to socially defined behaviours and characteristics typically associated with being either masculine or feminine.

Gender diverse: A term to describe people who do not conform to their society or culture's expectations for males and females. Being transgender is one way of being gender diverse, but not all gender diverse people are transgender.

Assigned male at birth: A person who was thought to be male when born and initially raised as a boy.

Assigned female at birth: A person who was thought to be female when born and initially raised as a girl.

Trans or transgender: A term for someone whose gender identity is not congruent with their sex assigned at birth.

Cisgender: A term for someone whose gender identity aligns with their sex assigned at birth.

Trans boy/male/man: A term to describe someone who was assigned female at birth who identifies as a boy/male/man.

Trans girl/female/woman: A term to describe someone who was assigned male at birth who identifies as a girl/female/woman.

Non-binary: A term to describe someone who doesn't identify exclusively as male or female.

Gender fluid: A person whose gender identity varies over time.

Agender: A term to describe someone who does not identify with any gender.

Brotherboy and Sistergirl: Aboriginal and Torres Strait Islander people may use these terms in a number of different contexts, but they are often used to refer to trans and gender-diverse people. Brotherboy typically refers to masculine-spirited people who were assigned female at birth. Sistergirl typically refers to feminine-spirited people who were assigned male at birth.

Gender dysphoria: A term that describes the distress experienced by a person due to incongruence between their gender identity and their sex assigned at birth.

Social transition: The process by which a person changes their gender expression to better match their gender identity.

Medical transition: The process by which a person changes their physical sex characteristics via hormonal intervention and/or surgery to more closely align with their gender identity.

Discover a
new favourite